LIBRARY OF NAVAL BIOGRAPHY

Joshua Barney

Hero of the Revolution and 1812

Louis Arthur Norton

Naval Institute Press
Annapolis, Maryland

Naval Institute Press
291 Wood Road
Annapolis, MD 21402

Library of Congress Cataloging-in-Publication Data

Norton, Louis A.
    Joshua Barney, hero of the Revolution and 1812/ Louis Arthur Norton.
        p. cm. — (Library of naval biography)
    Includes bibliographical references (p.) and index.
    ISBN 1-55750-490-3 (acid-free paper)
    1. Barney, Joshua, 1759-1818. 2. United States. Navy—Biography. 3. Sailors—United States—Biography. 4. United States—History—War of 1812—Biography.
5. United States—History—Revolution, 1775-1783—Biography. 6.United States—History, Naval—To 1900. I. Title: Joshua Barney. II. Title. III. Series.

E353.1.B26 N67 2000
973.3'5'092—dc21   00-039461

Printed in the United States of America on acid-free paper ∞
07 06 05 04 03 02 01 00   9 8 7 6 5 4 3 2
First printing

Frontispiece courtesy of the Maryland Historical Society

To my wife, Elinor, our children, Mark and Lauren,
and to Professor Emeritus William Davidson Geoghegan—
scholar, teacher, friend, and descendant of
Barney's sailing master, John Geoghegan

7

ᵛᵉ Contents ℛᵛ

⟡ Foreword ⟡

Joshua Barney lived during an age of adventure, and he certainly gar-
nered his share. Though best remembered for the courageous stand of
his naval gunners at Bladensburg as they tried to block the British
advance on Washington during the War of 1812, Barney by that time had
already survived enough adventures for half a dozen lifetimes. He had
first gone to sea forty-three years before, at the age of twelve. Later that
year he crossed the Atlantic for the first time, and three years after that,
at age fifteen, he became the commander of a merchant ship when its
captain died at sea. On arriving in Europe, Barney was forced by the
Spanish government to sail with his ship in an expedition against Algiers.
After returning home to Baltimore, Barney, still a teenager, fought
against Britain in the American War for Independence.

During a career spanning half a century Barney fought in four navies:
the Continental navy and Pennsylvania State navy in the American War
for Independence, the French navy in its wars against Great Britain, and
the Flotilla Service of the U.S. Navy during the War of 1812. The quarter
century between 1790 and 1815 was an era of constant warfare. In addition to his naval service, Barney commanded privateers flying the American and French flags, traded in the war-torn waters of the Caribbean
and Europe, held various government offices, and twice ran unsuccess-
fully for Congress. He made and lost several fortunes; won, lost, then
regained the admiration of his countrymen; and through it all was true
to his principles.

Barney was not a typical naval officer of the era by any means; indeed,
his career was far more interesting. In many ways it paralleled those of
John Paul Jones and Silas Talbot. Born between 1747 and 1759, all three
men went to sea in their early teens. After careers in the merchant

marine all three served in the Continental navy during the American Revolution but were forced to seek employment elsewhere when that body was disbanded following the American victory at Yorktown. Jones entered the Russian navy, Barney the French; Talbot and Barney became merchants after the war; and both Jones and Barney took great pride in their connection with the American flag. When, after a decade without a naval service, the U.S. government under the new Constitution established a navy and offered commissions to Talbot and Barney, each man felt slighted by his placement on the seniority list, reflecting a pride shared by the now-deceased Jones. Barney's sensitivity kept him from accepting a commission on the terms offered but did not in any way affect his patriotism.

Indeed, patriotism, a sense of adventure, an appetite for profit, a hatred of Britain, and a knack for survival guided Barney through his entire life. He was captured by the British half a dozen times and effected one of the most daring escapes of the age. As a privateer and an American naval officer Barney fought in a dozen engagements between ships at sea and won many more than he lost. During his nation's war against Great Britain he participated in the ill-fated defense of the Delaware and Chesapeake Bays against overwhelming enemy forces. As a merchant he navigated the equally treacherous politics of the French and Haitian Revolutions. Joshua Barney's many exploits earned for him a place among America's earliest naval heroes; indeed, he was the only officer to win acclaim in both the American Revolution and the War of 1812. His is a story well worth telling both for what it says about Barney as an individual and for the insight it provides into the American navies of the age of sail.

The Library of Naval Biography provides accurate, informative, and interpretive biographies of influential naval figures—men and women who shaped or reflected the naval affairs of their time. Each volume explains the forces that acted on its subject as well as the significance of that person in history. Some volumes explore the lives of individuals who have not previously been the subject of a modern, full-scale biography, while others reexamine the lives of better-known individuals, adding new information, a different perspective, or a fresh interpretation. The series is international in scope and includes individuals from several centuries. All volumes are based on solid research and written to be of interest to general readers as well as useful to specialists.

With these goals in mind, the length of each volume has been limited. The notes are placed at the end of the text and are restricted primarily to source references for direct quotations. A brief essay on "Further Reading" assesses previous biographies of the subject and directs readers to the most important studies of the era and events in which the person lived and participated. It is the intention that this combination of clear writing, fresh interpretations, and solid historical context will result in volumes that both restore the all-important human dimension to naval history and are enjoyable to read.

James C. Bradford
Series Editor

❧ Preface ❧

Here are our thoughts, voyager's thoughts,
Here not the land, firm land, alone appears, may then by them be said,
The sky o'er arches here, we feel the undulating deck beneath our feet,
We feel the long pulsation, ebb and flow of endless motion,
The tones of unseen mystery, the vague and vast suggestions of the
*   briny world, the liquid-flowing syllables,*
The perfume, the faint creaking of the cordage, the melancholy rhythm,
The boundless vista and the horizon far and dim are all here,
And this is the ocean's poem.

WALT WHITMAN, "IN CABIN'D SHIPS AT SEA"

Most notable historical figures slowly assume the significant roles designated for them by history. The remarkable accomplishments of Joshua Barney began in his early adolescence and became more intriguing as he matured into one of America's great naval heroes. His adventures make for wonderful sea stories that appear almost fictional. Though real, they are incredibly numerous for one man, and they illuminate the era of America's birth and contribute to the history of the American navy.

Of those men who won commissions in the nascent American navy or sailed as privateers, none was more clever, colorful, or competent than Joshua Barney of Baltimore. A man without formal education or military background, he had natural gifts of seamanship, leadership, and courage. At the age of fifteen, on the death of his sea captain brother-in-law, Barney found himself in command of a foundering vessel in the middle of the stormy North Atlantic. He completed the passage, proved his adeptness at business in a cutthroat market, and returned home with an impressive profit. At the start of the American Revolution he was a sixteen-year-old master's mate on the Continental navy ship *Hornet,* one of the first vessels to fly the American flag at sea. Shortly thereafter, he was promoted to naval lieutenant, an event that launched his remarkable career. As Herman Melville observed, it is in naval service where "the sons of adversity meet the children of calamity, and where the children of calamity meet the offspring of sin." (Melville, *White Jacket; or the World in a Man of War*, 82)

Barney took part in thirty-five Revolutionary War naval engagements. He lost five of these encounters, suffered imprisonment three times, and escaped twice using clever disguises. He was shipwrecked twice and put down one mutiny. The tales of Barney's incredible victories at sea, frustrating defeats, and cleverness as a prisoner constitute a series of remarkable anecdotes. His legendary triumph as captain of the *Hyder-Ally* became the subject of a popular poem and folk song of the late eighteenth century. This was one of the few American naval victories of the Revolutionary War and unique in defeating a numerically superior foe. As the War for Independence ended, Barney, though still a young lieutenant, commanded one of the few warships still under commission by the United States, shuttling secret messages between Congress in Philadelphia and Benjamin Franklin, John Adams, and John Jay in France as they negotiated the Treaty of Paris. During the 1790s Barney engaged in maritime commerce in an era of bitter warfare between the British and the French. At one point, captured again by the British, Barney stood trial for piracy. The charges were without merit, but the arrogance displayed by the British generated in Barney a deep-seated hatred for Britain and its navy.

As a member of the American delegation sent to Paris to express recognition of the new French republic, Barney was chosen to present the new government with the American colors in a moving fraternal gesture. His charm, ability, and handsome looks made a favorable impression on French officials—and ladies—during the Treaty of Paris negotiations and again during the recognition ceremonies.

Barney refused a coveted congressional appointment as one of the first six captains in the newly formed U.S. Navy based on a matter of personal principles involving his seniority on the list. Instead of entering the new navy Barney engaged in the West Indies trade until the French, in need of experienced senior naval officers, offered him a commission as commodore in their navy. Barney's acceptance proved to be a politically naive move because it placed him on the wrong side in the Quasi-War, which broke out between France and the United States in 1798.

Barney suffered some local reprobation because of his foreign service but regained his status as an American patriot by his distinguished service during the War of 1812. He helped plan the naval defense of the Chesapeake, and he commanded a battery of naval cannons that slowed the advance of an overwhelming British force toward the new U.S. capital city. Barney was severely wounded during the Battle of Bladensburg in an outstanding example of American courage and gallantry in the face of defeat. Although Washington was later captured and burned, the stand by Barney's men at Bladensburg was crucial in gaining time for the evacuation of the city that saved many historical relics from destruction.

Despite his impressive accomplishments, Joshua Barney's exploits have largely been forgotten. He first gained fame during the Revolutionary War, when naval victories were few and were not as revered as land battles. His greatest triumph came after Britain's defeat at Yorktown, the culminating point of the American Revolution. Perhaps Barney's youth and relatively low rank of lieutenant also affected his prominence in the history of the Revolutionary War. His second rise to prominence occurred during the Quasi-War with France, which often earns only a page or two in American history books; and worse, Commodore Barney was arguably on the wrong side in that conflict. His courage and tenacity in a military defeat on land during the War of 1812 became the stuff of legend. One might conclude that Joshua Barney was a man of distinguished valor who fought in the wrong military service during the right war, later rose to high rank on the wrong side, and, in his later years, gained fame in a losing cause. These curious social and historical ingredients were the likely recipe for his relative obscurity.

Barney's relationship with the history of the American flag is also remarkable. He was the first to use the banner for naval recruitment in Maryland; he served on one of the first Continental navy ships to fly the American flag; he was second in command of the *Andrea Doria* when that ship received the first salute from a foreign nation; he was given the honor of carrying the American flag into the National Assembly of France as the new republic received its first diplomatic recognition; finally, he served on the committee that designed and ordered the huge standard for Fort McHenry that inspired Francis Scott Key to write "The Star Spangled Banner."

Like all who live in the real world, Barney occasionally stumbled over the stones of reality. His many human frailties created the complex dimensions and textures that make him so fascinating. The story of this restless participant in so many conflicts mirrors the times in which he lived in America, France, and the West Indies when history was being influenced by Washington, Franklin, Adams, Jefferson, Morris, Monroe, Madison, Louis XVI, Toussaint, and Napoléon.

Unfortunately, history is generous to only a few. Remembrance of Joshua Barney has faded. Perhaps this happened because he was from Maryland, a state that did not at that time have the political clout of a Massachusetts, New York, Pennsylvania, or Virginia. Among the general public, he is not completely uncelebrated. His portrait hangs among the honored heroes of the American Revolutionary War in Independence Park in Philadelphia; much of his memorabilia is on display at the Daughters of the American Revolution Museum in Washington; and a large seascape depicting one of his most famous battles is on exhibit at the U.S. Naval Academy at Annapolis. The semblance of the man is known, but his story is in need of retelling. This new biography of Joshua Barney describes the highlights of the changing fortunes of his life. It also contains some of his own written words and much of the charming verse that was written about him during his life. The author admits to taking some minor license by adding a dash of prose coloration in order to provide life and excitement to some voyages or battle scenes. Taken all together, this is an attempt to remove the haze of time while preserving the patina of historical perspective. It is the author's hope that Barney's image may be polished to the brighter luster it deserves.

❧ *Acknowledgments* ❧

The first acknowledgments go to my eminent predecessors who recounted the life of Joshua Barney before me: Mary Barney, daughter-in-law of the commodore and author of the *Biographical Memoir of the Late Joshua Barney*; Ralph D. Paine, who wrote *Joshua Barney: Forgotten Hero of the Blue Water*; and Hulbert Footner, author of the scholarly *Sailor of Fortune: The Life and Adventures of Commodore Joshua Barney*. I wish to thank my wife, Elinor, for her patience, encouragement, and constructive criticism as this project took shape over many years. I owe a great debt of gratitude to Professor James C. Bradford of Texas A&M University for his insights into the history of the period and suggestions about writing style. In addition, I thank Ms. Katherine Viens, Director of the Old Colony Museum in Taunton, Massachusetts; and Mrs. Lauren Shafer for their editorial help and perceptive literary suggestions. I also am most grateful to my longtime friend Robert Andrews Kingsbury for his remarkable sense of detail and useful advice as a scholar of military history. These invaluable people provided the impetus for the many revisions of the manuscript. As is often said, writing a story is easy; it is the rewriting that taxes the author's skills.

I wish to give special acknowledgment for the early encouragement I received from Andrew German of the Mystic Seaport Museum and the inspiration I received from the faculty and students of Mystic Seaport's Munson Institute for Maritime Studies.

~ *Chronology* ~

20 Oct. 1777	Exchanged for a British officer
31 Mar. 1778	Captured by the British onboard the *Virginia*
May 1778	Imprisoned on a hulk in New York harbor
Aug. 1778	Exchanged for a British officer and given leave of absence from the navy; takes command of a schooner and is captured by a British privateer but released
Nov. 1778	Appointed first lieutenant of the privateer *General Mercer*
October 1779	Returns to Philadelphia in command of a prize, the letter-of-marque ship *Minerva*
16 Mar. 1780	Marries Anne Bedford in Philadelphia
July 1780	Joins the sloop-of-war *Saratoga* as first lieutenant
11 Oct. 1780	Captured by the British while sailing a prize to Philadelphia
15 Nov. 1780	Incarcerated on the notorious prison transport ship *Yarmouth,* and ultimately sent to Old Mill Prison in Plymouth, England
18 May 1781	Escapes from Old Mill Prison
19 Oct. 1781	The British surrender at the Battle of Yorktown
21 Mar. 1782	Returns to Philadelphia
25 Mar. 1782	Assumes command of the *Hyder-Ally*
8 Apr. 1782	Barney and *Hyder-Ally* capture the *General Monk*
16 May 1782	Appointed to command the refurbished *General Washington*
20 Sept. 1783	The Treaty of Paris is signed in France
6 Mar. 1784	Petitions Continental Congress for the rank of captain in the Continental navy
July 1788	Sails the miniature ship *Federalist* from Baltimore to Mount Vernon
14 July 1793	Barney's merchant ship, *Sampson,* is captured by three privateers

20 July 1793	Barney and crew recapture the *Sampson* and take their captors to Baltimore for trial
27 Mar. 1794	Congress passes the Navy Act of 1794, laying the basis for the U.S. Navy
5 June 1794	Declines a commission as one of the first six captains in the U.S. Navy
26 Sept. 1794	Presents the American flag to the French National Committee during the diplomatic recognition ceremony for the new Republic of France
1795	Appointed capitaine de vaisseau in the French navy
1796	Promoted to capitaine de vaisseau du premier
Dec. 1796	Visits Norfolk in command of the French frigates *Medusa* and *L'Insurgente*
7 July 1798	Start of the Quasi-War with France
2 July 1802	Leaves France for the United States
24 Dec. 1803	Attends wedding of Jérôme Bonaparte and Betsy Patterson
1806	Unsuccessfully seeks election to Congress from Baltimore City and County
4 July 1807	Offers services to President James Madison following *Chesapeake-Leopard* incident
25 July 1808	Anne Barney dies
24 Apr. 1809	Marries Harriet Coale
1810	Unsuccessfully seeks election to Congress from Baltimore City
Spring 1812	Moves to Anne Arundel County, Md.
18 June 1812	United States declares war on Great Britain
1813	Serves on committee that designs and orders the "star spangled banner"
20 Aug. 1813	Appointed acting master commander in the navy of the United States
26 Apr. 1814	Appointed a captain in the Flotilla Service of the U.S. Navy

10 June 1814	Barney's flotilla attacks British vessels of war
24 Aug. 1814	Severely wounded and captured at the Battle of Bladensburg
25 Aug. 1814	The British burn Washington
14 Sept. 1814	The British are repelled at the Battle of Baltimore
24 Dec. 1814	The Treaty of Ghent is signed
1 Dec. 1818	Dies near Pittsburgh, Pa.

Joshua Barney

❧ I ❧
MOLDING A MARINER

*J*oshua Barney assured his men that he knew navigation, how to use a quadrant, and how to do dead reckoning. The entire crew was older and probably more experienced than Barney, but they appeared either to have faith in the teenager's abilities or to admire his natural leadership qualities. The men grumbled a bit but, almost instinctively obeying orders, proceeded with their duties. The fifteen-year-old boy needed extraordinary courage because the January storms of the Atlantic were taking their toll. The barely seaworthy *Sidney* began to leak badly, almost coming apart at the seams. The men desperately worked the hand pumps and buckets to keep the ship afloat. Just as the merchant brig appeared certain to founder, it made its way past the Rock of Gibraltar and staggered into safe harbor. Continuing to Nice with the cargo would have to wait. The anchor splashed into the placid waters of the harbor, and Barney took a launch ashore to find assistance. The men left aboard pumped frantically under a capsized ensign hoisted as a signal of distress. Other vessels hastened to respond by sending fresh seamen to relieve the exhausted crew at the pumps and help jury-rig repairs.

In the middle of the eighteenth century, Great Britain's North American colonies were becoming partners in trade and an important source of raw materials and tax revenues for the king of England. Colonial society reflected that of Europe but had developed characteristics and cultural fabrics of its own as well. On the eve of the Revolution the colonies, like Great Britain, had several social classes. The lowest class was formed by the African slaves who worked in most of the colonies, including New England, but were concentrated in the South, where the labor-intensive plantation economy depended on them. Just above the slaves were English transported convicts or debtor immigrants from around the world. Most numerous of these indentured servants were the Irish, who were more easily trained and integrated into households because they shared the English language and many social and moral values. They worked hard for meager wages that went to pay for their transportation to America. Freedom from debt could be earned, but it took time. At the next level of society were sharecroppers, minor landowners, and migrant shellbacks with little education or social refinement. These poor farmers, fishermen, and sailors formed the closest thing America had to a peasant class. Above them was an emerging middle class comprised of merchants, shop-keepers, and artisans, people like Boston's Paul Revere and the Roosevelts of New York, who were highly skilled silversmiths to the wealthiest class. Members of the upper middle class owned large tracts of good land or were merchants who traded extensively. Their education and wealth gave them political influence. At the very top of the social ladder was a small, often European-educated aristocratic class that had extensive landholdings and considerable influence with the colonial governor and officials in London.

Joshua Barney was born on 6 July 1759 near Baltimore, Maryland, at that time a relatively poor village of only a few hundred people. The seaports on the Chesapeake Bay were just beginning to rise to prominence. Shipbuilding was becoming an important industry, and during the mid-eighteenth century shipwrights in Baltimore refined a French design to produce handsome, sleek, fast two-masted pilot schooners. These were the forerunners of the Baltimore clippers that won fame as privateer vessels and ultimately gave rise to the famous American clipper ships of the mid-nineteenth century. Barney's social status was solidly upper middle class, not far from the top layer of society. Each of his parents, William Barney and the former Frances Holland Watts, had inherited relatively prosperous farms, and thus the family had considerable landholdings. He was raised in the settlement on Bear Creek on Patapsco Neck, Maryland, as one of fourteen children. The family's farmhouse was built on the shore of one of the many inlets lining the Patapsco River, and Joshua's exposure to the water thus began very early in life. Although his family's wealth gave him a start toward financial security, Barney was to show a strong streak of independence. In 1769, at the age of ten, he wrote that he had "learnt everything that the [school] master could teach; wrote in a good hand and perfectly understood Arithmetic."[1] That observation may not be quite as arrogant as it seems, because many schoolmasters of the time had only limited education. They often moved from place to place, teaching in crude log structures that were poorly heated and ventilated and furnished with scanty educational tools. Out of frustration at the poor opportunities for education available to him, and displaying a sense of pragmatism beyond his years, Joshua made a considered decision and told his parents that he wanted to go to sea, eventually to become a shipmaster.

But the life of an ordinary young seaman was not for one of the class of the Barney family. As a prosperous farmer, William Barney probably considered such a life far beneath his son. Instead he arranged an apprenticeship to a Baltimore dry goods merchant. After only three months the merchant went out of business and the senior Barney then arranged to have his son work in a countinghouse in Alexandria, Virginia. Young Joshua knew that to succeed as a ship's captain he would need to be a skilled accountant and trader. On the other hand, he probably feared that a countinghouse would be a boring mercantile dungeon. He tried to please his father by toiling at the job for about a year, but at the Christmas holiday break in 1770 he decided that he had had enough and informed his parents that he would not return to the countinghouse. When the rebellious eleven-and-a-half-year-old reiterated his wish to go to sea, William Barney decided to let the obstinate youngster have his way. The hard life onboard a ship would either make a man of him or bring him to his senses. Thus, in 1771 the boy signed on as a hand aboard a pilot-boat schooner that plied the Chesapeake. Joshua was determined to make a success of this opportunity. A quick and energetic student, he learned to steer a course at the helm, sound the bottom, run out the log, raise and reef the sails, and generally mastered the rudiments of seamanship.

A variety of coastal trades flourished all along the eastern seaboard at this time. Timber, dried fish, and rum came from the North; agricultural products were brought up from the South; and molasses and sugarcane came in from the West Indies. This was also the era when pirates prowled the Caribbean as well as the Mediterranean. Those on the shore profited from salvaging wrecked ships and the occasional specie found in these hulks. Miserable, reeking slave ships cruised from the Guinea coast of Africa to the Chesapeake Bay to market their wretched cargo. By the early 1760s, East Coast ports were buzzing with mariners' complaints of harassment by the king's ships, humiliation from acts of maritime subservience, and what many considered unfair taxation. These seaports became the fecund breeding grounds for the revolution, and the receptive Joshua Barney absorbed the ideas he heard there.

After eight months as a pilot-schooner hand, young Joshua, now twelve, decided he was ready to cross the North Atlantic. An older sister had married Capt. Thomas Drysdale, the moody and often-domineering master of a small brig engaged in the Liverpool trade. Joshua, a likeable and spirited boy, persuaded his family to apprentice him to his hard-driving brother-in-law. Drysdale, who was a perceptive businessman, was quick to take advantage of the financial gain represented by having an unpaid family member as an apprentice mariner.

Barney's first trip to Liverpool in January 1772 onboard the diminutive brig proved a challenging initiation to life on the formidable North Atlantic Ocean. Apart from the loneliness that a young man might expect during the long separation from his family, he had to tolerate the dangers and indignities of a sailor's life at sea. Ships were swamped in heavy seas. Climbing rigging and manning the sails above a wildly pitching deck in an icy gale without safety devices was a terrifying chore. Life in the cramped forecastle (the forward living quarters near the ship's bow) among the aggressive, superstitious, and often ignorant sailors would have tested the will of even an older man. Packet ships traveled regular routes across the Atlantic carrying passengers, mail, and freight, which often included large amounts of dry food such as flour, salt, and sugar. Ships also carried extra sails, tarred rope, and spare masts, yards, and anchor cable; plus numerous barrels of water and salted meats. These bulky provisions took up a great deal of potential living space. The packet ships occasionally also had a chicken and duck coop for eggs, a cow or goat for milk, and pigs for fresh meat. The animals produced both a cacophony of sounds and a foul odor. The smell of bilge water, animal waste, rotting wood, and tarred hemp belowdecks vied with the odors of a particular cargo, and this plus the scurrying of rats in the dark made working in the hold a particularly unpleasant task. Finally, the sanitary facilities on eighteenth-century ships were extremely primitive. The seamen used leeward channels to urinate into the sea or clambered forward to the beakhead, or "the head," a wooden scaffold adjacent to the figurehead, to sit on one of the two or more boxes with holes in them to relieve themselves into the water below. These boxes were known as "seats of easement." Smaller ships had closetlike inboard heads (water closets) that required the use of a bucket of seawater to discharge waste through pipes into the sea. Bathing during the trip was at best rudimentary.

Seaman apprentice Barney was thoroughly battered by gales and ocean waves before he reached the welcome port in England. Captain Drysdale promptly sold the solidly built American brig at a profit, a not uncommon act after a Liverpool passage. The shipmaster and his charge then booked passage back to America on a Dublin packet filled to the gunwales with Irish redemptioners, people who had sold themselves into seven years of bondage in America to pay for their passage. The unfortunate passengers were confined below in the foul air of the hold, frequently under locked hatches. During this grueling two-month return voyage Barney worked as an unpaid member of the crew to continue honing his seamanship skills. When rumors emerged that an uprising was brewing among the passengers because of the terrible conditions, the captain placed armed sentries at the hatches, including Barney, to keep order until the ship reached the safety of Baltimore harbor. This was the young man's first exposure to controlling men by threatening the use of firearms.[2]

When Joshua Barney returned to Maryland in the late spring of 1772 he learned that his father, William, had died in a farming accident. Joshua, now thirteen, was thus forced to be even more dependent on his brother-in-law. After searching for employment along the Baltimore docks, Captain Drysdale was given the command of a substantial merchant brig, the *Sidney*, which he took on several voyages to Cádiz, Liverpool, and other ports in Europe. Barney's nautical skills advanced. When Joshua reached the age of fourteen, after a year working as a deckhand, Drysdale appointed him apprentice second mate. (This was also an inexpensive way to hire a second mate.) Because he was an apprentice, Barney's wages were to be retained by the ship's master, a legal ploy in the absence of child labor laws. Joshua eagerly accepted the responsible jobs of cargo and deck officer.

Just before Christmas, on 22 December 1774, the *Sidney* left Baltimore bound for Nice with a cargo of wheat. The ship sprung a leak off Virginia and had to put into Norfolk for repairs. Some of the cargo was damaged by the water, and this plus the profit lost in repairs meant the inevitable loss of the captain's quick temper. Drysdale quarreled with the first mate, who abruptly picked up his dunnage and left the ship. Christmas was a poor time to find a replacement, so the captain simply increased the duties of his teenaged second mate.

A few weeks into the Atlantic passage Drysdale became gravely ill with a fever of unknown origin. There were a few medicines onboard, but no one among the crew had enough medical knowledge to use them. The illness steadily worsened, and Drysdale died in his bunk in the captain's quarters. Joshua Barney's mentor, the husband of his sister, was buried at sea in a weighted shroud of sailcloth. The *Sidney*, now under the command of a teenaged boy, once again started to leak, but this time in the middle of the icy North Atlantic with an inexperienced crew and a perishable cargo. Logically Barney should have attempted to return by the shortest distance to Baltimore and salvage what he could. The fifteen-year-old skipper considered the alternatives and made the least rational choice. He resolved to complete the voyage to Nice and deliver the wheat to the consignees.

If command of a brig that was taking on water and a crew that was mostly his senior was not challenge enough, Barney's leadership soon met an additional test: a violent storm almost took the ship apart at its seams. After an exhausting round-the-clock effort at the bilge pumps by its crew, the *Sidney* limped into Gibraltar. Once the brig was able to drop anchor, crewmen from other ships rowed to their assistance and helped make repairs to the *Sidney*'s hull and keep it afloat. After many hours of heroic efforts, the *Sidney* was stabilized.

Barney had to petition the British Vice-Admiralty Court at Gibraltar for a damage survey of his ship before he could apply to local officials for permission to take his stricken vessel to Gibraltar's New Mole or King's Dock for an overhaul. Members of the court were astonished at Barney's story. Before them stood a teenaged apprentice who had taken over command of a transatlantic merchant vessel and crew and had survived a terrible storm. The ship was indeed in danger of sinking in their harbor, so the officials granted permission for the survey.[3] The *Sidney* was deemed salvageable, but the repairs would require months of work and many pounds sterling. The boy now faced a series of decisions. Should he take the advice of strangers, men who could easily take advantage of a young lad in a foreign port? Could he risk his men by going on to deliver his cargo at Nice in the leaky *Sidney*? Since he was not the captain who signed the original contract, what were his obligations to the owners in Baltimore and the consignees in Nice? If he could get a loan to make the repairs, how could he be sure of repaying the huge debt that was likely to ensue? Relying only on his warm personality and boyish charm, he made his decisions. Barney convinced the partners of Murray & Son, a Gibraltar commercial house, to lend him the then-prodigious sum of seven thousand pounds to cover dockyard expenses to get the *Sidney* in shape to complete its voyage. The British merchants expected repayment from the proceeds of the sale of the *Sidney*'s cargo in Nice and as security accepted a bottomry bond (a lien on the ship itself). This was an extremely generous and risky move on their part. Barney was legally a minor and not an official representative of the owners, who were unaware of Captain Drysdale's death. In a court of maritime law this bottomry note might be considered worthless.

The shipwrights and the crew finished refitting the ship in three months. The *Sidney* sailed for Nice with the junior Murray onboard as a fiduciary precaution ensuring repayment of the loan. In addition, Murray would protect the inexperienced Barney from the crafty merchants of Nice. At the time, Nice was under the flag of Sardinia and was renowned as one of the most difficult northern Mediterranean mercantile ports in which to do business.

Marine charts indicated that the harbor was too shallow to allow the *Sidney* to dock at the quay, so Barney went ashore by small boat to make contact with the receivers. The merchants who had ordered the wheat agreed to repay Murray & Son the seven-thousand-pound bottomry bond, and longshoremen began the tedious job of unloading the cargo into lighters in Villefranche, a small port a few miles east of Nice. As the grain warehouse started to fill, one of the merchants observed that Barney was a minor. This fact presented him with an opportunity to make a larger than expected profit. By international maritime law, Barney's signature on a receipt for the delivery of the freight was meaningless, and thus there was no need to pay him. When he learned of the merchants' intentions, the young shipmaster ordered his crew to seal the deck hatches. A confrontation was at hand. A mere apprentice mariner was defying influential Nice merchants! The merchants appealed to the governor of Nice, one of their countrymen, for a ruling, and, as expected, the provincial magistrate issued an order for Barney to resume unloading or face incarceration. The boy once again showed his spirit and refused to obey the order. An armed contingent of Sardinian soldiers arrested him and placed him in prison—the first of many imprisonments Barney would endure during his career at sea. The order stated that he was to be released without penalty only if he allowed the unloading to continue to the end, and there would be no payment to him or to Murray & Son when it was completed. This was morally intolerable, but as long as he was in prison Barney could do nothing about it. He desperately wanted to meet his obligation to the Gibraltar commercial house, so he agreed to accept the governor's terms . . . for the moment. After a delay in release as an attempt at intimidation, the young man was placed on parole and allowed to return to his ship. Once on the quarterdeck, Barney again ordered the holds sealed, then, in what turned out to be a brilliant tactic, defiantly hoisted the British ensign aloft for all the other ships in port to see. A well-armed force of infantry rowed to the anchorage site and challenged the small, unarmed crew. The Sardinian lieutenant in charge boisterously took command of the *Sidney*. Barney as captain strongly objected, stating that the troops had forcibly boarded the ship of a friendly sovereign nation and he was giving up command only because he feared for the safety of his crew. As he later wrote in his journal, he left the British "colors flying, that there may be no pretense hereafter of ignorance as to the nation to which this insult has been offered."[4]

The lieutenant, reconsidering his actions, became uneasy at assaulting a ship flying the Union Jack, symbol of the most powerful nation in Europe. He judiciously allowed Barney and his crew to gather their personal belongings and take their launch to another British vessel anchored nearby. Their fellow Englishmen received the deposed colonial seamen with great hospitality. Unfortunately, they were now men without a ship and under the charge of a novice captain who had incurred great debt with little hope of repaying it. At young Murray's suggestion, Barney decided to appeal to the British ambassador at the court of Sardinia in Milan. The road from Nice to Milan was one of the most formidable in eighteenth-century Europe, but Barney ignored the hardships of traveling it. His journal says only: "We crossed the famous Alps, so noted for snow and difficult travelling, on mules; we passed through part of Switzerland, and arrived at Milan."[5]

Sir William Lynch, minister of King George III in Sardinia, was a sympathetic and worldly man with a keen sense of justice; he was also apparently a man with a sense of drama as well as irony. With Mr. Murray in the background, the fifteen-year-old shipmaster from the colony of Maryland eloquently told his tale of being cheated and intimidated. The worst insult was the confiscation of a ship flying the British flag by an armed foreign contingent. Lynch was moved by Barney's story, and perhaps amused as well.

The ambassador quickly worded a strong letter of protest to the king of Sardinia, who immediately sent a royal courier over the same tortuous Alpine route to correct the series of misdeeds. When the courier returned with the news of his mission, Barney and Murray set out for Nice. On their arrival, the formerly arrogant governor ceremoniously greeted the teenager. With his cocked hat in hand, the regional administrator offered an effusive apology and the solicitude of his city. Barney was immediately given the promised seven thousand pounds sterling plus a generous reimbursement for expenses incurred on his journey to Milan. In fact, the governor suggested that Captain Barney might wish to propose a sum as an indemnity for the indignity suffered at his hands. Barney enjoyed the obvious discomfiture of the governor but refused any financial compensation. This, of course, made the magistrate even more uncomfortable because he desperately needed to regain the confidence of his king in Milan. Exuding personal charm, the governor persuaded Barney to write a letter absolving him of any future complaint on this matter. The young man did as requested, but one can image that he basked in the comic opera scene he had created.

After meeting with the governor, Barney's next order of business was to repay Murray & Son and to send the junior Murray, now a friend and fellow adventurer, back to Gibraltar. The captains of the British ships anchored in Nice, aware of the turn of events, made Barney the hero of the port, inviting him to many dinners and bestowing other maritime honors. It was reported that he participated in these celebrations with great modesty. In fact, Barney deported himself so well that the governor invited him to dine the evening before he set sail from Nice. Typical shipmasters spend their entire careers without achieving celebrity among their peers. Joshua Barney was obviously not going to be a typical shipmaster.

Additional profit for the voyage lay in finding a cargo for the *Sidney*'s return trip to North America. Barney decided that his next port of call would be Alicante, Spain, a southwesterly sail from Nice. The Alicante harbor was crowded with shipping of all sorts as the *Sidney* dropped anchor. Elegant two-deck warships gently swayed on tidal swells, their awnings spread and their gun ports open to catch any breeze for ventilation. Agile frigates together with schooners, brigs, sloops, supply ships, and a whole collection of small craft lay scattered in the anchorage as countless oared boats plied their way between vessels like so many water beetles. The Americans had never seen such an imposing concentration of warships, transports, and support ships. The quay seemed to vibrate with excitement.

The hurried activity signaled an expedition against the dey of Algiers, a leader of the Barbary corsairs who plagued the Mediterranean and its Atlantic approaches during much of the eighteenth century. Villainous sailors from the North African states of Algiers, Tunis, Tripoli, and Morocco captured ships, passengers, and sailors of non-Muslim nations. A Tripolian official justified the singular savagery of these pirates by noting that according to the local interpretation of the laws of the Prophet as written in the Koran, all nonbelievers were sinners. It was the right and duty of every Muslim to make war on them wherever they were found, and to make slaves of the prisoners.[6] The pirates' custom was to hold wealthy prisoners for ransom. Those who could not pay for their freedom were sent into slavery, often to row in the galley of a corsair. The corsairs preyed particularly on the merchant ships of nations that were either without great naval strength or unwilling or unable to pay tribute. Great Britain was a great naval power but paid tribute anyway to protect the trading vessels of its empire, perhaps believing that the corsairs played a useful role in keeping down competition by merchants of other nations.

Charles III of Spain had recently concluded that the corsairs were intolerable and ordered a campaign against Algiers, then the most aggressive of the four Barbary States. At Charles's orders an Irish mercenary, Gen. Count Alejandro O'Reilly, had assembled an army of thirty thousand for the invasion.[7] Spain needed ships to transport the troops and their supplies, however, so every ship that chanced into port was asked to serve the crown of Spain. Barney and the crew of the *Sidney* were offered a generous lease for use of their vessel, with no choice of refusal. In essence, the king of Spain impressed the ship and its crew. Joshua Barney, the young captain from Baltimore, was to take his orders from a Spanish flagship. In spite of the humiliation of impressment, the teenager was thrilled to be part of the huge convoy of gilded ships resplendent with colorful pennants, confident with their heavy armament, and aflame with the adrenaline needed to fight the impending battle.

On 1 July 1775, a few days before Barney's sixteenth birthday, the Spanish invasion fleet sailed from Alicante for the Bay of Algiers. The American Revolution had broken out at Lexington and Concord less than three months before, but events in North America were unknown to the assembled fleet. The whole length of the beach twinkled with lights from ships lying behind the cables off their bows. Every new arrival extended the array in what appeared as an infinite line.

But more than manpower and arms are required to win a land battle. The essential elements also include intelligence about the enemy, a simple plan, surprise, discipline, and an ability to maneuver on the field. A seaborne invasion also needs about a threefold numerical superiority in manpower. Unfortunately, the leaders of the Spanish force were ill prepared. After the armada arrived off Algiers, the flag officer, Adm. Don Pedro González de Castejón, and O'Reilly wrangled over their combined operation plan for a week. The element of surprise was lost. The Moors used this time to organize one hundred thousand troops to interdict the landing. After a naval bombardment of the shore, small boats began transporting contingents of infantry toward the beach. O'Reilly made the grave error of not providing sufficient ammunition for his men. Perhaps even more egregious was O'Reilly's failure to gather military intelligence concerning the strength and disposition of the enemy. The amphibious troops were rowed ashore in two separate divisions. The first wave met little resistance from the Algerians, who allowed the mercenaries to advance rapidly on the city of Algiers. In fact, the Algerians' retreat was a ploy designed to draw the attackers into a trap. The Moorish cavalry lying in wait counterattacked and swept down on the unfortunate troops. O'Reilly's troops retreated to the shore where the second division was in the process of landing, creating chaos. The men floundered on the beach in pathetic disarray. Turbaned men on horseback hacked at the confused soldiers before they could effectively reorganize. Within minutes the Algerian sand was stained with the blood of the hapless invaders. O'Reilly's entire force might have been annihilated except for the discipline and courage of a veteran Hibernian regiment. These fresh troops covered the first landed troops so that they could entrench, but the Algerian cannons and mortars found new enfilade positions. Eventually the remnants of the invaders were forced to evacuate to the waiting ships, leaving behind their dead and wounded. The Moors collected both the dead and the wounded and burned them all in a huge, sparking, smoky pyre on the shore. The carnage and the screams from those being burned alive spread fear among the Spanish troops waiting on the decks of the transports, even though they were a safe distance from the beach. Decimated by a well-prepared and numerically superior foe, O'Reilly's troops were forced to abandon the invasion and return to Spain.

On returning to Alicante with a portion of the battered remnants of Count O'Reilly's forces, Barney and the *Sidney* were given a lucrative cargo for their cooperation and trouble. After a brief layover in Gibraltar to visit the Murray family, Barney set out to recross the Atlantic. It was a long westerly passage, largely to windward, but it was respectably swift; as the sailors of the day would say, "the girls had hold of the tow-rope." As the *Sidney* approached land, a long cape appeared to larboard. A veil of cloud turned the distant flat Capes into smudged watercolors fading into an indistinct sky. The headland on the western shore reflected the sounds of the solemnly rhythmic tide. Beyond it lay the bay that cleaved the landmass of the Chesapeake, where the water seemed paler and more serene.

The *Sidney* reached the welcome shores of the Chesapeake on 1 October 1775, but not without one more disturbance. The British sloop-of-war *Kingfisher* intercepted the merchant brig and sent over a boarding party that treated Barney and his crew rudely. The king's men confiscated their firearms, thoroughly searched the ship, and examined all the ship's private papers. When the indignant young captain asked the reason for such a breach of maritime courtesy, he was informed about the Battles of Lexington and Concord that had taken place in April and the more recent June battle on Bunker Hill in Massachusetts. As representatives of George III, the naval officers had orders to suppress the rebellion now spreading throughout the colonies. Barney had favored American independence since his days on the pilot schooner, but he betrayed none of his delight to the British lieutenant. The *Sidney* was allowed to proceed to Baltimore because that port city had not yet joined the rebellion.[8]

After tying up to the wharf in front of Baltimore's familiar brick houses and wooden steepled churches, Barney made his way to the office of John Smith, the owner of the *Sidney*. Mr. Smith had heard nothing from the *Sidney* since it sailed in December under the command of Thomas Drysdale. Now, eight months later, before him stood an unusually mature lad of sixteen who claimed to be the master of his ship. When the boy identified himself as Joshua Barney, Smith recalled that the ship had an apprentice second mate by that name and asked what had happened to Captain Drysdale. Barney briefly related the events of the last eight months and placed the ship's log and other documents on the table before him. The owner likely read and reread the log of the unusual voyage, periodically looking up at the young man before him as he read. Mary Barney's biography of her father-in-law relates that in the end Smith welcomed the young man home with a warm smile and a hearty handshake. The shipowner said that he was proud of the lad's accomplishments and, indeed, pleased to have him in his employ.

~❧ 2 ❧~

THE CONTINENTAL NAVY

B y the middle of the eighteenth century the American colonies were developing an identity of their own and increasingly challenging the king's authority. In 1776, a perplexed Englishman described a strange flag that had lately appeared on the seas representing the United Colonies: "It is not probable that another instance can be found in the history of nations, where a revolting people placed upon their standard the emblem of the nation against which they were contending. It was a peculiar flag indeed; the thirteen stripes were emblematic of the union of the colonies, and the subjoined crosses represent the still-recognized sovereignty of England."[1]

With the death of Capt. Thomas Drysdale, Joshua Barney was no longer bound by maritime law to be an apprentice. He had passed the test of command and had excellent prospects as a merchant captain in the employ of Mr. Smith. However, the thought of joining the rebellion as a Continental naval officer was more intriguing than carrying cargo along familiar shipping lanes—lanes the British had begun to blockade to govern colonial commerce.

British, and to a lesser extent American, naval forces were vital in maintaining political control of territory. At the time of the Revolutionary

War, North American population centers were concentrated at seaports or on navigable rivers. Agricultural products were exported and manufactured products were imported by ship, making sea-lanes, estuary bays, and river channels the highways of commerce. By regulating these areas of transport the British could readily control much of the American economy and collect taxes to support the colonial government. On land, they were less successful. British officials had to travel on roads that were rutted in mud and rough from log and stone paving. Axles broke, carts overturned, and hitches frayed, limiting the size of the loads that could be carried. Most roads were little more than enlarged trails winding through dense forests that offered excellent cover for ambush. Control of sea-lanes and supply routes was the key to British control of the vast mainland. In order to subjugate the individual colonies militarily, King George's army commanded harbors with forts on promontories. Large, heavily armed warships, supplemented by a flotilla of smaller shallow-draft ships such as brigs, cutters, schooners, galleys, lugs, and barges placed in small waterways, interdicted movements of supplies to the rebel troops. In 1774, Lord Barrington, His Majesty's secretary of war, wrote, "A conquest by land is unnecessary when a country can be reduced first by distress, then to obedience, by our Marine."[2] Naval warfare played a significant role in the American victory, but, paradoxically, the Americans made only minor contributions to warfare at sea.

Before the Civil War, the people referred to *these* United States instead of *the* United States. Colonies or states had a great deal of autonomy. The individual colonies and their new national government, the Continental Congress, had little in the way of a navy. In fact, the colonies developed a conjoint American navy that combined individual colonial or state forces with one provided by the Continental Congress. In 1776, at the time the Continental Congress declared America's independence from Britain, the Continental navy listed 25 vessels mounting 422 guns. The British navy had 112 vessels that carried 3,714 guns; 78 of these ships mounting 2,078 guns were stationed along the coast of North America.[3] Many were ships of the line, large sailing ships that were used to fight in a line, the usual fleet tactic of that period. Ships fought in a line of battle, in single file, so their broadsides could have maximum effect. This strategy assumed that all the ships in the line would be able to sail at the about the same speed and hold the same course in the wind and current.

It also assumed that the ships would be equally armed so that no ship would be forced to fight a better-armed enemy.

Cannons were classified by the weight of the cannonball that each fired, ranging from 3 to 42 pounds; small swivel guns fired a half-pound charge; and carronades, short-range heavy weapons, were generally 32- or 68-pounders. The largest guns had a range of more than two thousand yards, about a mile. An exception was the long-barreled 6-pounder called "Long Tom," which fired a relatively light projectile well over a mile as harassment fire.

The conduct of naval engagements had become as standardized as the cannons. While the two lines of fighting ships engaged, frigates and smaller ships stationed behind the line of battle carried messages, repeated signals, picked up survivors clinging to wreckage, and pursued or harassed other enemy frigates if they tried to escape. That being understood, there was a gentleman's agreement that, during fleet actions, ships of the line did not fire on frigates. If a single ship of the line happened on a frigate and was fired on by that frigate, however, a one-on-one contest could properly ensue.

The tactics of the day matched ship for ship and cannon for cannon. Therefore, the idea of building an American navy to fight the enormous British navy was, as Samuel Chase of Maryland said, "the maddest Idea in the World."[4] Despite such opposition, the Second Continental Congress passed legislation to create a navy on 13 October 1775. By the end of the year this "Continental navy" consisted of two ships, four brigs, three schooners, and five sloops, plus several small merchant vessels that could be converted to carry cannons as well. These vessels were supposed to bridge the gap until a specially built squadron of thirteen ships—five with thirty-two guns, five with twenty-eight guns, and three with twenty-four guns—that the Congress had authorized in December 1775 was completed. The American merchant and fishing fleets contributed skilled seamen who had an intimate knowledge of the local waters but knew little about naval military skills and discipline. The colonists did have a small cadre of privateers, some of whom had served under letters of marque during the French and Indian War. In 1776 Congress licensed 136 privateers; by 1781 the number had swelled to 449. Various individual states licensed even more, and the ships and sailors of the "naughty privateer navy" were to prove crucial to the limited American success at sea during the Revolution.

Although the odds against the Americans seemed insurmountable, the British found themselves militarily stretched at the time. His Majesty had a large army to transport across a hazardous sea and distribute at strategic positions, and ultimately to reinforce and provision with food and munitions. This had to be done in an environment that was mostly hostile to the British. Ironically, most members of the British military stationed in North America considered the Americans to be sensible Englishmen who were more likely to opt for a political rather than a military resolution to the rebellion. As of January 1775, the British had just twenty-four vessels stationed in North American waters. Only four carried forty-eight guns or more, the largest being the seventy-gun *Boyne* stationed at Boston. While trying to subdue its rebellious colonies Britain became involved in naval struggles with France in 1778, Spain in 1779, and Holland in 1780. The French employed a navy of about one hundred ships of the line against the British in the American Revolution; the Spanish, seventy-seven; and the Dutch, forty-two. The need to fight these warships limited the number of vessels that could be spared to protect British interests in the vast, sparsely populated North American eastern seaboard. With the British thus fighting on multiple fronts, the Americans engaged them more easily on the sea of their choosing.

The creation of a Continental navy presented numerous problems to the Continental Congress. Capital had to be raised; a naval command system organized; ships designed and built; arms, munitions, and supplies purchased and manufactured; and, most important, trained manpower found to operate the vessels. The acquisition of experienced warrior seamen was the most difficult problem. Many of the first officers appointed to positions of command gained their status because they had political, economic, or familial ties to the Congress; leadership and seamanship skills were not considered of primary importance. This initial lack of good officers accounted for the budding navy's dearth of success compared with that of the Continental army. The latter had veterans who had fought in the French and Indian War. They knew British land tactics, and some were proficient in handling field weapons. These army officers provided leadership, and, if not winning decisive victories, they were clever enough to avoid a military disaster and hold their own against formidable odds. The maritime counterparts to these officers were the ex-privateers mentioned earlier. Privateers depended on surprise and the clever use of swift, maneuverable vessels. They avoided prolonged firefights because they were usually vulnerable in such situations. Instead, they depended on ingenuity, boldness, and good seamanship for victory. Against the most formidable navy in the world these traits would provide an advantage, but were they sufficient to bring victory?

An officer trying to earn a commission through the ranks in the fledgling American navy rather than procuring one through connections had an additional problem. There was a distinct pecking order among the colonies. In maritime affairs, the opinions of the strong New England colonies prevailed, and Yankee sea captains received most of the high-ranking command positions in the navy. John Paul Jones, a Scottish immigrant, had difficulty achieving high rank in the command system because he was considered a Virginian, a southerner and sojourner. The relatively middle class Joshua Barney from not very influential Maryland faced a similar problem.

It was service in the Continental navy, not in a privateer, that attracted Joshua Barney, so the young man traveled north to Philadelphia, the capital of the new nation and headquarters of the new navy. Lacking the political contacts needed to obtain an officer's commission, he explored the opportunities for a billet on the Delaware River waterfront. Impressed by Barney's experience and enterprise, the captain of the newly converted pilot schooner *Wasp* offered him the post of second mate. Capt. William Hallock, an immigrant from Bermuda and commander of the smaller ten-gun converted sloop *Hornet,* also needed an experienced man and sought Barney's service as master's mate. Sixteen-year-old Barney quickly accepted the higher rank, making him second in command to the captain, and was given the critical job of recruiting a crew, preferably in Baltimore. Armed with confidence from his recent voyage to the Mediterranean, Barney returned to his home port and began recruiting in a tavern frequented by sailors. Master's Mate Joshua Barney was the very symbol of a rebel leader: a handsome, enthusiastic recruiter in a public house on the waterfront of a town increasingly excited by the idea of revolution.

Barney had a singular, almost preordained relationship with the American flag during his life. His first encounter with it is related in a biography written by his daughter-in-law, Mary Barney: "Fortunately for his [Barney's] purpose, just at that moment a new American flag, sent by Commodore Hopkins for the service of the *Hornet,* arrived in Philadelphia—nothing could have been more opportune or acceptable.

It was the first American standard that had been seen in the colony of Maryland; and the next morning at sunrise, Barney had the enviable opportunity of unfurling it to the music of drums and fifes, and hoisting it on a staff planted with his hand at the door of his rendezvous."[5] During his later years Barney was fond of recounting the patriotic stir the new flag created. It had thirteen alternating red and white stripes, signifying the united thirteen colonies. In the corner was a canton of the combined crosses of Saint George and Saint Andrew. It was, in reality, the red British maritime merchant ensign with six horizontal white stripes oversewn on it to make thirteen stripes. The white stripes were to indicate a separation or independence from the mother country. This prototype of the American ensign was known as the flag of Grand Union. Barney claimed that showing the "Rebel Colors" was very effective in creating enthusiasm among those lining up to sign the articles for a cruise on the *Hornet.*

Barney was successful in recruiting a full crew for the *Hornet,* most of them with experience at sea as packetmen, coastal sailors, or fishermen. The master's mate and his crew boarded the sloop as it rode motionless above the twin of its own reflection, the ship's rattlesnake— "Don't Tread on Me"—ensign a patch of brilliant yellow against the pale blue sky. On 3 December 1776, John Paul Jones raised the new ensign, the Grand Union flag, to the masthead of the *Alfred.* A month later the *Alfred, Andrea Doria, Cabot,* and *Columbus* dropped down Delaware Bay to Reedy Island, where they were joined by the *Providence* and the *Fly.* Proceeding to Cape Henlopen, they rendezvoused with the *Hornet* and its sister ship-of-war, the schooner *Wasp,* on 13 February. With this humble armada of eight small vessels assembled, Commodore Esek Hopkins set sail for the Bahamas on 17 February.

A short narrative from Barney's autobiography gives what many secondary sources quote as an eyewitness account of the Americans' encounter with the British there: "We sailed together, and our rendezvous was at the Islands of Abico, [on arriving there] we proceeded directly to New Providence. The town & Fort surrendered to us with the ships & Vessels in the harbor, without making any resistance we secured all the cannon, Morter shells &c, that was there, and left the island. On return we had bad weather."[6] In fact, naval records of the time indicate that the *Hornet* collided with the *Fly* at sea before reaching the Bahamas and that both vessels missed the action at New Providence. Barney, who was aboard the *Hornet*, did not actually participate in the capture of the forts or town; however, his description of the operation is basically sound.

New Providence, the capital of the Bahamas, was in fact a small village sprawled along the water's edge behind Hog Island. Two forts guarded it: Montagu on the eastern shore and Nassau to the west. Most of the gunpowder was stored in Fort Nassau and protected by a civilian militia. The British military had been withdrawn except for one naval schooner, the *St. John*, which was careened for repairs. The American fleet of six vessels dropped anchor near the eastern end of the island and put ashore 250 sailors and marines in the first amphibious assault in U.S. history. After the Americans fired on the bulwark of Fort Montagu, the British answered by firing a few 18-pound shot that inflicted no damage. In short order a British officer of the fort came outside under a flag of truce to ask the commander of the American force who they were and what they intended. The British militia leader decided that shedding blood would serve no purpose and surrendered, and the Americans spent the night in the fort. Meanwhile, the British governor, Montfort Browne, became aware of the American threat. He ordered the captain of the merchant sloop *Mississippi Packet* to jettison his cargo of lumber and, under cover of darkness, load 162 barrels of Fort Nassau's gunpowder onboard for shipment to St. Augustine. The sloop successfully eluded capture by crossing a treacherous sandbar and avoiding the small American fleet. When Commodore Hopkins came ashore on 4 March he learned that the main target of the expedition, the gunpowder, was no longer there. Nevertheless, according to the log of the *Andrea Doria*, the Americans loaded "large Quantitys of Shel & Shott, 16 Morters of different Sizes: 30 Cask of powder & some Provisions fifty two cannon Eighteens twenty fore & Thirty two pounders loaded with Foynd Shott Double headed & Grape & several other Articles."[7]

The American fleet set sail for home on 16 March 1776 with its prizes and three prisoners: Governor Browne and two local officials. The *Hornet*, crippled from its collision with the *Fly*, made for the South Carolina coast with Barney onboard. As the badly damaged ship attempted to get past the sandbars off Charleston, the weather drove it out to sea. The *Hornet* finally arrived off the Cape of Delaware on 1 April 1776, and a pilot boat led the vessel to a place where its crew could make temporary repairs.

Barney had grave doubts about the courage of Captain Hallock, a deeply religious man who frequently sang hymns to himself and prayed but was slow in making decisions. His suspicions were soon confirmed. A pilot informed the Americans that the British frigate *Roebuck* was anchored in the roads while one of its tenders cruised near the Capes taking lesser-armed merchant ships as prizes. The pilot noted that this tender was vulnerable because it had fewer men and cannons than the *Hornet*. By destroying the tender the Americans could protect American merchant ship interests in the area. With the *Hornet* now repaired, Hallock carefully entered the bay. The king's tender quickly noticed what appeared to be a disabled American merchant sloop and promptly closed to engage and plunder it. The *Hornet* looked like easy prey. Its guns had been run inboard because of the recent bad weather and the ship looked like the merchant sloop it had once been. Barney kept as few crewmen as possible visible on deck to complete the deceptive picture. The rest hid behind the bulwarks next to their gun tackles, ready to surprise the enemy at close quarters. Just before the British were in range for a barrage, Captain Hallock descended from the poop. According to Barney, "I was running out our Guns & had a match in my hand to fire at her when our Captain order[ed] me not to fire as he had no inclination of *shedding blood*!!! when the tender immediately sheered off, by which means she escaped us, & our Captain was regarded by all on board as a Coward, indeed he had for several weeks before been constantly inclined to praying & to a religious turn."[8] Hallock abruptly fled the scene to escape Barney's wrath, but by now the tender had realized that the sloop was not as innocent as it appeared and turned out of harm's way to go in search of easier prey. The captain did not reappear from his cabin after being humiliated by his teenaged master's mate. The crew and lesser officers sided with Barney, and he assumed de facto command of the little ten-gun *Hornet* as it headed up Delaware Bay bound for home. Once the anchor was set in the harbor of Philadelphia, the pious Captain Hallock left the ship sitting on his sea chest with his hymnal in hand. Barney, who was now certain that the captain was a coward who would be unable to lead in the face of hostility, looked for an opportunity to transfer to another ship. After three weeks at anchor, the *Hornet* was brought into the shipyards for much-needed final repairs.

Barney still hoped to obtain a lieutenant's commission in the naval service, so he kept to himself his feelings about the cowardly Hallock, for such criticism might damage his career. Barney knew that he could not continue to serve under Hallock, so he asked to be transferred to the schooner *Wasp,* whose commander, Charles Alexander, a Scotsman, had a reputation as a fine seaman and courageous gentleman. According to its log, the *Hornet* was in Philadelphia 7–17 April 1776 with Barney still under the command of Hallock. Alexander was commissioned captain of the *Wasp* on 18 April and immediately set sail. Thus Barney's transfer must have been immediate.

After escorting a merchant ship bound for Europe out into the Atlantic, the *Wasp* returned to Delaware Bay with two British frigates, the *Roebuck* and the *Liverpool,* following close behind. The *Liverpool* gave chase to the much smaller but more maneuverable and shallower-draft *Wasp.* In order to elude the powerful enemy, Captain Alexander sailed the *Wasp* close to the poorly charted shore, a tactic that more than once would be effective against the British in the shoal-ridden bay. In short order the *Liverpool* struck a sandbar and had to wait for the next tide to float it free. Meanwhile the *Wasp* made for the safety provided by the Cape May Channel and two other American vessels, the brig *Lexington* under the command of John Barry and the *Surprise* under Capt. Lambert Wickes, avoiding a mismatch against the remaining British frigate.

After the next tide change, a lookout aboard the *Lexington* spotted the brig *Nancy* with all sails set being pursued by the *Liverpool.* The brig carried a precious cargo of arms and munitions, so the three small American ships felt compelled to disregard their own safety and charged to the rescue. Suddenly, the sails of the frigate *Roebuck* appeared on the horizon. The master of the *Nancy* saw that his ship could probably not elude capture, but thought he might save his cargo if he ran the ship aground close to shore. This he did, and the three American warships lowered small boats to help with the unloading. The *Wasp* had the shallowest draft of the trio of vessels and sailed close to the *Nancy.* The two British frigates wisely stayed in the deeper water of the center of the channel, delivering heavy cannon fire against the stationary targets. The Americans suffered heavy damage; an officer on the *Lexington* was killed and several crewmen were wounded.

Despite the rain of grapeshot, the Americans managed to transfer the greater part of the powder, bales, small arms, and kegs into the small boats and began hauling the vital supplies ashore. The British responded by sending their tenders filled with sailors and Royal Marines to capture the *Nancy* and what was left of its cargo. Captain Barry, in charge of a launch from the *Wasp* and the most senior officer present, ordered his

men to spill powder into the hold of the *Nancy,* light a slow fuse incon-
spicuously, and evacuate the doomed brig. The British bluejackets and
marines boarded and sent up a loud cheer, thereby announcing to their
mother ships that they had taken possession of the prize. As the British
seamen started a search of the spar deck and after cabin, the *Nancy* blew
apart with a deafening roar and disappeared within a white cloud punctuated by a flash of orange flame. Blasted spars, rigging, sections of timber, and deck planking whirled about. The ripple of the shock wave from
the explosion rolled across the water toward the assembled vessels like a
miniature typhoon. When the smoke cleared and the flying debris settled, little remained to be seen except charred flotsam.

In the confusion that followed, the swift *Wasp* escaped to the shallow
inlet of Wilmington Creek, but was still trapped. The frigates dared not
enter the uncharted shoals, and the *Wasp* dared not leave them. Joined by
the small brig *Betsy,* the British set up a blockade and waited for the
chance to take their revenge. Overnight, word of the entrapment of Captain Alexander and his schooner reached Commo. John Hazelwood of the
Pennsylvania State navy, who ordered a flotilla of galleys (armed barges
with sails and oars) to the mouth of Wilmington Creek to harass the
anchored British frigates. The ample draft of the frigates and the shoal-
laden water at the mouth of the creek affected the action. The keel of the
Roebuck came perilously close to the muddy bottom. According to Capt.
Andrew Snape Hammond's entry in the *Roebuck*'s log for 9 May 1776: "We
gave them chase immediately with all our Sail, and they as industriously
plied their Oars and Sails to avoid us: it falling little wind we were not able
to stem the ebb tide, and not having 6 inches water more than the ship
drew in the best ship channel . . . I was under the necessity of anchoring:
The Galleys rowed to a point of Land on the Western Shore and Anchored
also."[9] The *Roebuck* signaled its intentions to the *Liverpool,* and the *Betsy*
anchored nearby as protection. In the darkness of night and heavy fog, the
Wasp attempted to sneak past the three British ships. As the dawn burned
the fog into wisps, the tide changed. There was enough water in the channel to allow the *Roebuck* to raise anchor. In doing so, the British frigate
found itself abreast of the fleeing rebel schooner. Barney's journal records
his part in the events that followed. The *Roebuck* "immediately got underway & commenced firing at us, we received a heavy fire from her for near
one hour at half a miles distance, but she did us little or no damage; we by
rowing, sailing & towing got past the enemy & Joined the Gallies, which

had for some time been engaged; the action continued all day, the ships were much cut up, some Gallies could not come into action for want of men, I volunteered with a number of our men & went on board one of them, when she was rowed up to the Enemy the action became warm & the enemy were drove down before us as low at New Castle. Much might be said respecting this action, it was generally believed that the *Roebuck* might have been destroyed, whilst aground in the night by our fire vessels, but no attempt was made. . . . All the honour that was acquired in these two days was given to our little schooner."[10] This action would later be depicted in a painting by Irwin John Bevan.

After the *Roebuck* hoisted its sails to pursue the *Wasp,* Captain Hammond ordered the gunners to fire a broadside. The recoil from the blast retarded the frigate's forward motion, and the accompanying shroud of smoke from the burned powder temporarily blinded the gunners on the British ship. The *Wasp* took advantage of these two events and outran the much larger *Roebuck.* The British ship could do no more than fire its smaller bow-chaser cannons, which had a range of only half a mile. The gunners watched helplessly as their spent shot plunged harmlessly astern of the American vessel. The *Wasp* reached the cover of Commodore Hazelwood's galleys, which were now rowing into the bay. The galleys mounted relatively heavy cannons, while the *Wasp* was equipped with small-caliber weapons that were almost useless against a British frigate. Nevertheless, Captain Alexander stayed close to the galleys to offer assistance. The *Liverpool* weighed anchor in order to maneuver into an offensive position. After the rebel galleys had engaged the British frigates, Alexander noticed that the brig *Betsy,* which had not received the harassing cannon fire, was not joining the fight. Alexander confidently sailed directly at the vessel, subtly changed course to swoop alongside, interlocked the *Betsy* with grapples, and stormed aboard with Barney and a heavily armed boarding party of thirty men. The *Betsy* capitulated after a short struggle. A prize crew sailed the captured brig into Wilmington Creek and out of the reach of the British frigates. There the men watched from the shrouds supporting the *Betsy*'s masts as the distant British ships edged in as close as they dared.

The open-decked galleys were effective in keeping the frigates out in the bay, although their crews and armament suffered tremendous losses. Nevertheless, the galleys were in surprisingly good condition. Barney, as he noted in his diary, asked permission to take some gun crews from the

Wasp and reinforce one of the galleys that had dropped out of the fight. Alexander agreed, and Barney's galley attacked one of the frigates with renewed vigor. The beleaguered frigates had had enough of the two-day battle. They retreated to the relative safety of a point off Newcastle, temporarily abandoning the blockade of the small river because of the nuisance caused by the bold and aggressive behavior of the Americans in small boats.

Barney and his men remained with the flotilla of galleys until they reached Philadelphia. The brilliant tactics of the *Wasp,* the crew's valor in the *Nancy* incident, the capture of the *Betsy,* and the unselfish aid given to the stricken galleys made Alexander, his officers, and his men heroes of the fledgling navy. Captain Alexander made special mention of the meritorious conduct of Master's Mate Barney in his report of the conflict and urged that Barney be promoted. Soon afterward the sixteen-year-old lad was transferred to the sloop *Sachem* and ordered to supervise its refitting for naval duty.

A short time later Barney received a letter formally requesting him to report to financier Robert Morris, the president of the Marine Committee and one of the wealthiest of the patriots. He presented himself in Morris's office and took a seat across from the polished desk. Barney recorded what happened next in his memoir. "Mr. Morris after asking my name put his hands in his pocket & pulled out a paper which was a Commission as Lieutenant in the Navy (June 1776) which he gave me observing that the Committee had been informed of my good behavior at the Battle in the Delaware & that if I continued to act as I had done, he would always be my friend & should be happy to serve me (which has ever done)."[11] The avuncular Morris had found a protégé, and Barney had found a benefactor.

Like most ambitious young seamen, Barney probably had fantasized about receiving a lieutenant's commission, but the reality of its receipt may have engendered some anxiety. He was a month shy of seventeen and had been appointed to what was then the second-highest nonflag rank in the Continental navy, there being no grades between lieutenant and captain in those days. Further, he was not at all sure that he would ever be given a command. There was a shortage of American naval ships and an abundance of men with strong political connections applying for naval commissions. If a town or state raised money to build a ship, its leaders could influence the naming of the ship's officer contingent.

Shipbuilding in Maryland was still in its infancy, however, and few of the state's leaders were maritime-minded. It was, in fact, quite remarkable that a politically "unconnected" young man such as Barney had obtained a commission in the Continental navy at all.

Aboard the sloop *Sachem*, commanded by Capt. Isaiah Robinson, Lt. Joshua Barney first served as executive officer. The vessel had been a tender in the Royal Navy before its capture by John Barry on 17 April. After being taken into the Continental navy, the *Sachem* was ordered to sea patrol on 2 July 1776, only a few days before Barney's seventeenth birthday and two days before the signing of the Declaration of Independence. The first copy of the historic document was printed in the *Pennsylvania Evening Post* two days after the *Sachem* sailed. Without their knowledge, the officers and crew now sailed for a self-declared independent nation. A few days out of port the *Sachem* met the armed British merchant brig *Two Friends* en route from Antigua to New York with a cargo of sugar and rum.[12] The two evenly matched ships slugged at each other with cannon fire for more than two hours until the outlines of their masts and tattered sails were barely visible through the drifting smoke. By clever seamanship and raw courage both vessels survived, but each was badly damaged. The British brig suffered the worst from the encounter. Splintered and dismasted, it lost half of its crew to the Americans' fire and was forced to surrender. The crippled *Sachem* counted six men dead and more than twenty wounded. Robinson and Barney were the only officers left alive. The British brig's cargo of rum helped lessen the pain of the wounded on both sides of the action. In fact, little of the liquor made it back to Philadelphia. The *Two Friends* also carried a green sea turtle in its hold with the name of Lord North, the prime minister of Great Britain, carved on its shell. Barney took possession of this prize as a special gift for Robert Morris.

With Robinson wounded, Barney took command of the *Sachem* and its prize and ordered the two damaged vessels lashed together to form a large raft. After they made their way back through an ineffective blockade to Philadelphia, arriving on 7 September, Robinson and Barney were rewarded with transfers to a larger naval warship, the fourteen-gun brig *Andrea Doria*.

In a letter to Silas Deane dated 23 October 1776, Marine Committee members wrote that they wished to send the *Andrea Doria* to St. Eustatius, a Dutch colony, with a dispatch to be forwarded to William Bingham at Martinico. The voyage would prove to be a historic one.[13] Holland, Portugal, Denmark, and Austria generally forbade their subjects to supply contraband to the revolting colonies at the start of the Revolution. The Dutch government, generally pro-British, publicly condemned the Declaration of Independence and sympathized with Britain's efforts to extinguish the insurrection. On 20 March 1775 the States General, at the behest of the British, issued a proclamation prohibiting the export of munitions from Dutch harbors (European and colonial) to any vessel flying the English flag except by special license. This act was designed to prevent American ships, which were still technically British and thus allowed to fly the British flag, from purchasing arms for the rebellion. The embargo was to last for six months and was designed to cut America's supply of arms and to appease the British. Dutch traders were opportunists as well as astute businessmen, however, and most of them interpreted the law as a hurdle, not a roadblock.

St. Eustatius, or Statia, as it was more commonly known, lies at the northern end of the gently curving chain of Leeward Islands. At the time of the American Revolution it was a center of legal and quasi-legal trade. Many prominent New England families had made their fortunes by trading through the Dutch West India Company on Statia during the seventeenth and eighteenth centuries despite the concerted efforts of France and particularly Britain to control the port. Holland was a small maritime nation without a powerful navy, but it was renowned as a resourceful center for international trade. Although the Dutch had participated in a number of European wars, greater profit lay in neutrality. Thus Holland set up free ports where all nations were welcome. Statia was the North American conduit for trade between France and the New England colonies as well as the gateway to France's Caribbean colonies. It was the preferred trading port for American vessels, and although the sale of arms was officially prohibited, smuggling of illicit military arms was common. Statia's governor was sympathetic to the American cause and he participated in the profits being made from arms sales. Several Dutch firms quietly engaged in a clandestine traffic through French harbors shipping sizable quantities of military supplies to Statia. This well-stocked port, the cheapest source of European goods in the Caribbean, was both an economic and a political threat to Britain.

Flying the flag of Grand Union on the flagstaff by the taffrail, the *Andrea Doria* sailed for St. Eustatius in late October 1776 and entered its harbor on 16 November 1776. As the *Andrea Doria* backed its topsails to slow its headway in preparation for dropping anchor, Captain Robinson decided to make a noticeable entry into port. With Barney on deck, Robinson ordered his striped American Grand Union flag dipped. According to naval custom, when a nation's flag was dipped, an eleven-gun salute was the proper response. Abraham Ravené, the commander of the Orange fort, surmised that the unfamiliar flag was that of a rebel American warship but feared that returning a salute might offend the British. He hastily sent a message requesting instructions to Johannes de Graaff, the island's governor, whose home was near the fort. Ravené was directed to answer the salute. The booming cannon volley that followed would make history. This token of international courtesy would also turn out to be a diplomatic indiscretion. Until that momentous occasion the newly self-declared independent nation of the United States had not yet received formal political recognition by any European power. Such recognition was contrary to the foreign policy of the Dutch government, and when news of the incident reached neighboring St. Christopher, British officials sent a vehement protest to Governor de Graaff. The governor responded by saying that "this Port always made & still makes distinction between Merchant or Private Vessells and the Ships of War belonging to Sovereign States: the latter receive constantly, when they honor its Fortress with a salute Gun for Gun, as a distinc mark of Independancy."[14] The British governor of St. Christopher (St. Kitts), Craister Greathead, retorted that the *Andrea Doria* came "to an anchor in the Road of St Eustatius & with Colours flying known to be those of the Rebels called the Continental Congress Saluted with Thirteen Guns Their High Mightinesses Fort called Fort Orange & which Salute was afterwards with solemnity due to the Flags of Independent Sovereign States returned to the said Vessel by the said Fort, which Vessel was afterwards permitted to take in a Loading of Gunpowder & other necessities of war & Provisions at St Eustatius for the use of the American Rebel Army."[15] In his report of the incident to the British Foreign Office, Governor Greathead wrote: "The Impartial World will Judge between us, whether a salute deliberately returned by a Dutch fort to the Rebel brigantine *Andrew Doria*, under Colours known to the Commandant of that Fort to be those of His Majesty's rebellious Subjects, be, or be not, a Partiality in Favor of those Rebels and a flagrant Indignity offered to his Majesty's Flag."[16] This complaint went from the British Foreign Office to the States General of the Republic of the Netherlands. In his defense, the Dutch governor claimed that, not knowing the American colors, he had ordered the salute out of normal courtesy. He explained that he was not responsible for the treaty laws between Britain and the Dutch nation, and that he enforced the laws on the island as he understood them.

Capt. John Colpoly of the *Seaford* was sent to Statia on 14 December to present the formal protest of the British. He reported in a letter to Admiral Young, dated 31 December 1776, that when he entered the harbor, de Graaff said that he had hoped that Colpoly "would Salute the Fort, and that an equal number of Guns shou'd be returned. . . . I found an evasive answer was given on the subject of the Forts returning Salutes to Vessels, wearing the Colours, of the American Rebels. . . . His answer was, that Statia was a free port. . . . [A]ll Vessels under whatsoever Colours, were at liberty to come in there, and if the Fort was saluted, 2 Guns less was returned to all Mercht Vessels, to Kings ships an equal number." In conclusion Colpoly added, "Governor de Graaf is well known to have given more Aid, and Assistance, to the American Rebels than any other man in his Government, being by far, the most wealthy, & considerable Merchant in St. Eustatia, he of course, has been the best able to carry on the most extensive Illicit Trade with the Rebellious Colonists."[17] This was a devastating indictment that carried weight with the Admiralty.

The Americans viewed the incident with amusement. Baltimore's *Maryland Journal* for Wednesday, 22 January 1777, commented that the governor and the people of St. Eustatius had displayed their "partiality for the American States, now engaged in the Cause of all Mankind," and reprinted an article from the *Caribbean Gazette* of St. Kitts that said: "The *Andrew Doria,* saluted the Dutch Fort at St. Eustatius under piratical Colours, the officers of the Fort sent to receive his Honor's Orders, who, after mature Deliberation, commanded the Salute to be returned. . . . [T]he Affair was done deliberately, and the same Compliment repeated at the sailing of the Pirate."[18]

Britain's Parliament sent a formal complaint to The Hague on 21 February 1777 demanding that the Dutch government disavow the salute, dismiss and punish Governor de Graaff, and extend and enforce the West Indies munitions embargo. If satisfaction was not received within three weeks, Parliament threatened that Britain would recall its ambassador to the Netherlands. The Dutch government responded by calling de Graaff home to answer the charges at a formal inquiry. In the end the governor was neither dismissed nor punished, though the government did reaffirm the earlier embargo order in the West Indies against the export of military stores to the Americans and formally disclaimed acts of their officials that might be interpreted as recognizing American independence. De Graaff returned to The Hague eighteen months later to write a large, detailed volume in his defense. The governor was completely exonerated by the Dutch government and returned to Statia in 1779. On his return, de Graaff became even more a favorite of the revolutionaries. Two American privateers were named for him and his wife, and a portrait of him hangs today in the New Hampshire State House in gratitude for the "first salute" and to honor the Dutch armed neutrality that gave one belligerent such satisfaction and the other such total discontent.[19]

On his return voyage from the West Indies Captain Robinson had to contend with the British firsthand. While sailing off the western coast of Puerto Rico the *Andrea Doria* encountered the *Racehorse,* a brig assigned to the fleet protecting British commerce in the Caribbean. The evenly matched vessels soon closed to within cannon range and began exchanging thunderous broadsides. The American gun crews reloaded their cannons more quickly, and their shots breached the hull of the *Racehorse* and damaged its rigging. Lt. William Jones, the British ship's commander, was killed, and two junior officers and many of the crew were wounded. The *Andrea Doria* suffered a dozen casualties, but the physical damage to the ship was superficial and its guns remained operational. The badly damaged British ship struck its colors. Captain Robinson appointed the second lieutenant of the *Andrea Doria,* Benjamin Dunn, to serve as prize master of the *Racehorse* and sent workmen to the ship to patch its hull, fabricate new spars, and mend its sails.

Sailing northward toward Philadelphia a few days later, the two brigs engaged and captured a well-armed and heavily crewed snow (a subclass of brig), the *Thomas,* with little resistance and no loss of life. Barney took command of this second prize. The crew of the *Andrea Doria* was too small to man both prizes, so the Americans tried to coax at least some of the captured British crewmen to change their allegiance. This was not difficult because many British seamen were unwilling sailors who had been pressed into service. With offers of a share in the prize money, the persuasive Lieutenant Barney managed to recruit a large number of British sailors to join his prize crew. The three ships sailed

north from the southern latitudes, but as they reached the Virginia coast
a December snow squall blew the vessels out of sight of one another. On
Christmas night the wind drove them toward the shoals off Chincoteague Island. The keel of the *Thomas* struck the sandy bottom. The
vessel listed heavily, and the shoreward sea began crashing over the
ship's gunwales, making the seams of the ship creak in concert with the
surge of the wind and tide. The crew found temporary safety by clam-
bering up into the rigging. They clung to the swaying masts, spars, and
lines for a full frightening day. At one point a sloop washed ashore within
sight of them and was violently torn to pieces. Helpless to intervene,
Barney and his terrified men heard the piercing screams followed by
moans of resignation as some of the hands perished in the surf. As darkness fell again, the tide rose and the wind made a sudden shift so that it
now blew hard from the land, counteracting some of the force from the
breakers. When the pitching of the deck subsided, Barney got the crew
down from the rigging to man the capstan and weigh anchor. The snow
quickly righted itself and drifted back out to sea. Reefed sails were set,
and Barney and his exhausted crew found shelter in the Chincoteague
Inlet harbor. It took a week to repair the badly damaged *Thomas* sufficiently to continue on toward Philadelphia.

En route to Cape Henry in January, the hapless ship met with another
winter squall. When the weather cleared, the watch sighted the sails of a
British sloop-of-war. Barney ordered as much canvas aloft as he dared
on the foundering snow in an attempt to outrun the enemy. Faced with a
potential battle against their old mates and possible repatriation, the
British prisoners who had "volunteered" to join the crew became muti-
nous. Barney shot their leader in the shoulder with his pistol and threatened to do the same to the next man who refused to tend the sails. This
quieted the insurrection for the moment, but the barely seaworthy
Thomas was no match for the taut sloop-of-war that rapidly bore down
upon it. In a matter of minutes the British guns were within range of the
battered prize ship. Under the circumstances, resistance made no
sense. Thus, the twenty-four-gun *Perseus,* George Keith Elphinstone in
command, recaptured the snow. Captain Elphinstone's conduct thereafter is an excellent example of the chivalry that existed among the officer combatants at this early stage of the war.

The wounded leader of the recent mutiny aboard the *Thomas* thought
that he would have his revenge when Barney was taken into British

custody. He complained bitterly to Captain Elphinstone about his treatment by Barney, but the captain displayed little sympathy, noting that the British seaman had broken his promise to help bring the snow safely to port. On top of this, the mutineer had led an uprising against his captain and should have been ready to suffer the consequences of failure. Rather than punishing Barney for shooting a British sailor, Elphinstone reprimanded the seaman.

Captain Elphinstone put the prize crew from the snow ashore and held Lieutenant Barney and a small group of other Americans captured earlier to barter for some Scottish Highlanders held prisoner in South Carolina. The exchange was agreeable to the American commander in Charleston and was accomplished with ease. Unfortunately for Barney, there was a complication. According to the custom of the day, an officer could be exchanged only for a prisoner of like rank. There were no officers among the Scottish prisoners; thus, Barney remained in captivity.

The newly freed Scots complained of being held in close quarters for many months in humid South Carolina and protested about the poor food and treatment. As Barney was the only American left on the *Perseus,* the Scots began to abuse him physically. The young lieutenant avoided confrontations to the best of his ability, but a ship's purser among the Scots was particularly belligerent. He assaulted Barney with his fist and succeeded in landing a glancing blow. Barney returned the punch squarely, knocking the purser to the deck, then picked him up by the collar and threw him down the hatchway, letting him tumble to the gun deck below.

The crew of the *Perseus* quickly surrounded Barney to protect him, and the tempers of the hostile Scots on the spar deck cooled. Barney and the purser were brought before Captain Elphinstone, who became furious on hearing that the Scot struck an officer without provocation. He stated that the man had dishonored the Royal Navy by his actions and that a verbal apology was not enough. Elphinstone demanded that it be delivered on "bended knee." The proud purser refused to bow before Barney and was thus remanded to the ship's brig for an indefinite period. Captain Elphinstone expressed his personal apology and also that of the ship's company. He also stated that he deeply regretted not being able to include Barney in the prisoner exchange. He could, however, grant him a parole and accept Barney's word of honor that he would not bear arms against the king until an officer exchange of like rank could be arranged at some time in the future. Barney, naturally, agreed. As Barney left the *Perseus* both officers shook hands, wished each other well, and doffed their caps in the naval salute.

On landing at Charleston, Barney sought transport back to his base in Philadelphia. The only means available was by horseback. He started the long overland journey with three other naval officers who had been exchanged for British prisoners. Sailors are more at ease on rolling decks than they are on the backs of horses, and this was a particularly uncomfortable trip for all of them. Adding to the dangers, they had to cross and recross Tory lines to reach their destination. The young officers had to defend themselves unexpectedly on a number of occasions. Dusty and saddle-sore, they rode into Philadelphia nineteen days after leaving Charleston. Two were quickly assigned to ships, but Barney, by the terms of his parole, was indefinitely tied to the shore. From March to October 1777 the young lieutenant was incarcerated in a prison without walls, fettered by his word as an officer.

With additional maturity Barney realized that his formal education was insufficient to help him advance in his chosen profession, so he used the short interval in Philadelphia to study classical literature, read history, and learn a smattering of French. He also attended debates in Independence Hall, listening in fascination to the power struggles among the political factions.

The record says little concerning the activities of the *Andrea Doria* from March through September 1777, but events moved rapidly in the ship's home port of Philadelphia. On 26 September 1777 British forces under Gen. Sir William Howe captured the city. A month later, on 20 October 1777, a letter reached Barney from Captain Elphinstone stating that Governor Patrick Henry of Virginia had arranged to exchange Barney for Edmund Joshua Moriarty, a British navy lieutenant who had been captured by an American scouting party while ashore. When the exchange was formally completed on 2 November, Barney was legally released from the obligations of his parole. He rejoined the *Andrea Doria,* which was anchored off Mud Island as part of the American force trying to stop the British forces in Delaware Bay from linking up with those in Philadelphia. At about this time George Washington received intelligence that an attack on Fort Mifflin was likely to occur on 7 or 8 November. Responding to his warning on 8 November, Brig. Gen. James M. Varnum, commander of the defense of the Delaware, wrote to Washington describing the deployment of his forces, including "the continental vessells under Capt Robinson's command [which] will lay at the Mouth of the Schylkill and the Mouth of Timber Creek."[20]

Barney and his shipmates harassed the skirmishers and bombarded the enemy from their fixed positions, but the American forces were doomed. Outgunned and cut off from support, the defenders surrendered Fort Mifflin on 20 November 1777 and ordered the burning of the American vessels, including the *Andrea Doria,* to keep them out of the hands of the British. The American commander described the end of the *Andrea Doria* as follows: "There being no wind, the Continental Brig *Andora Doria, Xebechs, Repulse* and *Champion,* sloops *Race horse & Fly,* with the Province ships and two Floating Batteries, were set on Fire and burnt, which made a most terrible conflagration, to the great joy of our cruel & wicked enemies, and much to the depression of my spirits."[21] Those who could escaped in galleys to Bordentown on the Jersey shore. Thus, most of the ships of the original Continental navy, including two of those Barney had served in, were destroyed at about the same time, in the same way, and in the same place. Now the entire British force could concentrate on Fort Mercer. Realizing that their position was hopeless, the Americans abandoned the fort on 22 November. The next day a British man-of-war came up the Delaware to Philadelphia, signaling the passage of control of the Delaware waterway to the British, from the cape to the capital.

~3~

CAPTIVE AND PRIVATEER

With the Philadelphia fleet largely destroyed, the Marine Committee reassigned the surviving officers and crew to ships at other ports. Barney was ordered to join the twenty-eight-gun frigate *Virginia,* which was to sail out of Baltimore. In early December 1777 the young lieutenant led a unit of men across the frozen Schuylkill River at Valley Forge, where he stopped to pay his respects to the commander in chief of the Continental forces, General George Washington. It was Barney's first meeting with the famed man. Continuing on their way, the detachment of naval personnel trudged south on foot through the cold of that legendary winter. They were able to find shelter from the snow and freezing rain only for short periods. Incredibly, it took them almost a month to complete the approximately fifty-mile journey.

They found the *Virginia* tied up in the partly frozen Baltimore harbor as promised. A British fleet cruised just out of sight along the bleak gray Capes south of the port. Making for the sea through ice-choked Chesapeake Bay meant successfully slipping by or outrunning these well-armed maritime sentries. Barney, being familiar with these waters, was placed in temporary command of the *Virginia* for a patrol of the upper Chesapeake to monitor enemy ship movements. When the *Virginia* reached Tangier Sound he noticed a large sloop that was known to be from Baltimore. It was Barney's duty to warn American ships of the British presence, so he made for the sloop. He was almost directly alongside it when the *Virginia* received heavy musket fire and an order to strike its colors. Barney quickly hauled off to the sloop's stern and cautiously approached from the other side. From this angle he could see that there was a barge alongside with a detachment of British sailors disguised with blankets and tarred clothing. Barney's ship had only a pair of swivel guns, but he nevertheless aggressively moved in to challenge the enemy. After a short but heavy firefight, the officer in charge of the barge was wounded and his crew surrendered. Barney restored the sloop to the merchant captain and crew, who had been locked belowdecks, and placed the British captives under guard.

Laden with prisoners, the *Virginia* was now forced to give up its patrol and return to Baltimore. With his own treatment aboard the *Perseus* still fresh in his mind, Barney took especially good care of the wounded British officer, Lt. James Gray. He arranged for comfortable quarters and, under a flag of truce, sent for the lieutenant's clothing to protect him from the harsh winter. He received a note of thanks for his kind treatment from the young officer's commander, Capt. Matthew Squire of the *Otter,* who also sent an English cheese, a prized delicacy for the officers' mess.

On the last day of March 1778 the strong spring winds blew the larger British vessels off their stations in the Chesapeake Bay, giving the *Virginia* the opportunity to slip by the blockade and out into open ocean; but luck was against the Americans. Because of a piloting error the ship ran aground on the Middle Ground shoal. The next tide floated it free, but the *Virginia* had lost its rudder, making the ship virtually impossible to steer. To make matters worse, three British frigates came across the grounded American ship as dawn brightened the sky.

The incident that followed enraged Joshua Barney. With capture by the British inevitable, Capt. James Nicholson of the *Virginia* ran from his cabin in dishabille, ordered his personal boat into the water, and then rowed himself to shore, leaving his clothes, papers, and other possessions in his cabin. This cowardly act of abandonment left Lieutenant Barney abruptly in command of three hundred men who were about to be taken prisoner. The rudderless *Virginia* was at the mercy of the rapidly approaching enemy. Firing against the British would lead to wounding or loss of American life. The best alternative was to cut the *Virginia*'s cable and put up enough sail to drive the ship onto the shoal off Cape Henry. At least the Americans could deny the British the prize of one of their best frigates. Although officially he possessed the authority of command, Barney was only eighteen and was new to the ship. In addition, the morale of the men plummeted following Captain Nicholson's desertion. The crew disregarded Barney's order to cut the cable and, in the face of what appeared to be a terrible impending fate, broke into the purser's liquor locker to consume whatever alcohol they could find. The enemy took possession of the *Virginia* and its largely inebriated company without a struggle.

To Joshua Barney this was the worst disgrace of his naval career. He had envisioned the *Virginia* firing a final defiant broadside at the British as it started to break apart on the shore; to surrender without a fight rasped like a thistle against his pride. The crewmen of the *Virginia* were distributed among the three capturing vessels. Barney was taken aboard the *Emerald*, a prisoner of Capt. Benjamin Caldwell, who gave him a cabin and granted him the privilege of joining the officers' mess. Caldwell was extremely pleasant and gentlemanly toward Barney, probably because of Barney's kindness to Lieutenant Gray, which was known to the officers of the *Emerald*.

A second insult to Barney's self-imposed code of ethics occurred at midmorning on 2 April when Captain Nicholson came out to the frigate under a flag of truce to recover his clothes and personal effects. Barney could not remain silent. Risking a possible court-martial, he told Captain Nicholson what he thought of his actions in front of his captors, and he spared few words. The invectives were met by a stony silence. The humiliated Nicholson, showing no emotion, gathered his belongings, rowed back to shore, and disappeared into the morning sea smoke of the cool Chesapeake waters.

Joshua Barney's imprisonment aboard the *Emerald* was unusual, to be sure. He was treated almost as an honored guest. The ship stood off Hampton, Virginia, through April and May. During that time Barney was allowed ashore to visit friends for several days at a time with only his word as an officer that he would return to his captivity. In fact, Captain Caldwell, who must have been an extraordinary man, made friends with many people who lived in Hampton and sent his hosts small gifts and messages. Governor Patrick Henry at one point invited the captain to join him in a hunting party. Caldwell was flattered but said that it was improper behavior for an enemy officer and more than he dared to do. Governor Henry accepted his regrets and, in another extraordinary act of kindness, sent him a milk cow to stable aboard the *Emerald* and fodder to feed her.

The Americans at this point had few British seamen to exchange for American prisoners, so the British consolidated their naval prisoners into large men-of-war. Barney was transferred to the ship of the line *St. Albans* under command of Richard Onslow in mid May. Although Barney was treated with the courtesy accorded an officer, he and the lower-ranking fellow American captives found the conditions extremely cramped. The ship's company numbered about three hundred while the prisoner population was about five hundred. Barney, the senior American officer among them, reasoned that if he could persuade a few key members of the impressed British crew to side with the Americans they might be able to capture the *St. Albans*. After recruiting several crew members, he devised a plan to break into the arms locker and take over the ship. Just before the ringing of the ship's bell signaling a change of watch, a detachment of Royal Marines doubled the usual guard and locked the hatches. Barney was ordered to Captain Onslow's cabin, offered a glass of wine, and complimented on his cunning. The plot might have worked, Onslow told him, if a French seaman had not betrayed it. The captain asked Barney what would have happened to him if Barney had succeeded. Barney said that he would have received the kindness expected from a fellow officer, although there may have been the need for "a little restraint." Onslow then asked what he expected to do with his prize, which was stationed among a number of other British ships of the line. Displaying an aplomb that would become one of his primary characteristics, Barney declared that his grand plan was to capture the entire fleet. He was sure that most of the men of the regular ship's company would join the Americans once they had control of the *St. Albans*. This sixty-four-gun third-rater should easily take the *Virginia* and smaller ships as prizes. With this bantam fleet under his command, he intended to sail to the Chesapeake and decoy other ships on patrol by sending the British private signals aloft. His ultimate goal was to capture the *Emerald*, the *Solebay*, and the sloop *Otter*. Captain Onslow could only admire the imagination and audacity of the engaging young man.

Kind treatment was far from being guaranteed to British prisoners. Eventually Captain Onslow received orders to transport his captive American seamen to New York harbor for internment in the hulks, ships taken out of sea service from the Royal Navy or floating captured prizes not worth repairing that were used as prisons. The most notorious of the prison hulks at New York was the *Jersey*, a former ship of the line moored in shallow Wallabout Bay, a bend in the East River off Brooklyn. Its hull was rotten and wormy. The only ventilation for the men held belowdecks came from nine-inch slits cut in the two rows of boarded and barred gun ports. A heavily barred ten-foot barrier separated the prisoners from the guards on the quarterdeck, who confiscated any money or gifts sent to the luckless prisoners. The food was sparse and rancid. Disease was common and often fatal. Sanitation was almost nonexistent for the approximately one thousand men confined in the ship. The only exercise permitted was a few hours of pacing the deck under the watchful eyes of the armed guards. No light reached the men below except for that seen through the bars during the day. Depression was rampant, fostered by boredom in the extremely crowded conditions among the sick and dying. Few attempted escape because the sea offered its own hazards. The shore and beaches of Wallabout Bay were littered with unmarked graves of the almost eleven thousand Americans who had died as prisoners aboard the *Jersey*.

The horrors of imprisonment in the hulks became well known as the war progressed. This cruel type of confinement was reserved mostly for seamen, many of whom were privateers although they were often treated as pirates. The British treated captured soldiers far better because both sides had soldiers to barter in prisoner exchanges. General Washington wanted to exchange captured sailors as well, but except for officers this was against British policy. There was a relatively steady exchange of British and American soldier prisoners, although each might reinforce an army about to do battle with his former captors. The Americans, in some instances, treated their captives badly as well. The Connecticut village of Simsbury, for instance, had a copper mine in its northern section, now known as Granby. The convicts, Tories, and few British soldiers incarcerated there called it Old Newgate Prison in honor of its much larger and more formidable British counterpart. These unfortunate prisoners lived in similarly intolerable conditions but in addition were forced to work at hard labor.

In late May 1778 Barney found himself confined aboard one of the miserable hulks among the reeking sick and the dispirited. Death was a constant companion, relieving the suffering of those who were ill and terrifying those who were well. Lieutenant Barney was the only naval officer among this wretched collection of captive Americans. They lacked a leader, a role that Barney naturally filled. Easily gaining their respect, he began to enforce a degree of order and discipline. He put into effect a plan to divide the food and water, and had the men make crude attempts to clean the quarters. Adm. Richard Howe, the brother of Gen. Sir William Howe, was in command of the New York prison hulks. Although he appeared to be sympathetic toward the cause of the colonies, he permitted this barbarous situation to continue, either through cruelty or laziness, until it stained his reputation.

Howe's successor as naval commander at New York was Vice Adm. John "Foul Weather Jack" Byron. The admiral, appalled and disgusted at what he saw aboard the hulks, immediately relieved the crowding, appointed medical personnel to look after the sick and wounded, and instituted a prisoner military hierarchy to look after the complaints and needs of the men. Admiral Byron also felt that an American naval officer should not be confined aboard a hulk and had Lieutenant Barney transferred to his flagship, the *Ardent,* until an exchange could be arranged.

Before long the personable Barney had established friendly relations with the British flag officer. Invited to accompany the admiral on tours of the prison ships, Barney made suggestions about the proper management of men and facilities. The admiral knew that the prisoners would be more forthcoming and candid about their grievances to a young American officer whom they respected. When new prisoners were processed, Barney recorded their personal data and kept records for their hoped-for exchange.

The relationship between the captive naval officer and his jailer became even more unusual when Barney was allowed to use one of the admiral's boats to go ashore at his pleasure, the only stipulation being he must return to sleep aboard the *Ardent* every evening. One morning Barney was invited for breakfast with Sir William Twisden, aide to the admiral in New York. It is not clear where he got the clothing, but Barney appeared in the full dress uniform of a lieutenant of the Continental navy: blue coat, brass buttons, red lapels and waistcoat, and blue breeches. Once ashore, he walked slowly along a line of planked wooden buildings, carefully staying close to the wall to avoid any filth that might be thrown or accidentally dropped from the windows above. Carts and barrows clattered along the rough Dutch cobbles that paved the street. The tradesmen who populated the quayside by comparison to him seemed diminutive, greasy, and furtive. Indeed, Barney cut a splendid figure as an American naval officer, but New York, under control of the British, was a stronghold of the Tories. The previous evening there had been a severe fire not far from the place where he was to meet Sir William. The townspeople suspected that it was an act of arson perpetrated by a band of patriots. The sight of a uniformed American officer on the street by the still-smoldering ruin nearly caused a riot. The populace started to surround Barney, becoming increasingly belligerent and nasty. To a passing British naval officer who managed to extricate him from the hostile crowd, Barney explained that he was a prisoner of Admiral Byron and the invited breakfast guest of the admiral's aide. The officer suggested that if this unlikely story were true, the best place for him was aboard the *Ardent,* and Barney was rowed back to the flagship for his safety and renewed confinement.

Finally, the French navy captured a British lieutenant in an engagement with the *Mermaid,* terms of exchange were negotiated, and Barney was set free in Philadelphia. There was a very positive side to Barney's five-month imprisonment in New York harbor. Partly because of his leadership during this internment, conditions on the hulks improved greatly.

By the end of August 1778 Joshua Barney was again a free man. During the past year, however, the fledgling Continental navy had been devastated by the mighty British navy. Only five Continental vessels were still afloat: the twelve-gun *Providence* and four of the thirteen frigates built under the Continental Congress's act of 1775. There were few billets available for officers, so the nineteen-year-old Barney was given leave to recuperate in Baltimore. Perhaps out of boredom or perhaps in the hope of generating a little action, which he sorely missed, Barney accepted a local merchant's offer of command of an eight-man schooner armed with two guns. His ostensible assignment was to take tobacco to St. Eustatius. Foreign money was in demand, and a cargo of tobacco might fetch a few valuable guilders. This type of mission was a common cover for the transportation of papers or messages between governments in neutral ports, but it is not clear that the latter was the reason for Barney's acceptance of the assignment. Mary Barney felt that his act demonstrated "unselfish, generous zeal and intrepidity in service to others. It was impossible that he could hope to gain honor by such a command . . . but he believed that he might be useful, and that was motive enough for him."[1]

Shortly after leaving Baltimore but while still well inside the Chesapeake Bay, the tiny schooner found itself in a firefight with a fast British privateer. The larger ship carried sixty men and four guns. Two of the guns were heavy carronades, and the Americans were overmatched. After the early exchanges of fire, one American lay dead and two were wounded. There was no alternative but to surrender the schooner. Joshua Barney became a captive of the British for the third time and, counting his adventure in Nice, was imprisoned for a fourth time in four years at sea. As in the past, he relied on his charm and assumed a posture of ignorance and innocence. The privateer skipper found no profit, and some unwanted expense, in feeding merchant sailor prisoners and released them on Maryland's Eastern Shore while he made off with the schooner and its cargo. In a few days Barney and the remaining crew were back in Baltimore.

Another command was not soon forthcoming and within a few weeks the energetic Barney once again felt bored. Then, as luck would have it, relief appeared in the form of an old friend. While walking with his comrades on the quay he encountered Isaiah Robinson of the now-burned *Andrea Doria*. His former commander was looking for a first lieutenant and crew for a ship that he was fitting out in Alexandria, Virginia. Robinson had a letter of marque and invited Barney to join him in a new career as a privateer. Barney accepted with delight, pleased to have the chance to work with a man he greatly respected.

The quasi-naval enterprise of privateering, government-sanctioned piracy, was an important business through the eighteenth century and the early part of the nineteenth. When two nations, each possessing a merchant fleet, declared war, they had three options for waging war at sea. The first was to attack the enemy with a navy. The mission of a naval vessel was to seek and destroy or disable enemy ships; their capture was desirable and rewarded, but of secondary importance to putting them out of action. The second option was to issue letters of marque and reprisal to independent ships. Privateer commissions recorded the owner's name and the ship's tonnage, rig, armament, and number of crew. In many cases the captain and lieutenant paid a fee for their commissions. Privateer vessels captured the enemy's ships and their goods for the financial gain of the owners, captain, and crew. The rewards could be quite significant. The hands came onboard with the understanding of no prey, no pay. They were fed and quartered, but any earnings came from the prizes taken by the ship. This relative independence made some privateers unruly and haughty, difficult to control because they considered themselves not bound by usual maritime discipline. As a third option, a nation could work within a keen point of the law and encourage noncommissioned privateers to prey on enemy commerce. Letters of marque were costly and required some political influence to obtain. But a government that wanted enemy shipping interdicted occasionally winked at poorer captains who did not have the capital to obtain the official license. These rogue privateers were vulnerable, for if captured they would be punished as pirates. The line between them and true pirates, who operated completely outside the law, plundering any quarry they could capture, was a very fine one.

Privateers sailing under letters of marque issued by a revolutionary colonial government had no standing in British courts if Great Britain did not recognize the legality of the government using the commissions. On 27 July 1780, as the Revolutionary War progressed, privateers were all ordered to carry a commission from the secretary of Congress, making privateering a U.S. government–sponsored effort. The privateer captain was required to post a substantial bond to the government (state or federal) issuing the license—five thousand dollars for a vessel under one hundred tons and ten thousand dollars for heavier vessels. This did not seem to dissuade many ship captains, because 1,697 American vessels sailed under letters of marque during the Revolutionary War.

As a business venture, the risks of privateering were high. A privateer might find few prizes on the high seas, leading to financial failure. And captured prizes were vulnerable to recapture. The privateer crewmen could be seized and imprisoned in the feared prison hulks. Near-fatal battle wounds were common sequels of privateer incursions. These wounds often led to horrible diseases and slow and painful death. The dangers were well known, but evidently they were not an important consideration in the creation of the American privateer fleet. The potential rewards were too great. Privateering was an honorable and patriotic profession as well as a potentially lucrative enterprise. Half of all the money gained from prizes went to the shipowners. Therefore, investing in a privateer—or better yet, a fleet of privateers—could be a profitable, if highly risky, business. Many well-known merchant families made their fortunes and reputations from underwriting such gambles.

A privateer captain had to be an excellent seaman and leader. He also had to be enterprising, courageous, and quick thinking, but not foolhardy.

Excessive aggressiveness received little encouragement. The key to survival for a privateer was avoiding battles at sea. One relied on the swift-
ness of the ship and one's own cunning to gain the advantage over the
enemy's guns. A false flag, or *ruse de guerre,* was frequently employed to
ensnare a potential victim. In addition, some of the privateer's "guns"
were likely to be "Quakers," false wooden pieces (named for the nonbel-
ligerent Society of Friends) designed to look like guns to fool and intimidate a potential quarry.

The reward system consisted of shares that could be readily traded,
not unlike present-day stock certificates. The officers and men signed
articles of agreement that stipulated their rights to shares of prizes as
well as their responsibilities to the ship, the captain, and the owners.
The contract also carefully outlined the reward and punishment plans
for the enterprise. Those outfitting a privateer could sell or buy parts or
whole shares as they saw fit to raise money. This was sort of a "commod-
ity market plan" in that prices rose or fell with the season, the reputation of the captain or vessel, rumors of prizes to be taken, or the urgent
needs of the seller. A mariner could make as much money privateering
for a few months as he would make during several years of more peaceful employment. For many, the risks, a mere roll of sea-tossed dice, were
outweighed by the potential rewards.

The privateers' impact on the enemy was potentially enormous. Every
British vessel captured or sunk affected the nation's economy. The British
merchant fleet was under constant threat and could not guarantee delivery of supplies and needed goods during time of war. Men-of-war had to
be diverted to protect convoys from privateers. Insurance rates and other
costs of doing business rose dramatically. These expenses often changed
the fortunes of marginally profitable merchant ventures. American privateers captured or destroyed approximately three thousand British vessels
but did not disrupt British merchant commerce enough to influence the
outcome of the war. British privateers and naval vessels offset these losses
by capturing or destroying about eleven hundred American vessels.
Britain's depredations had a far greater impact on the American economy
because the United States had fewer ships and men at risk.

In November 1778 Joshua Barney entered the world of the privateers by
accepting appointment as first lieutenant of the *General Mercer.* Barney
was ordered to find munitions, cannons, and small arms for the ship and

to recruit a crew. These were difficult tasks; arms were scarce and most able-bodied men were either in the army or engaged in other employment. Barney succeeded in recruiting only thirty-five of the desired sixty-man crew, and these were not the best of seamen. The twelve cannons he purchased varied in size, which meant that cannon shot could not be exchanged between them if one was damaged during a firefight. Given his sparse crew and less than satisfactory armament, Captain Robinson decided to take on a lucrative cargo of tobacco and sail for Bordeaux, a relatively safe voyage that would give him the opportunity to fine-tune the ship and crew. It would also give him access to more men among their French allies and the chance to acquire fine French cannons.

The brig *General Mercer* left Baltimore in February 1779 intending to avoid contact with the enemy. Sailors stood in the crosstrees almost a hundred feet above the deck watching for ships on the horizon. On the third day at sea the watch reported white flashes of sails in the distance. As the thin morning light brightened under a gray sky, the hull of an approaching ship under full sail could be seen throwing out a broad wave from its bow. According to the sailor's crude measurements the ships were closing, but at a slow pace.

As the sun began to set, the approaching ship, the sixteen-gun privateer *Rosebud,* came to within hailing distance. Raising the Union Jack, its commander, Capt. Henry Duncan, put a speaking trumpet to his lips and asked the ship's identity. Captain Robinson replied only by hoisting the American flag. The captain of the *Rosebud,* again shouting through his speaking trumpet, ordered the *General Mercer* to haul down the American ensign and surrender. Captain Robinson responded by ordering his men to prepare a broadside from his nondescript battery of cannons. The crew, not well trained in gunnery, tied their handkerchiefs round their necks or heads, hitched up their trousers, and spat on their hands for good luck, or perhaps for a better grip. The men stared out through the gun ports as the early evening sunlight slanted in on their black cannons, their leathery, tanned bodies swaying unconsciously with the heaving of the vessel. They heard the signal from the quarterdeck to commence firing. The enormous roar of the cannons was accompanied by stabs of flame lighting clouds of white smoke. Within the clouds were black dashes, punctuation mark shadows of balls passing through on their way to a target.

A lucky American shot hit its mark, bringing down the enemy's fore-topsail. The tangle of rigging on the deck created confusion. The British fired a broadside in return, but with little effect. The damaged British ship was now slowed and could only follow, shooting bursts of fire every twenty or thirty minutes at the American's vulnerable quarter and stern. The *General Mercer* was slightly ahead of the *Rosebud,* but this meant that the British were out of range of the small-caliber cannons of the American ship. Lieutenant Barney suggested to Captain Robinson that they cut a new gun port by the sternpost and bring up a long 3-pounder to defend their vulnerable backside. When the *Rosebud* drew close to fire at what its captain thought was an undefended part of the ship, Barney's cannon barked, driving off the Englishman. The captain of the *Rosebud* decided to wait for dawn, and with it a chance to board. At first light the British privateer sailed in close to the stern of its American quarry, its crew in position and armed for boarding. On the *General Mercer,* Barney took command of the stern-chaser and with the help of the quartermaster and the helmsman loaded the cannon with a double charge of powder and grapeshot. At the last minute Barney decided to cram a crowbar into the barrel for good measure. When the cannon was fired, the crowbar spun through the air, cutting the *Rosebud*'s fore tack and weather shrouds. For safety's sake, the British privateer captain ordered his helmsman to wear away. Presented with the opportunity to deliver a broadside, the Americans fired with devastating effect, forcing the battered *Rosebud* to retreat out of harm's way. The American cannon killed or wounded eighty-two of the British ship's company. An account of this engagement was published in a New York newspaper, which accused the Americans of defending themselves unfairly by employing langrage (Barney's crowbar). Langrage consisted of nails, bolts, chain parts, and miscellaneous pieces of iron, and firing it was deemed unsportsmanlike by many eighteenth-century mariners, who held to a set of rules for marine combat that seem archaic by present standards.

The American merchantman-privateer arrived at Bordeaux with no further encounters. There the *General Mercer*'s captain increased the ship's armament to eighteen 6-pounders and its crew to seventy. After selling the tobacco cargo and taking on a load of brandy, the ship sailed for Philadelphia in early August. About halfway across the Atlantic it encountered an English privateer, the *Minerva,* in rough seas. Heading into the wind reduced the *General Mercer*'s roll, but torrents of water smashed over the bow and cascaded off the hatches, making the decks slick and dangerous. In these terrible conditions, the opposing ships could do no more than position themselves to a standoff for a day. Suddenly the storm abated and the wind dropped to only a hint of a breeze, and the two ships were becalmed within sight of each other. The British brig's sails luffed passively as it quietly reposed in the water about four miles ahead of the American ship. Captain Robinson ordered his small boats into the water, had them attach a towline, and, with the muscle of his rowers, closed on the enemy. Much to Robinson's surprise, the British surrendered without a fight. The British vessel had suffered twelve men killed and many wounded in a battle the previous day, and the spars and hull had been damaged as well. Isaiah Robinson now had a sixteen-gun brig with a seventy-man crew as a prize. Lieutenant Barney, put in command of the prize, supervised repairs and sailed the *Minerva* to Philadelphia.

Privateering was turning out to be a lucrative venture for the young man. Barney's share of the prize money was a fortune compared with his salary as a junior naval officer, and it gave him the means to achieve his next big milestone in life. Joshua Barney was a vigorous and handsome bachelor, five feet, eight inches tall with black hair, a dark complexion, and sparkling eyes. His radiant smile and self-confident manner made him very popular with the ladies. He was now also a man of relative means and thus an extremely eligible "catch" in the eyes of many Philadelphia matrons. Dividing his time between friends and relatives in Baltimore and the more elegant attractions of Philadelphia, Barney was in great social demand. Before long he fell in love. The object of his courtship was Anne Bedford, a young lady of great beauty and many personal accomplishments. The young man soon "struck his colors" and proposed marriage. His bride-to-be was the daughter of Gunning Bedford, a distinguished member of Philadelphia society, city alderman, former aide-de-camp to General Washington, and representative to the Continental Congress from Delaware. Joshua and Anne were married on 16 March 1780 with full parental approval. The happy couple enjoyed their month-long honeymoon, attending a perpetual round of parties in the hospitable Philadelphia area. When the attraction of the social whirl started to wane in mid-April, the couple left town and spent a week or two on the estate of Anne's brother in rural Delaware.

Barney was not yet twenty-one, but he had an unfaltering sense of responsibility. He decided to invest his fortune of a few thousand dollars of Continental script in a business enterprise in Baltimore. He made the

trip overland from Philadelphia by "horse and chair." In an act of innocence consistent with that of a trusting young sailor, the lieutenant left
the belted wooden strongbox on the "chair" overnight when he took
lodging. On his arrival in Baltimore Barney dismissed his driver, settled
into lodgings, and then to his horror discovered that the box had been
opened and that his fortune in paper money was missing. This theft was
a source of great personal embarrassment, and Barney did not divulge it
to his spouse for many years, though in his old age he would recount his
naiveté to his grandchildren as a lesson in ineptitude.

His fortune lost, Joshua Barney sought a billet aboard a naval ship in
order to earn the money he needed to support his new wife. After slightly
less than two weeks of inquiries he received orders to the eighteen-gun
sloop-of-war *Saratoga* as first lieutenant under Capt. James Young. Barney
was generally pleased with the assignment, but he considered it a demo-
tion in responsibility, and certainly it was a reduction in pay from his privateering days. In frustration he wrote to the Continental Congress:

July 26th, 1780
To the Honorable Delegates of the United States of America
in Congress Assembled:
  The Memorial of Joshua Barney most respectfully sheweth That your
  Memorialist hath served four Years as a Lieutenant in the Navy in the
  service of America during fifteen months of which time he hath been a
  Prisoner with the enemy. That he hath born the Rank on Board a Ship
  having more than twenty guns and is at the present directed to take the
  rank of First Lieutenant on Board the Saratoga, a vessel of inferior
  force. That by a resolve of your Honours the Pay of an officer is reduced
  in proportion to his reduction in point of Rank on board the Vessels of
  inferior force. That two Years' Pay is due your petitioner for his former
  services, which in the present depressed state of Currency is not worth
  his acceptance. That application hath been made to the board of Admi-
  ralty and Satisfaction can be obtained from that quarter without an
  order from your Honours. He therefore prays your Honours would fix his
  Rank and ascertain the pay he shall receive.
  Joshua Barney, Lt.[2]

The memorial, what we might call a memorandum today, was read
before the Committee on Naval Affairs of the Congress on 26 July 1780.

A favorable recommendation was made to the Admiralty, resulting in the following reply and resolution:

The Board of Admiralty to whom was referred the memorial of Lieu-tenant Barney of the Navy beg leave to report their opinion.

That any Officer who by virtue of this Commission or Warrant, hath served or hereafter shall serve on board any Ship-of-War of twenty guns and upwards belonging to the Navy of these States, and shall thereafter serve in the same rank on board any other Vessel of War of inferior force, such Officer shall receive the same pay as he was entitled to when serv-ing in a ship of Twenty Guns and upwards, any resolution to the con-trary notwithstanding.

(By order)

Francis Lewis

Order of Admiralty, Passed August 7th, 1780.[3]

The response settled Barney's title and salary, but not his arrears. Admiralty policy regarding ship duty, rank, and pay was unfair, but the Continental Congress was in poor fiscal condition. It had not paid offi-cers and men in the naval service for two years. Barney's advertised pay at this time was thirty dollars a month, but Continental currency was not worth much in the marketplace. Under the circumstances, the memo-randum from the junior naval officer to Congress was not mercenary or out of order; there was no formal chain of command at this time, and no one else to whom he might complain. With that painful episode now thankfully behind him, Barney made sure that his new wife was safe with her family in Philadelphia and reported to the *Saratoga*.

The sloop-of-war was fast but lightly ballasted, meaning that it sailed well only on the wind. Captain Young was able to make the most of his ship. He enjoyed seeing the sloop's bow buried in foam while the sails aloft strained the rigging. His crew ran up the shrouds and out onto the swaying yards like monkeys to answer Young's orders. As they filled with air the sails formed lofty white wings that seemed to lift the ship with a surge of power. The *Saratoga* could make about ten knots as it closed on its prey, its masthead pendant flicking like a coachman's whip dri-ving the ship onward. The intrepid band of American sailors found the hunting rather good. The *Saratoga*'s first capture was a merchantman, the sloop *Elizabeth* commanded by Capt. Lawrence Galghere. The prize was small, but its cargo of slaves, corn, and spars was welcomed in Philadelphia.

The next week the American ship came across three vessels, a brig and two small ships. Captain Young employed his usual strategy of showing the British flag, running alongside an unidentified vessel, hailing it, and then running up the Stars and Stripes, the new American flag, in preparation for battle. His initial quarry was the *Charming Molly* bound from Jamaica to New York with 230 puncheons of rum and several tons of sugar. As the Americans changed their colors, the *Saratoga* fired a broadside. The British quickly tried to load their cannons. Since the *Charming Molly* was a merchant ship, its crewmen were not used to combat, and in gunnery drill poorly coordinated. The merchant sailors bumped into one another, some standing momentarily at the wrong cannon while others groped at the unfamiliar equipment. Taking advantage of their confusion, the Americans, led by Barney, threw grappling hooks over the bulwarks, boarded the ship, and drove the crew into the holds below. The ship surrendered with no further resistance. The prisoners were taken aboard the *Saratoga,* and Barney was given command of the *Charming Molly* with a prize crew from the boarding party while Captain Young pursued the other two ships, which were still in sight. He overtook the first vessel at daybreak, another ship named *Elizabeth* under Capt. Thomas Taylor, carrying fourteen guns. After only little resistance on the part of the British, Young and his crew gained control. The *Saratoga* then turned on the brig *Nancy,* under the command of Capt. Thomas Eve, which had been sailing close by under the protection of the *Elizabeth.* The *Nancy* had only four guns and surrendered without a shot being fired. Thus, Captain Young had acquired two fine ships and a brig to show for two days of commerce raiding. The 1,900 hogsheads of rum found aboard would sell for three dollars a gallon, producing a fortune for that time. The ships and cannons represented a second fortune. The officers and crew of a Continental ship were entitled to one-half the value of a captured merchantman and its stores, and the full value of a ship of war or a privateer. The captain would receive two-twentieths of the value, and the officers would divide three-twentieths. In addition, Barney might receive a bonus of a set-aside for his gallantry in taking one or more of the prize ships. Doing the arithmetic, Barney calculated that he would be richer than he had ever imagined . . . once the crew brought the prizes to port.

The prize flotilla made for Philadelphia. Along the way, Barney noted that the *Charming Molly* was listing. Careful examination revealed that a seam had opened slightly from a shot that struck below the waterline. The *Saratoga* came alongside and assisted in making repairs. The *Charming Molly* was only minimally seaworthy, however, and had to proceed with caution, its pumps operating continuously. Before long the haze over the sea had separated the *Molly* from the *Saratoga*. On 11 October 1780, a few miles off Cape Henry near the mouth of the Chesapeake, the ship of the line *Intrepid* and the frigate *Raleigh* spied the *Charming Molly*. With only an eight-man prize crew, resistance would have meant the loss of life for no good reason. There was no use in fighting these two foes, so Barney's dreams of a fortune recovered vanished as the boarding party climbed over the rail and he found himself a prisoner of the British once again. Barney later learned that the *Saratoga* lost the other two prize ships, *Elizabeth* and *Nancy*, to recapture before returning to Philadelphia as well. This seesawing of events and exchange of prizes was typical for both sides. The *Saratoga* itself was tragically lost at sea with all hands, including Captain Young, the following March.

Joshua Barney was now about to enter yet another term of imprisonment as a captured naval officer, but this time he would not be so fortunate in his captors. Capt. Anthony James Pye Malloy of the seventy-four gun *Intrepid* believed that all American naval men were pirates and should be treated as such. He made the passage to New York miserable for Barney by forcing him to stand on the exposed quarterdeck for the entire journey. The young American officer was refused shelter or a change of clothing and was compelled to endure a snowstorm and accompanying knife-like winds for several days on end with only the lee of the deckhouse as protection from the harsh weather. Barney almost perished from exposure, and survived only to experience perhaps the worst level of inhumanity afforded to any American prisoner during the Revolutionary War.

"Foul Weather Jack" Byron, the genial vice admiral who had befriended Barney during his first imprisonment in New York, had been replaced by Adm. Sir George Rodney. The war was not going well for the Americans. The British held a large number of American naval officers, but there were few British prisoner officers to exchange for them. Most of the captive seamen were warehoused on the notoriously overcrowded *Jersey*. Barney and his prize crew were placed nearby in the smaller

Strombolo. The overcrowded prison ships were a continuing embarrass-ment for the local commanders. Therefore, Admiral Rodney ordered that seventy naval and privateer officers be put aboard the ship of the line *Yarmouth* for transport to a naval prison in England. On 17 November an order reached New York requesting an exchange of Captain Gill of the *Charming Molly* for Lieutenant Barney, but it arrived too late: The *Yarmouth* had sailed for Plymouth two days earlier.

Barney's fellow prisoners on the *Yarmouth* included Silas Talbot, a former Rhode Island artillery officer who had fought gallantly defending Fort Mifflin in the Delaware River below Philadelphia in 1777. About two years after that, on 17 September 1779, the Continental Congress had commissioned Talbot a captain in the Continental navy. Because there was no man-of-war available for him to command, Talbot accepted an offer from John Brown, an influential Providence merchant, to com-mand a privateer, the *General Washington.* Talbot captured two prizes with this new vessel, but his luck turned when he found himself in the midst of a fleet of British men-of-war. The *General Washington* ran before a gale but was ultimately captured by the *Culloden* in October 1780. The captured ship was renamed *General Monk,* and Talbot was sent to the *Yarmouth.*

The mid-November voyage across the stormy Atlantic on the *Yarmouth* was by all accounts a horrible experience. Its captain, a scoundrel named Skeffington Lutwidge, gained the distinction of being the man most despised by Joshua Barney. Henry Tuckerman's 1850 biog-raphy of Silas Talbot offers the following vivid account of the voyage:

In the midst of a hail storm [the prisoners] were marched . . . to the water's edge and put on board the *Yarmouth.* Not withstanding the extreme severity of the weather, they huddled together on the poop-deck, without the slightest refreshment until night when they were dri-ven into the hold, already nearly filled with casks of provisions, upon which loose planks were laid, the intervening space not allowing an upright posture. No light or air entered but what found their way through a scuttle only large enough to admit one prisoner at a time. Obliged to sit, kneel or crawl in this dismal abode, and deprived of the adequate means of respiration, they soon renewed the worst experience of the prison ship. Before morning there rose among them a desperate cry for water: a bottle was lowered, and such was the fierce struggle that ensued among the bewildered wretches, that scarcely one moistened his lips; and this miserable scene was again and again enacted. The air, at length, became so vitiated that a contagious fever broke out among the prisoners, and soon communicated to the sailors. Fear gained for the victims what pity had failed to yield. They were drawn up into squads, and placed in hammocks swung over the hog pens. By this process, continued through a winter voyage of seven weeks, these unfortunate men were alternately exposed to a putrid and suffocating heat and intense cold. . . . [T]heir appearance was frightful.[4]

If a man died, the others concealed it from their jailers as long as possible so that the dead man's food allotment would continue and could be shared among the survivors. Eleven of the seventy-one prisoners died in their own filth during that voyage, and even the most weather-toughened seamen suffered from severe illnesses and delirium.

When the ship reached Plymouth, fifty-three days after leaving Sandy Hook, and the hatches were unlocked, none of the poor wretches could climb out on his own. All had to be hoisted up by sling, and few could stand unaided when they were dropped onto the deck. The bright sunlight blinded and tortured eyes that had long been in darkness. The men shielded their faces with their hands or lowered their heads when the sun appeared from behind a cloud. Men who could stand gathered in twos and threes. Those able to walk staggered erratically across the deck, stumbling like patients emerging from some dark insane asylum. Bearded, disheveled, unkempt, and filthy, they were almost unrecognizable as once-proud American seamen. They seemed to have lost either the desire or the power to speak. The sight of their matted hair and beards, their sores running with pus, and their odor surely caused the officers and crew of the *Yarmouth* shame at the behavior of their captain, and at themselves for tolerating it.

The prisoners were moved to a nearby prison ship that was far more spacious. There they began to recover from the poor treatment at the hands of Captain Lutwidge. After a brief recuperation period they were transported ashore in small boats under heavy guard. This was probably more to hide them from the people of Plymouth than to prevent them from escaping. Once assembled in a courtroom for trial, they were placed before a quasi civil/military tribunal and questioned about the "allegiance they owned to His Most gracious Majesty" and their "revolt."

All were convicted of treason against the Crown for being "found in arms and Rebellion on the High Seas in various ships commissioned by the North American Congress." Sentenced to Old Mill Prison, located on a promontory between the town of Plymouth and the Plymouth docks, they joined some two to three hundred Americans already in custody.[5]

The Old Mill Prison complex consisted of several stoutly constructed gray stone buildings surrounded by double walls about twenty feet apart. The prison had two adjacent compounds, one for Americans and another for French and Spanish prisoners. The European inmates received slightly better treatment because they were designated prisoners of war, while the Americans were considered either lowly pirates or traitors to the Crown. The only access to the prison was through two eight-foot-tall iron gates. Sentries stood at these gates and patrolled the walls that overlooked the prison yards and the road to the prison.

The new inmates met old shipmates who had been incarcerated there for a year or more. These seasoned prisoners cast a pall of hopelessness and despair on the newcomers. Escape from this fortress was difficult. Exchanges were few. On the other hand, the warden of the prison, a reasonable but bureaucratic man, allowed a certain amount of commerce between the prisoners and townspeople as well as with the guards. Prisoners could purchase food to supplement the prison diet, clothing, and small personal items with money sent by their families. Many guards remembered pleasant experiences serving "over seas" in North America or had family there and were amicable toward the American prisoners.

One of the prisoners, William Russell, kept a journal of the events in the prison and on 4 July 1781 recorded that many of the Americans decorated their hats with either thirteen stars and stripes drawn on pieces of paper or the motto "Independence, Liberty or Death." Just before one o'clock in the afternoon, they drew up in a military line in the yard to give thirteen cheers in the traditional navy huzzah for the United States of America. Their allies, the French prisoners, answered over the walls in a like manner, and all celebrated with what merriment they could muster under the watchful guards. Barney did not participate in this celebration, for he had made a daring escape a month and a half earlier. Two entries in Russell's journal describe the event:

May 18, 1781: Lieutenant Joshua Barney made his escape over the gate at noon, and has not been missed yet.

May 19, 1781: A tailor brought a suit of cloth[e]s to the prison for Lieutenant Barney by which means his escape was discovered and we were mustered. The Agent says he saw him at twelve o'clock this day and has ordered us to be locked in the yard all day, dinner excepted. The way we concealed his escape was when we were counted in the prison, to put a young boy out through the window and he was counted twice. So much for one of our Old Mill Prison capers![6]

Russell's account is at slight odds with the tale of Barney's escape as told by Mary Barney. It is possible that she or her father-in-law may have taken some minor romantic license in recounting a few details of the escape, but her description of it is far more detailed than Russell's. According to Mary, Barney had tried to escape shortly after being interned, and being caught was sentenced to thirty days in solitary confinement secured by double heavy irons. Thinking that Barney would try to escape again, the warden ordered the guards to watch him closely. Realizing this, the lieutenant was especially discreet as he laid his escape plans. First he pretended to injure his ankle while engaged in an athletic activity with the men in the prison yard. In full view of the guards, fellow prisoners bathed and dressed the wound. Thereafter he hobbled about on an improvised pair of crutches. Barney seemed unlikely to attempt an escape until he had recovered, and the guards relaxed their vigilance.

Next, the crafty lieutenant started to wear a dreary greatcoat, a sort of oversized duster, in the prison yard. This costume made him blend into the general prison population and covered whatever garments he wore underneath. The merchants who frequently came to the prison had a profitable business furnishing goods for the prisoners' needs. Barney asked a tailor to make or alter a British naval officer's uniform for him. Junior British officers wore a blue tailed coat with a white lining that showed at the lapels, brass buttons, and a black cocked hat with a cockade (a knot of ribbon worn as a badge of rank). Somehow the outfit was smuggled into the prison. Barney then enlisted a small group of friends to help in his plan. One was a very tall fellow with broad shoulders who was asked to loiter near the gate so that he would be in position when needed. Next, Barney had a boy called "Slender," who had been a powder monkey, practice slipping through the window bars. Slender's job was to retrieve Barney's greatcoat at the proper moment and, later, to act as a substitute for Barney at roll call so that the lieutenant would not be missed. As a final precaution Barney cultivated friendships with some of the guards. He became particularly close to a sergeant who had served in America and had enough confidence in this relationship to ask the Englishman for help in his escape.

On the day of the planned escape, 18 May 1781, Barney limped on his crutches over to the prison gate. The guard who was his friend was on duty between the two gates from noon until two o'clock. Barney whispered the prearranged signal: "Today?" The soldier responded, "Dinner!" signifying that the time to try the escape was one o'clock, when most of the guards would be at lunch. Barney returned to the barracks, donned the secreted officer's uniform under his greatcoat, and alerted his conspirators. As they took their stations in the yard, Barney purposely walked without the usual limp across the prison yard. He went directly up to the large—almost gigantic—friend who had positioned himself next to the wall. A guard patrolling the outer wall was temporarily distracted by a commotion on the other side of the prison yard. The sergeant gave Barney a wink that indicated the coast was clear. The young lieutenant then rapidly placed one foot into the stirrup formed by the hands of the tall, strong friend. He jumped onto his accomplice's shoulders, and from there onto the inner wall of the prison. Quickly and silently he dropped to the ground on the other side of the inner wall. The greatcoat was tossed back into the yard, where Slender put it on and limped away. Barney nonchalantly passed the sergeant four guineas with a return wink. Now, disguised as a uniformed British naval officer with the appropriate well-practiced bearing, Barney strolled past the sentries on the outer wall and through its gate without a challenge, exchanging the courtesy of a smart naval salute.

After the short walk into Plymouth Barney made his way to a "safe house" run by sympathizers to the American cause. At first the people who ran the safe house thought that a British naval officer had discovered their divided loyalties. Once convinced that Barney was an escapee, they hid him until darkness, then moved him to the house of a respected clergyman of Plymouth where he would be safe. Much to Barney's surprise, three Americans from the Eastern Shore of Maryland were already guests at the pastor's house. The two gentlemen and their servant had been passengers on a ship captured by the British. As noncombatants they had been taken to England and placed under loose surveillance. Now they were awaiting the opportunity to slip out of the country and back to America. The good news for Barney was that they had sufficient funds to take him with them.

The imaginative lieutenant persuaded the Americans that he could lead them all to safety. They accepted his plan and provided funds for the purchase of a fishing smack, which was tied at the Plymouth fishing quay. On the eve of the planned escape the two gentlemen and their servant, dressed in old attire suitable for fishermen, boarded the vessel and pretended to retire for the night. Just before dawn the next morning, Barney joined them. He wore another coarsely woven greatcoat described as a "fear-nothing," plus a large, water-repellent oiled tarpaulin hat and a black handkerchief knotted at his throat. The greatcoat tied at his waist with an old rope end gave him the appearance of a very salty fisherman indeed. Under this costume he wore his recently acquired British naval officer's uniform.

Dawn broke through the morning fog at the quayside as Barney, the only man of the group with experience at handling a sail or a line, cast off the smack's lines from the quay, hoisted a jib, set a closely reefed mainsail, and eased the smack into the shipping channel. The tide and winds were favorable. As the sun rose, the coverlet of fog neatly folded back and the smack sailed past the breakwater at the mouth of the harbor. With the light becoming brighter, Barney ordered the two American gentlemen below into the tiny cabin. The appearance on deck would be that of a fisherman and his mate out for their morning fishing expedition. There were many ships-of-war "pacing about," and Barney eyed them warily as if they were huge sentries on the wall of Old Mill Prison. His plan appeared to be working. No alarm had been sounded about his escape, and none of the ships in the harbor showed any interest in a common fishing boat. Finally, they passed the last of the warships and entered the open English Channel. Barney shouted below for his companions to come up on deck, but there was no answer. The two Americans were seasick. An old salt's remedy of the day was to consume pork fat, and Barney ordered the servant to fetch some from the galley. Unfortunately, the servant, whose name was Jem, was also seasick, lying with his face next to a leeward scupper. This made Barney the only man onboard who could handle the smack. That would not be a problem if the wind held and they did not encounter any curious British vessels.

After a few hours at sea Barney spotted a sail on the horizon. He watched carefully as it approached the fishing boat. To his dismay the ship identified itself as a privateer out of Guernsey and ordered the smack to heave to. Barney had no choice but to obey. The armed vessel sent over a jolly boat with a young officer in charge who demanded to know what cargo the fishing boat was carrying and its destination. Barney knew that his ruse as a Plymouth fisherman would not carry any credence at this point because he could not imitate the local working-class dialect. Thinking quickly, he spoke as a gentleman, stating that he had nothing onboard except three passengers and he was bound for France. The astonished officer asked what his business was in France. Barney replied that he was not at liberty to divulge this; then, untying the rope around his waist and the knot of his handkerchief, he removed his oversized hat, pulled back the folds of the greatcoat, and displayed the uniform of a British naval officer. The young officer of the privateer was impressed and respectfully saluted by lifting his cap. He deferentially begged the lieutenant's pardon and rowed back to the ship.

Barney's anxiety temporarily turned to confidence, but after a few minutes the jolly boat returned, this time carrying the captain of the privateer. The discerning skipper was very much aware of the many schemes of the smugglers and spies who ran the channel waters. He climbed over the rail of the smack and greeted Barney with great official courtesy, then politely inquired what business might bring a disguised but uniformed British naval officer into enemy waters without any armed support. The captain said that he was sorry to detain the unidentified naval officer from completing his mission, but he required some proof or documentation that the lieutenant was on government business. Perhaps the lieutenant could produce confirmation without revealing any official secrets? Barney replied that showing the captain such proof might compromise the secrecy of his extremely vital Crown business in France. If he was to be successful, secrecy was essential.

The captain remained polite but steadfast. Under the circumstances, he said, it would be necessary to return Barney and his passengers to England. This was not the response Barney had expected. He felt the frigid finger of impending doom touching his shoulder. Exhibiting a calm front over his agitated stomach, however, he said, "Do as you please, sir, but remember that it is at your own peril. All I have to say is, that if you persist in interrupting my voyage, I must demand that you carry me directly on board Admiral Digby's ship at Plymouth." This was a dangerous but brilliant ploy. Barney knew that British privateers were very reluctant to venture near men-of-war, particularly admirals' ships. The Royal Navy was very short of able seamen and more than willing to impress the crew of a privateer when the opportunity arose. In order to subtly make the threat of possible impressment more apparent, Barney went out of his way to praise the seamanship of the privateer's sailors and their neat, navylike appearance. The captain was unyielding, however, and left an officer and two men aboard the smack to ensure that it would follow the privateer back to Plymouth.

The return trip was against the wind, making it difficult for the smack to follow the more seaworthy privateer back to Plymouth. At times the larger ship was almost out of sight. If the two American gentlemen and the servant had not been seasick, the four Americans might have overpowered their guards, recaptured the smack, and escaped into the darkness. It was no use for Barney to try it with just himself, however. Evidently, though, Barney had made his point about the vulnerability of the privateer's crew. After transferring his captives to the privateer, the captain ordered both vessels to drop anchor in Causen Bay about two leagues (ca. six nautical miles) away from Admiral Digby's flagship. He was still puzzled about Barney's true identity but treated him with the respect that was due a British naval officer.[7]

The captain ordered his personal gig lowered and was rowed the considerable distance to the admiral's ship to speak directly to the commander. Meanwhile, Barney's companions had recovered enough to be distressed at learning that they would likely be tried as conspirators for abetting the flight of a prisoner. Barney, who had no intention of remaining tamely on the privateer, persuaded them that if he were not in their company, the authorities would not be harsh on the Americans.

In the captain's absence much of the privateer's crew went ashore. The men who remained onboard appeared impressed by Barney's shiny brass buttons, so Lieutenant Barney continued to act like a British naval officer, pacing the decks with practiced bearing while carefully looking for an opportunity to slip away. He found one. A small skiff was tied up under the stern of the privateer. Barney feigned drowsiness, remarked that he needed a nap, and pretended to fall asleep near the stern rail on the quarterdeck. At around noon the crew cued up for dinner. Seeing that they were distracted, Barney rolled over the rail and dropped hand-over-hand down the stern line to the boat below, painfully scraping his leg on the rough hemp rope during the descent.

A strong onshore wind was pushing the stern of the ship in the direction of the village of Causen. Barney could see that his descent had been observed from the shore, so he decided to scull shoreward to allay any suspicion. As he landed, some of the men on the beach helped him secure the boat and draw it up above the tide line. Maintaining a military voice of authority, he gave directions to a group that included the local customs officer, who started asking questions about the fishing smack. The official wanted to know where it had been taken and what it had aboard, assuming, quite naturally, that Barney was part of the force that had taken it as a prize. Barney disregarded the questions and pointed to his bleeding leg. Stating that he wished to have his wound treated, he asked where "his men" were. The answer came back that they were last seen at the Red Lion Pub at the west end of the village. He thanked the customs official and limped down the village high street, maintaining a proper military demeanor. The rutted road took him past the Red Lion, which he managed to skirt without notice. As he came to a bend in the street just beyond the tavern, a crew member from the privateer suddenly came upon him strolling in the same general direction. The crewman, who had no reason to believe that Barney was anything other than the naval officer he was pretending to be, greeted him cordially. The two men exchanged pleasantries, the seaman saying that he was pleased to see the lieutenant ashore. During their brief conversation the sailor mentioned that some of the men had talked about asking Barney for information concerning joining the Royal Navy. They wanted to serve with fine officers like him. As Barney answered the man's pointed questions he gained the impression that privateering, at least with their present captain, had not been profitable for the crew. Barney continued to engage the sailor in conversation, pointing out additional opportunities of naval service and using him as a "cover" as he walked through the village. The sailor was uncomfortable talking to an officer and felt the need of his fellow crewmen for support. Presently he stopped and asked where Barney was going. Barney answered, "To Plymouth. Come on; you might as well come with me to join the navy." Not one to make quick decisions, the seaman said that he had to talk it over with his mates, but he wished the lieutenant luck as they parted company. One wonders why Barney told the sailor his destination since his true identity would soon be common knowledge. It may have been an attempt at reverse logic; if this is where the cunning man said he was going, those looking for him might conclude that there was little chance that he would actually go there.

When the good-natured, if slow-witted, tar excused himself to disappear into a public house, Barney quickened his pace. Any subsequent encounter with a crewman from the privateer was not likely to have such a benign outcome. Deciding that his best chance for escape lay in leaving the highway, Barney jumped through a hedge that bordered the road. On the other side was a park surrounding an elegant château, which he would later discover was the home of Lord Edgecombe. Before long Barney came to a large, well-tended formal garden. His leg wound was now causing him great discomfort, so he rested for a few minutes in the shade of a large old oak tree. It was not long before a crusty old gardener discovered the fugitive and asked what he was doing on private property. Barney replied that he was an officer from the privateer in Causen Bay on his way to Plymouth. He explained he had crossed the hedge and the park with the hope of finding a shortcut. He had hurt his leg in a careless accident, and he wanted to walk as little as possible. The gardener said that there was a toll of half a guinea for trespassing onto the estate. Barney replied that as a seaman he was not aware of such tolls or fines for going overland. The lieutenant turned on his considerable charm, making the gardener forget his demands and become a helpful friend. He led Barney to a back portion of the grounds that bordered the river that ran through Plymouth. When they arrived at the riverbank they saw a shallow-draft wherry being navigated by a butcher who was taking two sheep to market downstream. Barney negotiated a ferry ride across the river for sixpence. This enabled him to avoid the public ferry and circumvent Old Mill Prison, where he had started this adventure. By nightfall he found himself back under the hospitable roof of the kindly, trusted cleric in Plymouth.

Two years later, Barney made a postwar visit to Lord Edgecombe's estate and sought out the old gardener in order to pay the man the half guinea the lieutenant felt he still owed. The old man was both astonished and pleased to see him. Ironically, it turned out that the guard at Mill Prison who had helped him to escape was the man's son. The father and son had talked about the pleasant young American many times since then. Barney was so amused and pleased that he gave the gardener the entire contents of his purse rather than half a guinea, plus his address in America so that if he or his son were ever to visit they might be his guests.

❧ 4 ❧

HOME

The *Hyder-Ally*

When he reached Admiral Digby's flagship, the captain of the British privateer found that the alleged Royal Navy officer he had in custody was an impostor. Admiral Digby had received word that an artful American naval officer had escaped from Old Mill Prison, and he reasoned that the man the privateer had captured was probably the same fellow. Congratulating the privateer captain, the admiral ordered him to place the American prisoner ashore under armed guard so that he might be returned to Old Mill. When the triumphant captain returned to his ship, he was confounded to find that Barney had fled some time ago—and in one of his own boats. Admiral Digby would certainly not be pleased to hear that, and he might retaliate by seizing the privateer and its crew. The captain still held the two American gentlemen and their servant, but they were a liability to feed and quarter. The privateer therefore ordered them put ashore, confiscating their fishing smack as a meager reward for this misadventure, and quickly sailed away from the Plymouth area.

The Americans traveled the same road to Plymouth that Barney had taken earlier and reached the minister's residence to find that Barney had preceded them. The lieutenant was pleased to see that his companions had been released unharmed, as he anticipated. The four men enjoyed sharing the story of their mutual escape from the privateer. Though amusing in its retelling, the capture and release had been profoundly serious at the time. During a hearty reunion dinner, their recounting and laughter were interrupted by a town crier who strolled by the vicarage shouting, "Five guineas reward for the apprehension of Joshua Barney, a rebel deserter from Mill Prison. All loyal subjects are to assist in his arrest." A handbill that soon appeared in town said that Barney was to be considered dangerous. The lieutenant's appearance together with that of his uniform was described in some detail on the bill. Barney had no difficulty persuading his former colleagues that, for their own safety, he should continue his escape alone. The cleric had a son who was about Barney's size, so an elegant coat and trousers were slightly altered to fit the American. A ruffled shirt, silk stockings, the hat of a dandy, and a powdered wig completed the new disguise. Because of his excellent manners and striking features, Barney could easily pass as an English gentleman. All that was required was a reasonable impersonation, and the American naval lieutenant relished the challenge. His companions from Maryland gave him a letter of credit to aid him if he made it to London.

After a fond farewell to his comrades and an another expression of gratitude to his hosts, the young lieutenant climbed into a post chaise for yet another escape, this time in a more stylish disguise. A sentry challenged Barney's driver as they reached the gate of the town. The army private shoved his lantern into the cab and peered at the lone passenger. His orders were to keep a sharp watch for the American fugitive. Barney, playing a scene out of light opera, assumed a look of arrogance and indignation. He barked at the soldier for his insolence in stopping him for such a foolish business, then smiled, saying that a gentleman must be allowed to pass. Raising his tone slightly, Barney threatened to speak with the soldier's sergeant about the affront, suggesting a punishment the sentinel would long regret. The intimidated sentry wilted under Barney's threat, and with the crack of the postilion's whip, the post chaise rolled quickly down the road.

The first scheduled stop was about forty-five miles away in the pleasant town of Exeter. Arriving at about dawn, Barney ate a hearty breakfast in an inn where he made the acquaintance of a "young female of modest, and interesting appearance" who was following the same route to

Bristol that Barney was taking.[1] Using a little charm, he persuaded her to let him pose as her brother, should any query be made about him, because he was traveling on a secret mission and must remain incognito. She readily agreed. Once again his charisma had worked its magic.

Barney arrived in Bristol without incident. There he contacted an Englishman who was a friend of his comrades from Maryland. The Englishman introduced him to the affable Mr. Clifford, an agent for the American government. Confident now that his escape would be successful, Barney rested for several days. The two men determined that Barney should go to London, where he would find a sympathizer, an American by birth who was an official in His Majesty's Customs. Mr. Clifford made an impression of his personal seal in wax for Barney to show as identification and a sign of entitlement to protection and assistance. Contact was made in London, and he and the customs official quickly became good friends.

Barney thought that he should not be denied the opportunity to see the sights of London simply because he was a fugitive. The best hiding place, after all, is often in the open where no one expects to find you. Therefore, the two new friends audaciously attended a service at Westminster, went boating on the Thames, and even watched King George drive by in his gilded state coach on his way to Saint Paul's Cathedral. Barney later said that he was not very impressed at the sight of His Majesty.

Barney knew that Henry Laurens, a wealthy merchant and planter from South Carolina, was being held prisoner in the Tower of London. Laurens, one of America's most notable diplomats, had been captured while traveling to Holland with the draft for a treaty between the Continental Congress and the Netherlands. He attempted to scuttle the papers by throwing them over the side of the ship *Mercury*, but they did not sink. The British retrieved them and realized that they had captured a political prize as well as a prize vessel. Barney desperately wanted to visit Laurens, but this was considered too brazen for a man in his position to attempt.

Finally, the time came for Barney to cross the English Channel and make the final leg of the escape to either a neutral country or one allied to the United States. The least-guarded route was that of the continental mail packet that regularly sailed to Ostend. Barney rode by stage to Margate and found the small vessel that was to make the channel crossing. The sea was particularly rough as they left the safety of the harbor, and Barney was pleased to be on the deck of the rolling packet. He noticed a handsome private coach lashed to deck rings between the deckhouses. Nearby, four well-matched horses were tied to jury-rigged stalls made from assorted timbers. He wondered about the owner of the fine equipage. None of the passengers that he had seen board, the usual mix of merchants and artisans, appeared able to afford such luxury. When he took shelter in the passenger cabin the mystery was solved. All of the cabin's occupants were completely absorbed in dealing with their own mal de mer. On plush overstuffed pillows in a corner lay a woman who seemed to be in a faint. When the vessel lurched wildly, the poor woman was thrown to the deck. The other passengers, in various stages of misery themselves, appeared oblivious to her. Although the lady was desperately ill, Barney could not help noticing that she was both beautiful and well dressed, and that she had an appearance of grace and breeding. When he came to her aid, the woman addressed him in cultured French. She had left her cabin to find a steward when her strength failed her, she told him. She had tried to rest on the cushions but had been thrown to the floor. Barney picked her up in his strong arms, carried her to her stateroom, and placed her safely on her bunk. He then had a pantry-man make a cup of hot mulled wine to treat her seasickness. Whether this was an alternative remedy to the pork fat prescribed during his fishing-smack adventure for the same malady or one that he reserved for fine ladies is not clear. In any case, the lady appeared grateful and thanked him.

When the tired and battered passengers arrived safely at the pier in Ostend the next morning, Barney politely inquired about the health of the elegant lady passenger. She was exhausted, but pleased at the fine-looking young man's concern. She was under the impression that he was a physician. The lady addressed her liveried servants in Italian, asking them to look after the horses, which might also have suffered during the difficult voyage. Then the mysterious woman invited Barney to join her at dinner. He accepted with thanks and during the meal told her that he was an American naval officer. She was amused at her mistaken assumption of his profession and thereafter addressed him as "Monsieur le Capitaine." Much to Barney's chagrin, the lady would not identify herself by name. During the dinner conversation she told him that she was an Italian citizen who had been living in London. She was on her way to Brussels by way of Bruges, where she was to meet a friend on personal business. During the dessert course she asked Barney his destination. He replied that he was going to Amsterdam by way of Brussels. On hearing this, she invited him to join her in her private carriage for the journey.

Their first stop was at Bruges. There, an elderly gentleman in the uniform of an Austrian major general greeted her with great deference. The lady and the distinguished officer conversed in Italian quietly, then the major general gave her a sealed packet to take with her in the carriage. Barney did not speak Italian, and this discussion was thus lost on him. When they arrived in Brussels the lady asked Barney to wait with her and share her accommodations in a hotel for two days until she could make a rendezvous. The mysterious rendezvous ultimately took place at an exquisite house located in an exclusive part of town. An elegantly dressed porter greeted them and ushered them into a reception room where diplomats and high-ranking German officers sat in formal chairs or stood in clusters near a splendid fireplace. All stiffened noticeably and bowed as Emperor Joseph II of Austria entered the room. The emperor took the lady's hand and spoke to her with affection. She introduced Barney to His Imperial Majesty as an American naval officer who had shown her much kindness in making her journey safe and enjoyable. The emperor addressed Barney, apparently thanking him, but Barney did not understand his German. The lady spoke to the emperor in a private chamber for more than a quarter of an hour, then asked Barney to accompany her back to their hotel. She explained that the emperor was traveling incognito to provinces within his protectorate (including Belgium) and that Barney was not to mention this meeting to anyone. She unfortunately had to leave immediately for Italy and thanked him once again for his many courtesies. With that they parted. If Barney knew the lady's true identity, he never divulged it, or the statecraft and intrigue he had observed. It was his first personal encounter with royalty, and it left a lasting impression.[2]

Barney spent the next two days alone in Brussels before he could arrange transportation to Amsterdam. The trip had its rewards because he was able to tour the lovely cities of Antwerp, Rotterdam, and The Hague on the way. In Amsterdam he met John Adams, minister plenipotentiary of the United States, who was there to complete the treaty of alliance with Holland that had been interrupted by the capture of Henry Laurens. Adams had heard of the young man and received him courteously. During their conversation Barney related the story of his capture by the *Intrepid* and the events leading up to his present meeting. The crusty New Englander was delighted with the story and commended him for his resourcefulness and bravery. Adams mentioned that there was a newly commissioned American frigate at the port of Amsterdam that was expected to sail for the United States shortly and gave him a note of introduction to the captain, Commo. Alexander Gillon, requesting a gratis passage home for Barney. The ship was the *South Carolina*, of the South Carolina navy, and Gillon cordially accepted Lieutenant Barney as a passenger but warned that he was about to sail.

The *South Carolina* had originally been built for the Continental Congress, but the British ambassador, Sir Joseph York, had lodged a protest with the Dutch officials, who responded by blocking the ship's delivery to the Americans. Instead it was sold to the duke of Montmorency-Luxembourg, who entered an agreement with Alexander Gillon, a successful merchant from Charleston, South Carolina, who had come to Europe to purchase supplies for the Continental Congress and ships for his state's navy. Gillon would sail the ship as a privateer, and the duke of Luxembourg would receive a quarter share of the prizes taken.

For two years after Gillon leased the vessel it sat idle at Texel Roads near Amsterdam. Always short of funds, Gillon let the ship fall into disrepair. The chronically shorthanded crew was mostly made up of American sailors, ex-prisoners who had escaped from various British jails. Gillon's practice of keeping the men onboard with no liberty privileges, but within sight of the land only two miles away, produced a very disgruntled crew. Despite a huge debit and threats of seizure by creditors, he had managed by mid-1781 to gather a sufficient crew, assemble enough provisions, and make the necessary repairs to put to sea safely.

Barney boarded the *South Carolina* on 12 August 1781, and the vessel soon sailed for North America on its maiden voyage. Misfortune immediately visited them in the form of a violent North Sea storm that was to claim many lives and ships. One of the passengers on the vessel was the multitalented John Trumbull. The Yale-educated Trumbull, only a year or two older than Barney, had served briefly as aide-de-camp to General Washington before becoming more interested in art than war and deciding to study in England to perfect his skills. Before long, Trumbull's politics became known and the artist-author was imprisoned. After his release was arranged, he traveled to Holland seeking passage to America.

Trumbull's memoirs give a vivid account of the great North Sea storm that pummeled the *South Carolina* shortly after it sailed.[3]

The obvious course was to return to the relative shelter of Texel Roads, but Commodore Gillon dared not do that for fear of being imprisoned for unpaid debts. Entry into the English Channel would make the *South Carolina* easy prey for British cruisers. Anchoring was not a good option. The wind was so fierce that the ship was likely to be blown onto the lee shore. The only other possibility was to sail to the northeast under shortened sail. At that point an extremely heavy fog engulfed them. Now the shallow water and shifting sands off the coast of Holland became a real danger. The *South Carolina* spent an anxious morning among the shoals, and by the afternoon it was noted that the ship's weather chain plates (iron plates fixed to the hull to hold the lateral rigging of the masts) had suffered damage from the stress. The crew had to close-reef the topsails under the most arduous of conditions. When this was finally accomplished they were in sight of Heligoland, the headlands and mouth of the River Elbe, where the coast turns due north. At ten o'clock in the evening an even more intense squall struck. Blowing from the north, the gale set the *South Carolina*'s sails aback, stopping the ship's forward progress and rendering it unmanageable. The officers lost their self-confidence, and the crew was in a state of confusion and panic.

At this point Barney stepped forward. Trumbull wrote, "Happily for us, Capt. Barney was among the passengers—he had just escaped from Mill Prison in England. Hearing the increasing tumult aloft and feeling the ungovernable motion of the ship, he flew on the deck, saw the danger, assumed command, the men obeyed, and he soon had her again under control." The wind shifted several more points to the northeast, so by tacking to the west Barney was able to relieve the dangerous strain on the mainmast and the ship safely rode out the storm. The artist noted that on the following morning a Swedish seventy-four-gun ship and the twelve merchantmen comprising its convoy were found wrecked on Texel Island with all hands lost. As they were to learn later, the *South Carolina* was also assumed lost among the immense tangle of jetsam that was a graveyard of ships.

In fact, the *South Carolina* sailed north around the Orkney Islands of Scotland and then south below Ireland. During this northerly run the ship was caught in a typical North Sea heavy gale. This time several dozen cannonballs broke loose from their locker and rolled from side to side on the gun deck inside the ship, crashing into everything, men or objects, in their path. Chests, furniture, and supplies in canvas bags were all crushed to varying degrees. The only way to stop the shot was to snag them in sailor's hammocks thrown on the deck.

The *South Carolina* managed to sail on to the Bay of Biscay. Despite all the punishment the ship had taken, Gillon was able to take one small prize along the way to help pay for the voyage. The badly damaged *South Carolina* was forced to put into the Spanish port of Coruña to seek food, water, and other stores. Barney, Trumbull, and a number of other passengers, having lost all confidence in Gillon, left the *South Carolina* there.

Barney and Trumbull took passage to America on the twenty-gun privateer *Cicero*. Its captain, Hugh Hill, put to sea for the first leg of the voyage along with two prizes that mounted sixteen guns each. They were told that an English ship and two brigs were in the area and were advised to keep a sharp lookout. At sunset the *Cicero* came across what appeared to be that very force. The Americans loaded their cannons, armed a boarding party, and sailed alongside. They hailed the ships in English, got no response, and then tried French. The reply was an annoying silence. Captain Hill ordered a massive broadside that sent the "hostile squadron" scurrying in multiple directions. A small boat was lowered from the largest of the vessels and a party crossed to the *Cicero* under a flag of truce. It turned out that the Americans had attacked a convoy of Spanish ships bound for the West Indies. The ships had suffered severe damage to their masts and rigging, but fortunately no one was killed or badly hurt. Apologies were made and the Americans assisted with repairs. The trio of American ships then escorted their unfortunate victims back to the safety of Bilboa. As the *Cicero* was taking on additional cargo for a passage to Beverly, a messenger arrived from Madrid "with orders to unhang the rudders of all American ships in the port until the bill for repairs of the wounded ship, damage to her consorts, etc., were paid."[4]

The owner of the *Cicero*, the house of Cabot of Beverly, Massachusetts, was good for its bills, but it took months for currency to be transferred and the accounting to be verified. During this time, word reached the stranded Americans of the British surrender at Yorktown on 19 October 1781. Good news traveled surprisingly fast as ships exchanged important information with each passing vessel. The war was not yet officially over, but the victory of the United States now seemed certain. The

Cicero finally set sail for the Atlantic crossing in November. When they reached Beverly in mid-December, twenty-two-year-old Joshua Barney was the center of attention. The Cabots had heard all about the exploits of the young mariner. The passengers had developed affection for the young man and made sure that his extraordinary story was spread among those ashore. Shortly after he had settled into temporary lodgings, the Messrs. Cabot offered him the captaincy of a fine, well-equipped, twenty-gun privateer and the privilege of choosing his own grounds on which to sail it. (It is not clear what Barney's obligations were, if any, to fulfilling the terms of his naval commission.) It was flattering indeed for such a very young man to be offered his first official captain's title plus the financial opportunities that such a position afforded. But he had been away from his wife for more than a year, and had suffered much during that time. Barney reluctantly declined the generous offer in favor of time to rest and be with his family.

His route from Beverly to Philadelphia took Barney though Boston, where a northeast blizzard stranded him for weeks. Barney possessed some notoriety in this highly social town and before long had made the acquaintance of several other men who had been prisoners at Old Mill Prison. They formed a strong bond that only shared hard experience can produce, and the renewed acquaintances led to evenings with John Hancock and Samuel Adams. Moved by his meetings with these legendary patriots, the young lieutenant found the time spent in Boston most pleasant and formed fond memories for his later years.

Winter refused to loosen its icy grip on New England that year. Barney befriended another man who wished to go to Philadelphia and the pair journeyed overland by sleigh. With the help of a pair of good horses and sturdy runners, they made it to Princeton, New Jersey, and the edge of the snowy ground cover. Here they changed to a more conventional wheeled vehicle. Finally, on 21 March 1782, Lt. Joshua Barney arrived at Alderman Bedford's townhouse in Philadelphia. When the door opened, the light from the street fell on the face of his wife, whom he had sorely missed. This was an intense moment of elation for Barney. His biographer daughter-in-law colored this affectionate scene with the following sentence: "To add to his present felicity, his blushing wife presented him a young stranger, already able to lisp those earliest endearing, heart-touching monosyllables: 'Ma! . . . Pa!'" This was Mary Barney's first description of the young boy she would later marry.

The happy reunion with his family, the respite in Philadelphia, and the ending of the Revolutionary War would seem to presage the end of Barney's naval career. They were, in fact, merely the prologue to the legend of Lieutenant and Commodore Joshua Barney.

For most casual students of American history, the Revolutionary War ended with Lord Cornwallis's surrender to General Washington at Yorktown on 19 October 1781. While this was the last significant land battle, the war at sea continued for another seventeen months. By the spring of 1782 the Continental navy had only two frigates left, the *Deane* and the *Alliance,* and half a dozen smaller vessels. The *Saratoga* had been lost at sea; the *Confederacy* had surrendered without a struggle; and the British ships *Iris* and *General Monk* had captured the proud frigate *Trumbull* the previous summer. Particularly humiliating was the fact that the *Iris* was the American ship *Hancock* captured and renamed. Similarly, the *General Monk,* a trim sloop-of-war, was the refitted ex-privateer *General Washington* from Rhode Island, the same vessel that Capt. Silas Talbot had been forced to surrender to the *Culloden* almost two years earlier.

As Lieutenant Barney assessed the prospects for resuming his career in the Continental navy, he learned that the list of unassigned naval officers numbered twenty-two captains and thirty-nine lieutenants. The likelihood of finding a billet appeared slim. However, Daniel Smith, secretary to the Pennsylvania Commissioners for the Defense of the Delaware, heard of Barney's return and recommended granting him a commission as a captain in the navy of Pennsylvania and assigning him command of an armed vessel. The prospect of commanding a ship all his own was both gratifying and flattering. A Pennsylvania commission, though not a federal navy rank, would allow him to continue the fight against the British and might lead to a higher position more quickly. It was not unusual for officers to accept a command in a state's navy while waiting for an assignment in the regular navy; thus Barney became a captain in the Pennsylvania State navy.

During early 1782 the British blockade of the Delaware River was nearly impenetrable. A network of various-sized armed vessels interdicted all shipping. Many of the British fleet were small, flat-bottomed craft called refugee boats because Tories manned them. These vessels would hide in marsh creeks and tiny coves, then swoop down on passing ships before their defenses could be mustered. Delaware's wide coastal marshlands contained many inlets, creeks, and river mouths that offered shelter to the raiders before and after raids. The shallow-draft vessels also carried British soldiers and marines to raid farms and villages. The raiders burned the houses of American rebels and took their livestock. The refugee boats were supplemented by a moving picket line of larger ships; the most effective of these were a whaler called the *Trimmer* from New York, the British frigate *Medea,* and the sloop-of-war *General Monk.* When the Continental Congress and Pennsylvania's navy failed to drive off the British blockaders, Philadelphia merchants took action. They purchased and armed the best vessel available at quayside, the one-hundred-ton *Hyder-Ally,* a merchantman owned by John Willcocks and named for a Moslem ruler who led a courageous but unsuccessful revolt against the British in India.[5]

Four days after Barney arrived back home in Philadelphia he was recruited to command the ship, and on 25 March 1782 the twenty-two-year-old assumed the direction of the *Hyder-Ally*'s conversion into a warship. The job consisted of cutting gun ports in the ship's sides, strengthening the bulwarks against cannon shot, reinforcing the decks to withstand the weight of heavy cannons, and providing accommodations for the more than one hundred sailors needed to operate the sails and guns. Barney and the merchants managed to find sixteen 6-pounder cannons and had them mounted. The *Hyder-Ally*'s rigging was restored, and spare sails were made. Stores, including black powder, shot of various kinds, and small arms, were procured. At the same time Barney chose his officers and crew from a relative abundance of unemployed experienced sailors in the Philadelphia area. Justus Starr was his first lieutenant, Luke Mathewman was appointed his second, and the lieutenant for the marines was named Scull. The latter was a Bucks County resident who enlisted a formidable band of marksmen. The marines took great pride in their abilities and seemed to enjoy military discipline. The rest of the crew drilled to become proficient in the art of naval artillery.

A favorite means of capturing the imagination of the populace during the Revolutionary War was to pen a patriotic poem (no matter how bad) and set it to a familiar tune to be sung in taverns and on village greens. These poems served as genre "rap songs," rhythmic adventure stories. At that time a substantial part of the population was illiterate or only semiliterate. Listening to a rousing poem sung to well-known music was a popular form of entertainment. The journalist and sometime "patriot poet" Philip Freneau wrote a fifteen-stanza poem for Barney's recruiting effort that promised wealth, drink, women, and masculine adventure to those who enlisted. Some sample stanzas give the flavor of the antique advertising used to sway mere boys to become fighting men.

The Sailor's Invitation

Come all ye lads that know no fear,
To wealth and honor we will steer
In the Hyder-Ally Privateer
Commanded by bold Barney.

Accept our terms without delay,
And make your fortunes while you may.
Such offers are not every day
In the power of the jolly sailor.

Who cannot wounds and battle dare
Shall never clasp the blooming fair;
The brave alone their charms shall share
The brave and their protectors!

While timorous landsmen lurk on shore,
'Tis ours to go where cannons roar—
On a coasting cruise we'll go once more,
Despisers of all danger.

And fortune still, that crowns the brave
Shall guard us o'er the gloomy wave—
A fearful heart betrays a knave!
Success to the Hyder-Ally![6]

The promise of potential financial reward was crucial in raising funds for a bond and recruiting a crew. On 2 April 1782, Joshua Barney and William Allibone posted a bond of twenty thousand dollars for the vessel, a near record for the time. Records list the *Hyder-Ally's* owners as Thomas Fitzsimmonds, Francis Gurney, and William Allibone.[7] For some unknown reason, perhaps a clerical error or an effort to make him appear more mature, the letter of marque issued to Barney as master of the *Hyder-Ally* gave his age as twenty-five. Actually he was still three months shy of twenty-three. With the primary paperwork in order, Barney cast off on 7 April 1782 to meet his fate in Delaware Bay.

The elapsed time from his appointment as captain to the ship's departure, including the ship's refitting and the recruiting and rudimentary training of the hundred-man crew, was an astonishing fourteen days.[8] That he accomplished so much so quickly is a testament to Barney's reputation and leadership. He had served as captain on small vessels and prize ships before, but this was his first formally appointed command. It would be a lonely position, with no help from companions in the wardroom and without the freedom from responsibility that the subordinate officers enjoyed during off-duty hours. In the teeth of a fierce gale, the still air of the becalmed, or the thunder and fire of an enemy broadside, when advice might be most needed, there would be none. All direction had to come from the captain, who held the power of life or death over his one-hundred-man crew. The assumption of responsibility must have brought Barney both exhilaration and trepidation, emotions shared by many before him.

The owners of the *Hyder-Ally* ordered Barney to escort a convoy of seven merchant ships to the mouth of Delaware Bay. Once there he was to remain near the Capes and protect other ships against the refugee boats and small privateers common to the area. Barney had not yet had the opportunity to fully assess the handling characteristics of his first command, so the cruise would also give him an opportunity to get to know both his ship and his men. A fair wind brought the flotilla to Cape May with little difficulty. Just as sundown approached, the wind died and the convoy was forced to anchor in sheltered water just inside the cape. Out in the Atlantic, the British frigate *Quebec* and the sloop-of-war *General Monk* cruised between Capes May and Henlopen. After a lookout on the *General Monk* spotted the American convoy in the fading light, the British force anchored in the Cape May Channel in order to block the egress of these ships out to sea. The presence of the British went undetected by the Americans.

That evening Capt. Christopher Mason of the *Quebec* and Capt. Josias Rogers of the *General Monk* laid detailed plans to capture the Americans. The *Quebec,* a large ship that drew a great deal of water, dared not attempt to cross the shoals at the mouth of the bay and would thus sail around the Overfalls, a mid-bay shoal, to block a likely escape route. The *General Monk* would attack the American vessels, confident that it could handle the *Hyder-Ally,* the only American ship with significant armament. At daybreak the British captains were pleased to see three British privateers passing the entrance to the bay. Only one, however, the brig *Fair American*, responded to the British Admiralty signal hoisted aloft and sailed to join them.

At ten o'clock Barney became aware that three ships were advancing toward him from the sea. An hour later a lookout identified them as a frigate, a sloop-of-war, and an armed brig. At the change of the noon watch it was clear that the frigate was going to stand off Cape Henlopen while the brig and sloop sailed up the Cape May Channel to engage him. Barney ordered his convoy to weigh anchor and return up the channel, staying as close to the shore as possible because the British were unlikely to follow them into shallow, poorly charted waters. The *Hyder-Ally* would act as their rear guard.

Accounts of the scramble to safety indicate that confusion reigned as the tightly bunched ships began hauling in their anchors and setting sail in haste. The *Charming Sally* quickly ran aground on the Overfalls shoal and became an early prize for the privateer. The ship's crew fled ashore in small boats or leapt from the bowsprit to swim to safety. The *General Greene*, armed with twelve guns, disobeyed Barney's order to flee and stayed behind to stand and fight alongside the *Hyder-Ally*. The battle would at least be even at two against two. Barney had his crew heave heavy unneeded equipment overboard to lighten the *Hyder-Ally* and give it added speed and maneuverability. He then tacked back and forth in the wake of his escaping charges to present a target for the approaching enemy while acting as a cover for the departing American fleet.

The *Fair American* led the *General Monk* into the engagement with the Americans, firing two broadsides as it passed the *Hyder-Ally*. The broadsides made great clouds of smoke but inflicted little damage. The cannonballs whipped and whistled past the ship into the sea to make monuments of spray. The *Hyder-Ally* did not respond. The *General Greene* tacked out of harm's way to avoid contact, but the quarters were too tight and it ran aground off Cape May Point. The *Fair American*, being a privateer, sailed past the *General Greene* in hope of catching the fleeing convoy of rich prizes. Barney's defensive strategy of sailing close to shoals and the shore worked. There was a ripple of water over sandy flats in the bay off Egg Island. As the tide started to ebb, breakers began to form as they caught the surface of the soft, sandy bottom. The *Fair American* did not heed the warning and its keel buried itself with a jolt into these flats, taking the privateer permanently out of the action. There were now one British and two American vessels aground on various shallows near the mouth of the bay.

The as-yet-unidentified sloop-of-war slowed long enough to drop a small boat with orders to take control of the abandoned *Charming Sally*. Then, quickly and smartly resuming its speed and point of sail, the sloop headed directly toward the *Hyder-Ally*. The *Hyder-Ally* tried some evasive tactics, but the nimble sloop covered them and gained sailing advantages. As the sloop approached, Barney noted that it had twelve gun ports on a side versus his own ship's nine, and that its decks were crowded with sailors and its crosstrees filled with many marines. He had a novice crew that had been at sea together for only one day. Even if he could successfully escape his pursuer, a more formidable challenger was guarding the deeper water on the opposite side of the bay. Rather than discouraging Barney, the difficult situation seemed to ignite his imagination and embolden him.

The young American captain had not ordered his gun ports opened even in the face of the two earlier broadsides fired by the *Fair American*. The captain of the British aggressor assumed that Barney did not intend to put up a fight but was acting as a moving target and screen so that his convoy of merchantmen might escape to Philadelphia. He decided that the best strategy to take the *Hyder-Ally* was to come alongside and board. The sloop-of-war had a great advantage in crew size, speed, and maneuverability. And although the captain had no way of knowing it at the time, his men were vastly superior in training and experience as well. Barney had only surprise and adroitness on his side. To capitalize on these he ordered his men to load all cannons with a combination of round shot, grapeshot, and canister rounds. They were exhorted to stay hidden until the *Hyder-Ally* was within pistol range of the British sloop. The guns squeaked and rumbled toward the closed ports. At precisely the correct moment, the ports were opened and the first shots found their mark. The *Monk* replied with its bow guns because they were the only ones facing the foe. Barney ordered the *Hyder-Ally* quickly to port so that it was standing directly athwart the bow of the *General Monk,* then ordered a full raking broadside. The planks of the deck vibrated under Barney's shoes as the broadside rolled with a series of brilliant flashes lighting a cloud of gun smoke, its voice echoing among the hills of the shore. The short-ranged, deadly carronades fired next, producing a high-pitched bark that sounded like a sharp crack. There followed a strange silence as the powder smoke of the cannons drifted with the wind across the bay toward the target. The stillness was broken by a cacophonous postlude of screaming from frightened seabirds flying in every direction. The broadside shredded the *General*

Monk's sails and rigging. The main topmast was damaged, the main top-gallant leaned at a dangerous angle, and the *Monk's* sails were pock-marked with punctures and fluttered like rags in a gale.

Finally, the two ships maneuvered alongside each other, only a few yards apart, and proceeded to slug it out broadside for broadside. The *Monk's* 6-pounders had been rebored to fire 9-pound shot. These guns overheated, and some capsized from the recoil on their inadequate gun carriages. Many of the *Monk's* men were injured as they tried to right the hot cannons. The carronades, with their lower center of gravity, did not suffer this fate. In addition, six of the "guns" were Quakers.

During the deafening exchange the two ships drifted even closer until they were within earshot of each other. Barney strode aft, hands behind his back, his sword flapping against his side. He ordered his cannon crews to reload with grape and canister shot but to hold their fire. He told the rest of his men to prepare for hand-to-hand fighting but to stay under cover. His Bucks County sharpshooter marines were in position at their posts aloft on the fighting platforms. The captain then told his helmsman to "follow my next orders by the rule of the contrary." Patiently waiting until the *Hyder-Ally* was about a quarter of a boat length in front of the *Monk*, Barney suddenly yelled at the top of his lungs, "Hard a-port your helm. Do you want him to run aboard of us?" This order was easily heard on the *Monk*, whose captain ordered "hard a-port" to cover this tack. When the *Hyder-Ally* abruptly turned to starboard as the *Monk* turned to port, the jib boom of the latter became tangled in the *Hyder-Ally's* fore rigging. Barney immediately ordered dockhands to secure the Englishman's jib spar to his own ship's rigging, thereby preventing the *Monk* from backing away. Then the resourceful lieutenant commanded his gunners to fire a broadside of antipersonnel shot. This neutralized most of the remaining British cannons by wounding their gun crews. It also devastated the men preparing to board.

The roar of the battle intensified in pitch as the two ships ground together yardarm to yardarm. The broadsides merged into a continuous bellow of iron against iron. Boarders and repellers alike gave feral yells, either to frighten or to gain false courage, as men prepared to storm the bulwarks of the grappled ships. The momentum of the colliding ships drove them hard and fast together with a tremendous crash, and a flash of sparks from the scraping chain plates was followed by the sounds of spars splintering in the brutal embrace. The snapping rigging and thrashing of ripped sails made cracking sounds like a hundred drover's whips. To this clamor was added the rolling thunder of plunging canvas, rigging, and yards falling heavily onto the deck. Barney's men fought their way amidships, where the piles of debris and cordage and broken spars formed a nautical jungle. The savage hand-to-hand fighting was punctuated by animal-like sounds and flashing images of frenzied faces contorted in hate. The collage of individual deadly actions combined to produce a portrait of terror. Those who had been killed lay sprawled in the bloody attitudes of death. The survivors, away from the prongs of the attack, found themselves shouting with adrenaline-induced excitement or mute with the stony cold of shock.

Captain Barney climbed on the stout, rectangular binnacle box that housed the ship's compass for a better view and directed the fighting through his speaking trumpet from this unusual vantage point. After a few minutes the binnacle was shot away from under him, but Barney escaped serious injury. He had the surviving 6-pounders turned around from the port side to add firepower to starboard. Their recoil tackle was lashed to any strong point on the deck, and the gunners were ordered into action against the hapless British. Under the command of the gunnery officer, Lt. Luke Mathewman, they fought with the muzzles of their cannon almost rubbing together. The Bucks County marines rained lethal musket shots on the deck below. After the battle, it was discovered that almost all of the British killed by musket rounds had entry wounds from above. After a scant twenty-six minutes, the one-sided conflict ended.[9] As evidence of the ferocity of the attack, the small mizzen-staysail of the *General Monk* was taken down with 365 shot holes in it.[10]

Years later, Barney recounted his many memories of the battle. In particular he remembered that a musket ball passed through his hat as he stood on top of the binnacle, producing a slight scalp wound. Another bullet tore a hole in the back flap of his new captain's coat. This was the only time he recalled cursing during the battle. Barney noticed that one of his inexperienced young crewmen became frightened and refused to serve his cannon, standing like an immobile puppet without a puppeteer to give him life. An officer threatened him with a cook's ax and was about to deliver a blow when Barney's binnacle/observation platform was shot away. The officer dropped the ax and ran to Barney's side, thinking that he was wounded. Meanwhile, the frozen sailor found his courage or his sense and returned to his gun. Later, a marine called down to Barney to "watch that fellow in the white hat." He then fired a single shot that made the man leap into the air and drop like a limp bag of flour to the deck. "That's the third I've made 'em hop, cap," said the Bucks County sharpshooter.

The *Hyder-Ally* fired thirteen broadsides during the twenty-six minutes of battle, excellent shooting even for an experienced crew. The murderous fire left the deck of the *General Monk* in shambles. Its rigging and shrouds hung like black-tarred vines on mangled trees. A British midshipman, one of the few men of any rank left standing, struck the sloop's colors. It was not until the battle was over and the Americans started to tend to the wounded and prisoners that Barney learned that he had recaptured the 250-ton *General Washington*. It is not evident that Barney took any particular satisfaction in recapturing of Silas Talbot's former ship. Ironically, the lives of these two men had crossed again, if only indirectly.

The British suffered severe losses. The *Monk*'s first lieutenant and surgeon were dead, and the purser, boatswain, and chief gunner were badly wounded. Captain Rogers was severely wounded in the foot. Altogether, the encounter with the *Hyder-Ally* cost the *General Monk* twenty dead and thirty-three wounded out of a crew of 136. The *Hyder-Ally* logged four killed and eleven wounded in one of the most brilliant American naval victories of the Revolutionary War. The *Monk* had been a serious threat to American shipping. During the approximately two years Rogers had command of the *General Monk* he took, or assisted in taking, sixty vessels. Barney's capture of the British captain and his ship was thus a major achievement made even more remarkable by the fact that the Americans had been significantly outgunned. The underdog *Hyder-Ally* carried only sixteen 6-pound cannons as opposed to the *Monk*'s twenty 9-pounders. The difference in the weight of their shot per broadside was therefore 96 pounds (16×6) versus 180 pounds (20×9).

With the end of the battle came the task of unlashing and extricating the sloop's bowsprit from the *Hyder-Ally*'s fore rigging and making badly needed repairs. They were able to repair the *Monk* only enough to move it with great caution. Barney now had to anticipate engaging the *Quebec*, which was within telescope range of the action about two nautical miles away. The *Hyder-Ally* was damaged as well, but little of the injury was aloft. The American ship should still be able to sail under control. In order to deceive the *Quebec*, Barney ordered the British ensign run up on both ships. Logically, the *General Monk* should have triumphed, particularly in so brief an action. In addition, a copy of the British signal book was found in the *Monk*'s cabin, giving the Americans the ability to answer any signals from the distant *Quebec*. Barney wanted to go after the *Fair American,* which was aground nearby and extremely vulnerable, but he soon thought better of it and put the *Hyder-Ally* in a position covering the stern of the prize ship *General Monk*. The captain of the *Quebec* apparently assumed that the *Monk* was going to mop up stragglers in the American merchant ship convoy and elected to stay on his blockade station at the mouth of Delaware Bay.

Before the day ended Barney had overtaken six of the members of his convoy, now safely anchored farther up the bay. Leaving the *Hyder-Ally* anchored among them off Chester, Barney sailed his prize, the *General Monk,* back to the port of Philadelphia. A thirteen-gun salute and a swelling crowd of well-wishers greeted his arrival.

Captain Rogers of the now deposed *General Monk* was in serious condition with his foot badly crushed by a cannonball. Four years older than Barney, he was a rising star in the officer corps of the British navy. Rogers had been in service in North American waters since the beginning of the Revolutionary War and, like Barney, had served as second in command of some of the better-known vessels, including the frigate *Roebuck* under Capt. Andrew Snape Hammond. Barney remembered the military courtesies afforded to a defeated enemy that he had enjoyed in his early imprisonments. The behavior of the British captain had gained his respect, and he wished to show similar civility toward his new prisoner. Once the prize ship had docked in Philadelphia, Barney had Rogers gently carried ashore on a litter made from a hammock and his wound cared for at the home of a Quaker woman who was locally known for her nursing abilities. The Englishman recovered but thereafter walked with a limp, a lifelong reminder of that fateful engagement.

It takes years for history to allocate significance to events. In the years to come Joshua Barney's naval victory near the close of the war became celebrated in story. In his 1845 *The History of the Navy of the United States of America,* James Fenimore Cooper wrote that the defeat of the *General Monk* by the *Hyder-Ally*

has been justly deemed one of the most brilliant that ever occurred under the American flag. It was fought in the presence of a vastly superior force that was not engaged; and the ship taken was, in every essential respect, superior to her conqueror. The dispropor-

tion in metal between a six-pounder and a nine-pounder is half;
and the *Monk,* besides being heavier and a larger ship, had the
most men. . . .

The steadiness with which Captain Barney protected his convoy,
the gallantry and conduct with which he engaged, and [the] persever-
ance with which he covered the retreat of his prize, are all deserving
of high praise. Throughout the whole affair this officer exhibited the
qualities of a great naval captain; failing in no essential of that distinguished character.[11]

Once the prize ship *General Monk* was safely docked at Philadelphia,
Barney returned to the anchored *Hyder-Ally* and the remainder of the
fleet. There is no mention of what happened at this point, but one can
safely assume that the British were humiliated by their defeat and tight-
ened their patrols at the mouth of Delaware Bay. On 21 April the *Hyder-
Ally* still had not gotten its convoy to sea, and went instead on a local privateering excursion. The next day, Barney captured a refugee boat with a
crew of twenty. The small craft, armed only with one 6-pounder and four
swivel guns, bore the strange name *Hook-'em Snivey.* (The term *snivey*
was a slang expression of that time for something nasty or mean. Therefore, the vessel's name meant to catch and play with a prey in a cruel or
wicked manner, somewhat like a cat.) The fact that the river commissioners of the Supreme Executive Council of Pennsylvania formally
recorded this relatively insignificant capture attests to their high regard
for their heroic captain.[12] This minor operation was the last the *Hyder-
Ally* would see under the command of Joshua Barney.

Folk poetry and music formed part of the fabric of revolutionary American life, and a poem about the adventures of Captain Barney and the
Hyder-Ally became a popular folk song of the day. The tune has been
lost, but Mary Barney saved the words, attributed to Philip Freneau, in
her 1832 biography of Barney. The colorful doggerel exemplifies the
poetic license taken in such works.

Song on Captain Barney's Victory over the Ship General Monk
  O'er the waste of waters cruising,
  Long the General Monk *had reign'd,*
  All subduing, all reducing—
  None her lawless rage restrain'd!

Many a brave and hearty fellow,
Yielding to this warlike foe,
When her guns began to bellow,
Struck his humble colors low!

But grown bold with long successes,
Leaving the wide wat'ry way,
She, a stranger to distresses,
Came to cruise within Cape May:
"Now we soon" (said Captain Rogers)
"Shall the men of commerce meet;
In our hold we'll have them lodgers—
We shall capture half their fleet.

"Lo! I see their van appearing—
Back the topsails to the mast—
They toward full are steering
With a gentle western blast:
I've a list of all their cargoes,
All their guns, and all their men!
I am sure these modern Argos
Can't escape us one in ten.

"Yonder comes the Charming Sally,
Sailing with the General Greene—
First we'll fight the Hyder-Ally—
Taking her is taking them:
She intends to give us battle!
Bearing down with all her sail!
Now boys! Let our cannon rattle!
To take her, we cannot fail."

Captain Barney, then preparing,
Thus address'd his gallant crew:
"Now, brave lads! Be bold and daring!
Let your hearts be firm and true!
This is a proud English cruiser,
Roving up and down the main:

We must fight her—must reduce her,
Tho' our decks be stre'd with slain.

"We with our sixteen sixes
will face the proud and daring band:
Let no dangers damp your courage,
Nothing can the brave withstand!
Fighting for our country's honor,
Now to gallant deeds aspire!
Helmsman! Bear us down upon her
Gunner! Give the word fire!"

Then yard-arm and yard-arm meeting
Straight began the dismal fray;
Cannon mouths each other greeting,
Belch'd their smoky flames away:
Soon the langrage, grape and chain-shot,
That from Barney's cannon flew,
Swept the Monk, and clear'd each round-top,
Kill'd and wounded half the crew.

Captain Rogers strove to rally
His men, from their quarters fled,
While the roaring Hyder-Ally
Cover'd o'er his decks with dead!
When from their tops, their dead tumbled
And the streams of blood did flow,
Then their proudest hopes were humbled
By their brave inferior foe.

All aghast and all confounded
They beheld their champions fall,
And their captain sorely wounded,
Bade them quick for quarters call.
Then the Monk's proud flag descended,
And their cannon ceased to roar—
By her crew no more defended,
She confess'd the conquest o'er.[13]

It is strange that the poet included neither Barney's "orders by the rule of the contrary" to the helmsman nor his direction of the sea battle from atop the binnacle. Perhaps this offbeat order was not well known at the time of the poem's writing, or perhaps it was fantasy that became "fact" in the retelling of the story over the years. War stories start simply but, like the repeated passage of a rumor, become embellished as they are recounted over time. Nevertheless, this event was one of the most celebrated naval victories of the Revolutionary War, which had few such victories to celebrate. It was the pivotal action that made Joshua Barney famous. On 13 April 1782, five days after the report of the battle, the Pennsylvania legislature passed a resolution praising the captain and his crew.[14] In addition, a special presentation sword was given to Barney by Governor John Dickinson. Unfortunately, the impressive piece, Barney's proudest possession, was stolen in Paris some years later. The replica Barney ordered to replace it is still on display at the Museum of the Daughters of the American Revolution in Washington, D.C. He was so proud of his victory in the battle that some years later, while he was in the employ of the French government, he commissioned a French artist, L. P. Crepin, to make a large seascape of the encounter between the *Hyder-Ally* and the *General Monk*. When he returned to the United States Barney presented the painting to the secretary of the navy. It now hangs in the Museum of the U.S. Naval Academy with a concise description of the battle scene.

The decisive victory of the outmatched *Hyder-Ally* over the *General Monk* gave the emerging nation a sorely needed act of heroism in which to display military pride. Because the incident occurred subsequent to the Battle of Yorktown, however, after which the British had lost the will to fight against the rebellion, it is not well remembered today.

Contemporary portrait (1774–75?) of Joshua Barney by Charles Wilson Peale. *Courtesy of the National Park Service, Independence National Historical Park, Philadelphia*

The Taking of His Britannic Majesty's Ship "General Monk" of 20 Guns, Captain Rogers, by the American Ship the "Hyder Ally" of 16 Guns, Captain Barney, in Delaware Bay, the 8th of April 1782, by Louis Phillipe Crepin (1782–1851), Paris, France. *Courtesy of the U.S. Naval Academy Museum*

U.S. Navy engraving of Joshua Barney, by J. Gross, from a drawing by
W. G. Armstrong, after a miniature portrait by Jean Baptiste Isabey.
From Ralph D. Paine, *Joshua Barney: Forgotten Hero of the Blue Water*
(New York: Century, 1924)

Portrait of an elderly Commodore Barney in his study, from a painting by Alonzo Chappel (1827–87). Johnson, Fry and Company, New York, 1862. *From the author's collection*

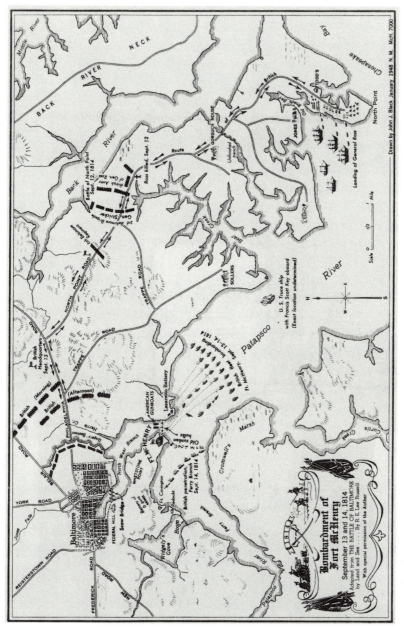

Map of Baltimore and Baltimore Harbor. The route of the British landing forces is shown on the right. The general positions of the British warships are shown at left center off Fort McHenry. Barney was born on the northern shore of Bear Creek (right center). *Courtesy of the Geography and Map Division, Library of Congress*

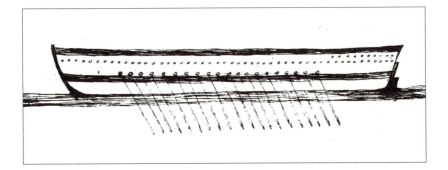

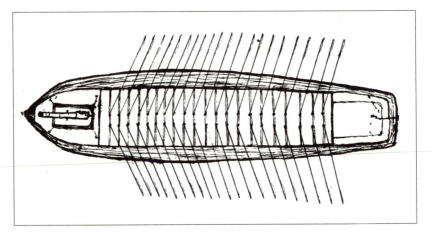

Barney's drawing of a row galley used in the defense of the Chesapeake Bay, dated 4 July 1813. *Courtesy of the U.S. National Archives and Registration Administration*

Galley Attack on the Delaware River. Watercolor by Irwin John Bevan (1852–1940). The gunboat in the center is attacking the *Roebuck*, which had temporarily run aground. Joshua Barney commanded a gunboat during this episode on 9–10 May 1776. *Courtesy of the Mariner's Museum, Newport News, Virginia*

British prison hulk *Jersey* at anchor off Brooklyn, New York, in 1777. This 1908 wash drawing by R. G. Skerret is from a drawing by an unidentified prisoner. *Courtesy of the U.S. Naval Photographic Center, Washington, D.C.*

Battle between the Schooner "Rossie" and the Ship "Princess Amelia" on the 16th of September 1812. Lithograph by A. Weingartner of New York (no date). From George Coggeshall, *History of the American Privateers, and Letters-of-Marque during Our War with England in the Years 1812, '13, and '14* (New York: printed by the author, 1856); Connecticut State Library

Sword presented to Commodore Joshua Barney
by the City of Washington 1844
Courtesy of William Joshua Barney

Sword presented to Joshua Barney by the city of Washington for his gallantry at the Battle of Bladensburg on 24 August 1814. From William
Frederick Adams, *Joshua Barney: United States Navy, 1767–1812* (Springfield, Mass.: privately printed, 1912); Connecticut State Library

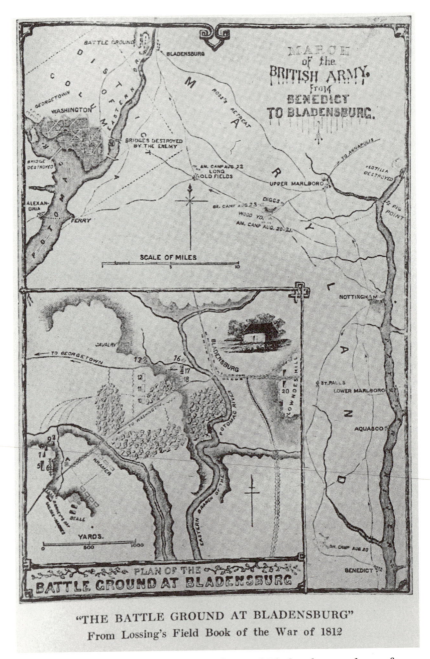

"THE BATTLE GROUND AT BLADENSBURG"

From Lossing's Field Book of the War of 1812

Woodcut of the battle plan of the defense of Bladensburg redrawn from contemporary documents. From J. Benson Lossing, *Field Book of the War of 1812* (New York: Harper and Brothers, 1869)

❧ 5 ❧

FINALE
End of a First Career

With uncommon haste the navy of Pennsylvania changed the name of the *General Monk* back to *General Washington* and ordered Joshua Barney to supervise its repair and refitting. Pennsylvania intended to use the ship for the defense of the Delaware and made no mention of returning it to the navy of Rhode Island, in which the ship had started its service career. On 16 May 1782 Captain Barney received a new letter of marque from the Pennsylvania Supreme Executive Council and formal assignment to the Pennsylvania ship *General Washington*, 250 tons' burden, carrying eighteen guns and 120 men.

Barney's first orders from the Marine Office and the Pennsylvania commissioners were given to him in a sealed packet. The cover letter, from his friend Robert Morris, instructed him not to open the packet until he was "clear of the Capes." If captured, he was to "sink the dispatches, which you will keep in readiness for that purpose."[1] In conjunction with sailing from Philadelphia Barney was asked to lead a convoy of sixteen vessels, including privateers and merchantmen, out of Delaware Bay. This was an imposing responsibility for such a young man, and being in charge of this large squadron entitled him to the title of commodore. Barney's Continental navy rank was still lieutenant, however, and he never referred to himself as commodore at this time, though some who knew him honored Barney by addressing him with the title.

When the convoy reached the Capes, the sails of three British frigates patrolling the area were visible. Barney considered signaling the other ships in the convoy to form up for a skirmish with the enemy because the Americans had a numerical advantage. Although still impulsive, however, he was maturing with his new responsibilities and thought better of it. His orders were to take the *General Washington* to sea, so he let the British vessels go. The convoy fled back upriver to safety and Barney's ship sailed forth alone to engage in a game of hide-and-seek with the British frigates. The fall of darkness helped to keep them at a safe distance; at daybreak the commodore was able to sneak past the patrol and escape to the open ocean. Once free of the confines of the bay, he was delighted to find that the *General Washington* had exceptional speed and maneuverability. Safely offshore, Barney opened the secret orders. They instructed him to sail to Havana and contact Robert Smith, an agent for the United States. Smith, in turn, was to speak to merchants in Havana who engaged in trade with the United States and inform them that in return for a 2 percent "freight tax" the *General Washington* would transport funds to Philadelphia for them. Barney would receive one-half of 1 percent as a "commission" for physically collecting the money and another portion for the expenses of the voyage. The French government would provide a frigate at Le Cap Français, on the island of Hispaniola, to act as an escort. The written orders from Morris concluded: "You are on no account to risk your ship or delay your voyage by chasing vessels, making prizes, or engaging, unless in the last necessity; and then, I am confident you will do your duty, so as to command again the applause of your country."[2] This meant that for the first time, Joshua Barney was to employ his warship not in combat operations against the enemy but as a transport vessel; he was to depend on speed and stealth rather than guile, grit, and guns.

The passage was disconcertingly slow; the vessel's wake seemed to dangle like a limp tail dragged behind the stern. The only excitement during this dreary leg of the voyage came when Barney blatantly disobeyed his orders and captured a brigantine with a cargo of rum. He placed a prize crew onboard and ordered them to follow the *General Washington* to Le Cap Français.

Off Turk's Island a tempting brig crossed Barney's path. Since he would not have to go out of his way to engage it, and thus would not significantly delay his voyage, he rationalized attempting another capture. The brig tried to escape, but the *General Washington* was too fast. As Barney came alongside, he hailed the brig, but its reply was not intelligible. When the brig "clawed off" (purposely let wind out of its sails) and dropped astern of his ship, Barney decided to intimidate his foe by ordering a single shot fired over the brig. The guns and crew of the *General Washington* had long been ready, but Barney's order was misunderstood and they fired an entire broadside that fell harmlessly astern of its target. The brig was now alerted and, through excellent seamanship on the part of its captain and crew, maneuvered into position to rake the *General Washington*. Barney berated his sailing master for his poor performance and eventually evened out the contest by gaining advantages on all points of sail. The two ships were closely matched in weight of cannon shot, the enemy having sixteen 9-pounders at its disposal. Unfortunately, Barney's cannons were the same rebored pieces that had given Captain Rogers problems when the ship was the *General Monk*. During firing, six of the weapons capsized and had to be repositioned. This meant they were out of action for many precious minutes when they might have been in range and facing the target. Barney ordered his sailing master to bring the ships yardarm to yardarm so the Americans could attempt boarding. Once again the brig managed to extricate itself from harm's way. The fight continued into the night until a shot from the brig splintered the top half of the mizzenmast of the *General Washington*. Barney was furious because the shot hit just as he had the advantage he had sought. He was sure the brig was about to strike its colors, but to save his own ship he was forced to bear away. The brig wore off (turned about with the wind coming from its stern) to leeward like a graceful white gull soaring in silence, then heeled steeply to take the wind under its stern as the sails filled to its thrust. An exasperated Barney had to watch helplessly as an enemy on the verge of capture escaped.

The fight was over, and Barney's command was a crippled and vulnerable ship. It now became obvious that he had exhibited poor judgment in attacking the brig and endangering the completion of his primary mission, an example of Barney's frequent blindness to the spirit as well as the letter of his orders. In his own defense, Barney felt that the captain of a privateer had a responsibility to his crew, who could make their fortunes by capturing prizes, not by delivering messages. This attitude made Barney popular with his men, who liked his "cheerful intrepidity."

The man took foolish and unnecessary risks, but they were predictably in character. His bad luck in the skirmish was replaced by good fortune as he made it to a friendly port without any further encounters.

Just before the *General Washington* set sail for Cuba, one of the most important naval battles of the Revolutionary War had taken place in nearby West Indian waters. On 12 April 1782 a British fleet commanded by Adm. Sir George Rodney defeated a slightly inferior French fleet under Adm. Count de Grasse at the Battle of the Saints between Dominica and Guadeloupe. The English victory foiled plans by Admiral de Grasse, hero of the Battle of the Virginia Capes, to unite his fleet with Adm. Solano's Spanish fleet at Hispaniola. Rodney's victory gave Britain naval dominance in American waters as the American War of Independence drew to a close. The majority of the vessels in the French fleet escaped undamaged, and although it lost this battle, the French navy emerged more successful than it had in previous wars with the British. And because the Royal Navy could not deliver a final crushing blow in their victory, the French realized that the British were not invincible. Psychologically this event likely set the stage for the next conflict between these powers, the wars of the French Revolution and Empire.

By the time Barney arrived off Le Cap Français, now known as Cap Haitien, only a remnant of the French fleet remained in the small harbor. After anchoring in the harbor Barney presented his letters to the American agent and began repairs to his ship. The damage the British brig had inflicted required a new mainmast, mizzenmast, and main yard. The captured brigantine with its cargo of rum made port shortly thereafter and was sold. The revenue was distributed, and the crew had a pleasant, if short, liberty in the tropical port. In only six days the *General Washington* was made ready to sail again. Before putting to sea Barney asked the French for the promised escort, and the sixty-four-gun *Eveillée* was assigned to accompany the *General Washington* to Havana.

The two ships made the treacherous passage in just short of four days. Barney's business in the Cuban capital went smoothly. The American ship took aboard $600,000 in negotiable tender from various private businesses in the area. For his services Barney received what was then a tidy fortune. In addition, he organized the American ships in Havana harbor that had been waiting for an opportunity to sail home with some degree of safety.

The convoy comprising the *General Washington,* the ship of the line *Eveillée,* and assorted merchant ships left Havana six days after Barney arrived there. The trip was uneventful as far as the mouth of the Chesapeake, where the convoy split up. Several merchantmen departed there, but the *General Washington* and the *Eveillée* continued on toward Cape May, New Jersey, and Philadelphia. Just outside the Capes of the Delaware a British ship of the line and two frigates came into sight. The *Eveillée* stood back to cover Barney's stern as the *General Washington* sailed on ahead. One of the British frigates took advantage of a favorable wind and quickly drew to within cannon range of the French warship. The guns of the *Eveillée* proved effective and forced the pursuing frigate to take in sail. This greatly reduced the pursuer's momentum, and it never again came close to either ship before abandoning the chase. As darkness descended, the *General Washington* and the *Eveillée* took shelter off the Capes. Barney ran up a signal releasing the French vessel from its escort duty with his thanks. As was the naval tradition when two allied vessels parted, it is likely that the happy sound of three huzzahs rose from each deck.[3]

On his way to port Barney once again disobeyed his orders to avoid engaging the enemy. Slowly cruising up the bay under the cover of darkness he sighted a forest of bare masts and yards, a covey of small Tory refugee vessels anchored for the night. He ordered his ship to come about, his seamen to silently assume battle stations, and his gun crews to load their cannons with grape and canister. The *General Washington* sailed in a slow, stately manner among the smaller vessels and opened fire from both sides. The surprise and the effect of the fire were devastating. In a matter of minutes the Americans managed to rid this part of the Delaware of Tories for the rest of the war. In addition, the *General Washington* took the sloops *Sally* and *Boreas* plus the schooner *Happy Return* as prizes for the benefit of its captain and crew.

The next day Barney sighted another fleet of vessels anchored by the channel and called his crew to battle quarters, only to discover that it was the same fleet of merchantmen that the *General Washington* had escorted to the Capes thirty-five days earlier. Although armed, they had been too intimidated to leave the safety of the bay. The Americans were surprised to see Barney because they had assumed that the British had captured him and that the *General Washington* was sailing toward them flying false colors. A pleasant but brief reunion ensued.

When the *General Washington* tied up at the pier at Philadelphia on the following morning, Barney immediately reported his success to Robert Morris. The financier was delighted by the rapidity of the round trip plus the much-needed money raised by the expedition and carried onboard. In rapid succession Barney landed the revenues and disposed of the prisoners and prizes. Before long he could return home to see his wife, Anne, and son, William. The following day, true to his code as a naval officer, he visited his former adversary Captain Rogers, who was still recovering from his wounds at the home of the Quaker nurse.

During the summer of 1782 Barney found himself ashore with little to do. The war was winding down, and raids on the Delaware were less of a problem. The Pennsylvania commissioners charged with its defense decided that they needed money and sold the *General Washington* at auction for £7,550 but retained the *Hyder-Ally* for privateer duty. A day after the sale, the Continental Congress resolved to purchase the *General Washington* for the Continental navy for use as a dispatch vessel. Barney returned to public service as the ship's commander, still with the rank of lieutenant.[4] The refitted *General Washington* mounted only eight guns, with four in the hold in case of emergency, and had a smaller crew of forty. At the time, Robert Morris urged Congress to authorize the building of six ships a year to create a real American navy. Barney hoped to be among the cadre who would command the vessels, but Congress rejected Morris's advice and took no action. Therefore, although he was addressed as captain, Barney's congressionally approved promotion to that rank did not come until 6 March 1784, and he remained a lieutenant for another year and a half.

Now that the British had been forced to accept the notion that colonists could demand and win the same rights and privileges as Englishmen based at home, they wished to end the conflict and grant independence to the Americans. The Americans, however, were bound by their alliance with France not to make a separate peace. The French, in turn, had an agreement with Spain to negotiate with Britain only if the return of Gibraltar was on the bargaining table. The defeat of the French fleet by Rodney and the weakened position of the Spanish fleet made a compromise of each country's demands more likely. The preliminary peace talks between the belligerent parties had started in Paris. The war was essentially over on land, but at sea, the British continued to prey on American shipping and to press American sailors into their navy. This formed the seed of the next conflict.

Barney's orders from the Marine Office, dated 7 October 1782, instructed him to carry diplomatic papers to Europe. Being well aware of the impulsive character of his courier, Morris cautioned Barney that "as your safe and speedy arrival is of great importance, you will take care not to chase any vessel, but to avoid as much as possible everything which can either delay or endanger you."[5] For once, Barney respected his orders and sailed directly for France. On reaching Europe he met John Adams, Henry Laurens, John Jay, and Benjamin Franklin, who were engaged in treaty negotiations with the British. Franklin took a particular liking to Barney. The seventy-six-year-old Philadelphia Quaker and noted diplomat admired youth, enthusiasm, fearlessness, and good looks, qualities Barney possessed in profusion. Franklin dined with the naval lieutenant, a man who was his intellectual inferior but who had marvelous tales to tell of bloody battles and the changing fortunes of war. These were still a source of pride for the American patriots, and Franklin enjoyed conversing with the charming and adventurous naval hero.

Franklin was a favorite of the court at Versailles, and he promised to introduce Barney to the great and influential people of French society. Among the first he met was Marie Antoinette. The queen apparently was so taken with the appearance of the young American officer that when he was introduced, instead of offering her hand, the usual custom of royalty, she held up her cheek to be kissed. According to accounts of the meeting, her ladies-in-waiting showed a similar disposition, and Barney obliged. Barney said little about that night except that the evening was "very American" because many French officers in attendance had fought alongside Americans during the Revolution.[6]

Although Barney was apparently a strikingly handsome man, there is no evidence that he was a lothario. Nevertheless, an unconfirmed story about his success with the ladies passed down from generation to generation in the Barney family is both charming and credible. Barney's attractiveness to women apparently produced envy among his cohorts, and they parodied him in song and verses titled "Barney Leave the Girls Alone." The tune has been lost, but the words remain:

Judy leads me such a life! (Repeat.)
The devil n'er had such a wife;
What can the matter be?
For, if I sing the funny song of Dolly put the kettle on,
She's mocking at me all day long;
What can the matter be?

Mr. Barney leave the girls alone! (Repeat.)
Why don't you leave the girls alone,
And let them quiet be?

Put the muffins down to roast, (Repeat.)
Blow the fire and make a toast;
We'll all take tea.
Barney you're a wicked boy (Repeat.)
And you do always play and toy
With all the gals you see.

Mr. Barney leave the girls alone! (Repeat.)
Why don't you leave the girls alone,
And let them quiet be?

Barney rock the cradle, O! (Repeat.)
Or else you'll get the ladle, O!
When Judy harps to-day.[7]

The "Mr. Barney" of this song was popularly believed to be Joshua. Because the piece appeared in an anthology written in Baltimore in 1830, this seems likely, but the name may also refer to a generic "Barney" rather than the dashing young American naval officer.

After a series of secret negotiations with the British and a loan of six hundred thousand livres from the French government, the Americans were on the verge of signing a peace treaty. Ordered to sail to Philadelphia with the news on 17 January 1783, Barney was given a formal handwritten passport from King George to allow him to pass British blockades. The officious, historic document invoking the royal "We" survives.

GEORGE R.

George the third by the Grace of God King of Great Britain, France and Ireland. Defender of the Faith &c. To all Admirals, Vice Admirals, Captains Commanders, of Our Ships of War or Privateers, Governors of

Our Forts and Castles, Customers, Comptrollers, Searchers, and to all and singular Our Officers, Civil and Military, Our Ministers and loving subjects whom it may concern, Greeting. Our Will and Pleasure is and We do hereby strictly charge and require you, as We do likewise pray and desire the Officers and Ministers of all Princes and States in Amity with Us to permit and suffer the Vessel called the Washington *commanded by Mr. ———Barney belonging to the United States of North America, to sail from either of the ports of France to any Port or Place in North America without any Lett, Hindrance or Molestation Whatsoever; but to the contrary offer the said Vessel all such Aid and Assistance as may be necessary.*

Given at our Court at St. James the Tenth day of December 1782, In the Twenty-Third Year of our Reign.

By His Majesty's Command
Tho: Townshend
Ship *Washington*—Pass[8]

Barney was chased by three British ships as he entered the Delaware Capes in a heavy winter offshore breeze. The lieutenant was determined not to be boarded by the ships or to engage them in combat. Barney's hubris as an American naval officer made him too proud to use his pass unless forced to do so. Instead, he ordered as much sail aloft as the *General Washington* could handle and kept close to shore. Barney had the advantage of knowing the shoal waters better than the British, who had no pilot aboard. At night he anchored in only three fathoms of water where the British dared not follow. The next morning the *General Washington*'s rigging was covered with ice, but the British apparently had sailed by without seeing their prey against the darkened wooded shore. Barney's crew chipped the ice off the lines and spars and the *General Washington* slipped safely into the Cape May Channel, heading north to Philadelphia and the completion of their momentous mission. On 12 March 1783 Captain Barney arrived with official word of the provisional peace treaty that had been signed on 30 November 1782. The news had taken about three and one-half months to cross the Atlantic, but Barney's arrival was an important historical event. Sailing under an unused pass from his former sovereign, Joshua Barney brought the first marvelous news of capitulation and the granting of independence by the British to the United States of America.[9]

The citizens of the new nation called the United States feasted on speculations of an impending peace liberally garnished with hopes and rumors about its progress. Ratification of the treaty could not be completed until France and Spain signed the instrument. These two allies were adamantly against the Americans making a separate peace with their old enemy. Ironically, the authorizing signatures were affixed to the document on 20 January 1783, only two days after Barney sailed from L'Orient, France, for North America. Admiral Count d'Estaing was accorded the honor of delivering the *official* report of the signing of the Treaty of Paris to the general population in Philadelphia. The sheriff read a proclamation of peace ending the long war on the steps of the courthouse of Philadelphia on 16 April under the flag of the United States of America.[10] Joshua Barney had played a significant part in raising the banner that symbolized the freedom of his people. His intimate association with the flag would continue throughout his career.

The war was over, but the American government was in dire financial straits and having great difficulty meeting its debts to its soldiers and creditors. On about 1 June, Robert Morris ordered Joshua Barney to sail the *General Washington* to France to deliver an appeal for 800,000 livres to His Royal Majesty through the American minister, Benjamin Franklin. Barney's first European landfall was at Plymouth, England. The young captain took particular pleasure in sailing his own command into the harbor of the town where only two years before he had been hunted as an escaped fugitive. After delivering some dispatches ashore, Barney visited the clergyman and family who had befriended him. He was pleased to learn that their complicity in his escape had never been discovered. He also personally thanked the guard who had helped him, and at that time discovered the man's relationship to Lord Edgecombe's gardener, who had also aided in his escape. The lieutenant invited all of them and their friends to a grand party aboard the *General Washington*. The ship was dressed with signal flags, decorated to look its finest, with every lantern polished and lit for the warm summer evening. Many years later Barney reminisced to Mary Barney that "this was one of the happiest days of my life!"[11] The admiral in charge of the port of Plymouth asked to inspect the ship. As he left, the exhilarated flag officer suggested to Barney that he might have made a good officer in the Royal Navy—this to a man one month short of twenty-four years of age who had been stalked as an escapee and threatened with hanging.

Barney's next stop was L'Orient, where after anchoring the *General Washington* he traveled as fast as possible to Paris to deliver his dispatches to Franklin. He had a pleasant reunion with the old gentleman, who had become his friend, and Franklin asked Barney to dine with him, John Jay, and Henry Laurens. After dinner Franklin requested that Barney "fight his battles over again" with one more recounting. During the next few days Barney renewed old acquaintances in Paris with Count d'Estaing and Count Rochambeau and took a short leave to enjoy some of the amusements for which Paris was so renowned. Once Benjamin Franklin had gathered the necessary information and written a dispatch to Robert Morris, Barney hastened to L'Orient to board his ship for the return voyage. This time he was to carry the distinguished commissioner Henry Laurens as a passenger for Poole, England. During the voyage Barney told his important guest that he had been a fugitive from Old Mill Prison when Laurens was being held in London and had attempted to find a way to visit Laurens during his incarceration in the Tower of London. Amused at Barney's temerity, Laurens told him that he had made the correct decision to keep his cover. The two former prisoners of the British became friends, both taking comfort in the political changes that were rapidly occurring. Barney arrived in Philadelphia to report to Robert Morris on 20 September 1783. This, by coincidence, was the day of the official signing of the Treaty of Paris in France.

Cuts in defense spending usually follow the signing of peace treaties, and the events of 1783 proved no exception. The French, who had generously helped finance the war, began to pressure Congress for repayment of the monies advanced to the United States during its time of need. One of the great drains on the economy of the new nation was its tiny navy. Robert Morris, the superintendent of finance, estimated that it cost six hundred dollars a month to keep the *General Washington* at sea. Several states were hinting that they would no longer contribute to the national treasury. The superintendent thought that cutting all expenditures for maritime protection would make a great saving. Therefore, he recommended that the *General Washington* be put up for sale.

Before the ship was to be sold, however, Congress sent the *General Washington* on a final mission, to carry Capt. John Paul Jones to France. Congress had recently appointed Jones a diplomatic agent to collect money owed to American sailors for prizes sent to European ports during the war. The *General Washington* sailed for Europe on 10 November 1783 carrying not only Jones but also two French generals who had served in the American Revolution and Major Pierre Charles L'Enfant, who later designed the city of Washington. L'Enfant was an agent for the Society of the Cincinnati, an organization of Revolutionary War army and naval officers of which Barney later became a member. The French major, a spirited and courtly officer, became everyone's favorite companion during the voyage. The other insouciant Frenchmen occupied themselves with thoughts of returning to their homes as triumphant warriors. By contrast, Jones was extremely reserved in his relations with the other passengers. He was serious and somber, hardly speaking, and when he did converse, his manner was morose.[12]

It is likely that Barney and Jones were acquainted, and they may even have been friends . . . at least in arms. They had served on different vessels in the squadron of Commodore Hopkins in 1776. Barney's ship, the *Hornet,* was late to join the command and left early after an accident, but both officers had sailed out of Philadelphia in 1777 and 1783, and it is probable that they met during at least one of those years. The two men had much in common but more in contrast. Barney was twelve years Jones's junior and still a lieutenant in the navy. He had an abundance of charm, good looks, and the vigor of youth, and easily made friends wherever he went. Jones, by contrast, was lonely and introspective. Both men disliked many of the incompetent politicians who ran their military lives and shared the traits of bravery and pride—pride in the sense of the prerogatives of naval rank and privilege, a vestige of the British model of naval command. During this transatlantic voyage they apparently became much closer. Barney was to recall spending many hours striding the deck conferring with his comrade and listening to his views on warfare.

Barney's orders from Morris were to land Jones anyplace in Europe that he chose. John Paul Jones astonished everyone by asking to be landed in England, where he was believed by many to be a pirate and was actively vilified in the press. Barney advised Jones against the plan, particularly since his only hope for reward lay in France; only imprisonment or death lay in England. The headstrong Jones was adamant in his decision. Apparently he was under orders to deliver dispatches to a certain unnamed person in England and was not concerned about personal danger. Jones later explained that "the packet boat [*Washington*] was forced by contrary winds to enter at Plymouth, and [as] I was entrusted public dispatches of importance I immediately took the mail carriage for London and was so diligent that five days after my departure from Plymouth I reached Paris and delivered my dispatches."[13] The *General Washington* sailed on to the port of Le Havre in mid-December.

Under orders to stay with his ship in Le Havre for three weeks, Barney bid his grateful French passengers farewell on the quay. He soon received letters from Benjamin Franklin and John Paul Jones. The diplomat sent a note inviting Barney to be his guest in Paris and also requested the delivery of a Christmas present containing tobacco and snuff that had been packed by his daughter, Mrs. Benjamin Franklin Bache of Philadelphia. In the same post, Paul Jones informed Barney that he had arrived safely in Paris and asked him "to favor me by forwarding my little trunk that I left in your cabin, and a small case that is in the care of Mr. Fitzgerald, by the same conveyance with those articles for Mr. Franklin." Jones also wrote that he expected "immediately to be presented to the King, and after that ceremony, when I have had some conversation with the ministers, I will write . . . [about] the Prize Money."[14]

Barney received his official dispatches from the American minister on the very day that the three-week stay at Le Havre was completed. His orders were clear, so he immediately set sail for the United States without learning the outcome of Paul Jones's quest. A few days out from port, the *General Washington* encountered a fierce gale that disabled the ship. Repairs were made at sea, and the *General Washington* limped home, arriving in America at the beginning of March. The once-proud ship approached the shores of America like the old saw of the sea, "patch upon patch and a patch over all." The winter of 1783–84 was one of the coldest on record. Much of the Chesapeake was frozen all the way to Cape Henry. Barney fought his way up the bay as the *General Washington* became a battered icebreaker with sails. His men suffered from frostbite, and the ship lost an anchor when a cable sheared from the pressure of the ice. Barney managed to find safe refuge in Annapolis, which was serving as the nation's capital at the time.

Having successfully completed his special mission, Barney decided that it might be an opportune moment to petition for promotion. This timing may have been on the advice of John Paul Jones, and the date on the letter delivered to the president of Congress indicates that it was probably composed during the homeward voyage.

His Excellency
Thomas Mifflin Esq.

I beg leave to lay before your excellency and the Hon'ble Congress a short Memorial wherein I wish for the Indulgence of that Hon'ble Body to state my long Services in the Navy of the United States under the Commission of a Lieutenant in which character I have served since early in 1776, from which I have been upward of three years a Prisoner. It will be needless for me to trouble you with the nature of my Services by Land and Sea in the course of the War, and as my intention is to remain in the Navy and my present command is that of Captain, I should be happy if Congress in its great wisdom would grant me a Commission in that class. I have unfortunately at several times of promotion been a prisoner when younger officers [in time of service] have had the honor conferred on them. Should Congress think proper to grant me this indulgence I shall as in duty ever pray &c.

And Your Excellency's Most ob't Serv't
Joshua Barney
Annapolis
March 6, 1784[15]

In spite of its eloquence and convincing arguments, Congress took no action on Barney's memorial. The decision had already been made to disband the navy. On 16 March, the agent of marine reported that the repairs needed by the *General Washington* would be costly but necessary if the government wished to try to recover some of its initial investment. Since the treasury was badly depleted, the work would have to be delayed, thereby allowing additional structural deterioration. Once the repairs could be made, the *General Washington* was to be sold at auction to reduce the nation's debt.

Joshua Barney never openly expressed his reaction to this rebuff, but it must have hurt him badly. He hastened overland to rejoin his family in Baltimore for the support he badly needed. This journey almost cost him his life. The snow was extremely deep, standing in huge drifts across the trail. While attempting to traverse a stream, Barney and his horse broke through some thin ice and were saved only after very difficult maneuvers from passersby.

After a month Barney received orders from Philadelphia to ready his ship for sale. His first assignment was to bring the ship from Annapolis to Baltimore for an appraisal. Barney knew that, for the sake of safety, the *General Washington* was in desperate need of repairs. On 11 May Robert Morris sent him a copy of the resolution of Congress directing the sale at Baltimore and telling him what he was to do with the proceeds. The proposed sale was hardly a surprise. For Barney, the most difficult aspect of the ship's disposal was that with it, he would be automatically retired from active naval service. When the sale was completed, Barney went to Philadelphia to say good-bye to Morris, who was very moved to see their long relationship come to an end. He generously offered Barney a loan to set himself up in business and extended his services as an adviser in commercial matters. Barney graciously declined.[16]

In a touching letter Barney received about this time, Henry Laurens wrote, "Your discharge from the service of the public, an act of necessity and with your own approbation, cannot obliterate the honor you acquired, nor wither the laurels which you gained in that service. The ploughshare now is preferable to the spear. You are on shore making a better provision for your progeny. . . . I am persuaded that you could not remain a day unemployed."[17]

⚜ 6 ⚜

MERCHANT AND POLITICIAN

*J*oshua Barney, now twenty-five years old, had spent thirteen years at sea, most of them in the service of his country. The life of a sailor was all that he really knew. Now he was cast ashore into the treacherous shoals of business and politics. A quaint saying known as the fisherman's philosophy may apply to Barney at this time: "Sometimes you think you are going to make a fortune, but you never do; sometimes you think that you will starve to death, but you never do either."

In the fall of 1784 Barney became a Baltimore businessman with his brother-in-law Capt. John Stricker. Barney supplied the capital to underwrite the venture, and Stricker brought to the partnership his many business and social contacts in Baltimore, Havana, Hispaniola, Spain, France, England, and Holland. At first it seemed that the new firm would succeed, but before long Barney discovered that more than capital and contacts were needed to establish a successful business. Luck was important, too. The new firm sent a large shipment of cargo to Havana that was sold at a substantial profit, but a local agent squandered the Baltimore partners' money and declared personal bankruptcy. On another occasion the firm imported casks of fine French wine but could find no buyers. They reshipped the wine to the West Indies, but the cargo spoiled on the way, turning to vinegar before it could be sold.

As the business floundered through 1785, Barney became bored and began to dabble in politics at the local level. In 1786 he was appointed to the Board of Special Commissioners "for the leveling, pitching, paving and repairing streets, and the building and repairing of bridges." Baltimore was growing into a significant city. There was a need for Barney's leadership skills, particularly in the bridging of Jones's Falls, an important project over a waterway bisecting the town. Unfortunately, the hero of the *Hyder-Ally* did not find this an exciting enterprise, and he avoided most of the board meetings.

Barney then became a silent partner in an importation business venture that nearly bankrupted him. He sued his former agent in Europe for remuneration, but the legal fees consumed most of the settlement. At this point he prudently decided to cut his losses. With the funds he was able to salvage from his commercial ventures Barney purchased a large tract of undeveloped land in Kentucky as an investment for his rapidly growing family. In January 1787 he had just fathered a handsome son, his third, who was christened John. In November of that year Barney went to visit his land in Kentucky, traveling by horse across the Alleghenies and by barge down the Ohio River. The winter he spent in the western foothills of the mountains was one of the few periods of contentment he had known since leaving the sea. In the west Barney was among independent men who relished the challenges of life. During his time on the frontier he developed his riding and shooting skills far beyond those of a Maryland country gentleman. On returning to Baltimore, Barney found that his family had grown by the addition of a daughter, Caroline, born on 21 December 1787.

While Barney was in the west the Constitutional Convention meeting in Philadelphia had drafted a new document meant to establish a stronger central government. In the spring of 1788, when Barney returned to Baltimore, he found a populace deeply divided over the merits of the new Constitution. The arguments for and against ratification had been sharply drawn and were the constant topic of conversation. Because Maryland was a small state and was thus in danger of being outvoted in the Congress by states with greater populations and economic resources, some of Maryland's delegates to the Philadelphia convention had championed states' rights. One of their representatives, Luther Martin, became a renowned spokesman for the Antifederalists.

Joshua Barney, on the other hand, ardently embraced the Federalist cause. During his years in the navy he had witnessed the impotence of Congress laboring under the old Articles of Confederation. Sailing first under the flag of the federal navy and later for the smaller navy of a state, Barney had experienced firsthand the difficulties entailed in fighting for a nation with a weak and divided government. Also to his taste, the Federalists envisioned a more global role for the United States and a strong navy. Therefore he actively campaigned for the election of delegates to the state convention who were in favor of ratification. Barney attended town meetings almost every night, gaining his first exhilarating taste of politics.

Barney exerted his charismatic leadership through his bearing and commanding voice, not through oratorical flourish. He spoke in the vernacular and with the directness of the sailor, a manner that proved to be an excellent way of communicating with the common people. As with most important political issues, passionate arguments over ratification divided families and neighbors. On one occasion after presenting his arguments, Barney received a blow to the head from a member of the opposition that temporarily ended his electioneering and almost his life. Although the scar from this blow in the defense of his beliefs faded, it remained a source of deep emotional pain for the remainder of his life.[1]

The Federalists triumphed in the election, and Maryland's state convention ratified the Constitution by a lopsided vote of sixty-three to eleven. Baltimore's Federalists celebrated with a great parade with flags, bunting, and guns firing seven shots, one for each of the seven states that had ratified the Constitution at that point, followed by the familiar cheer-salute of three huzzahs. The local newspaper, which had printed letters fanning the debate, described the celebration in glowing terms: "We are persuaded that nothing for grandeur, brilliancy, decorum and unanimity has ever equaled it since the first settlement of Maryland."[2]

The grand and historic parade was divided into sections. First in the line of march were local dignitaries, then came the intellectuals of the community, the members of learned professions. The members of artisan guilds followed them. A special place of distinction in the procession was reserved for those who had served in the Revolutionary War. Since Baltimore was a seaport, the city's most prized citizens were the captains and men who served at sea and the shipwrights and stay makers of the port. A select group among them rode on a float drawn by four stout draft horses. The float was a miniature fully rigged ship called the *Federalist*. Its captain was Baltimore's redoubtable Joshua Barney. The working replica was fifteen feet long, and its captain had supervised the vessel's construction by the best local shipwrights. As the appropriate shrill notes sounded on a silver pipe to signal commands, the well-known hero had the small crew raise the sails as if they were at sea. The float was a focal point that delighted the crowd at the memorable event. The odd assortment of marching musicians, prominent citizens, veterans, and floats ended their procession on a hill on the south side of Baltimore overlooking the harbor. In honor of the occasion the site was renamed Federal Hill, a name it retains to this day.

The diminutive ship was "anchored" on top of Federal Hill next to a tent where the crowd was served a local brew. According to Mary Barney's biographical sketch, the refreshments "made the welkin ring with shouts of 'Huzzah for the Constitution'!" Thirteen toasts, one for each state of the union, followed this tumult. The crowd then descended to Mr. Stark's tavern and a ball put on by the ladies of the town. The evening's festivities culminated in a bonfire on Federal Hill later that evening. In addition to delighting the citizens of Baltimore, the grand celebration helped move the states that had not yet ratified the Constitution.

A few days after the celebration Barney had the *Federalist* carted to the harbor and launched. The miniature ship was not a theatrical set piece but a working vessel that proved seaworthy even when the captain took it out into the Chesapeake Bay. Elated by the reception he received from ships in the harbor and people onshore, Barney decided to sail to Annapolis, the state's capital, some thirty miles to the south. Annapolis was an older port than Baltimore and well known for its urbanity and hospitality. When Joshua Barney tied up at the town wharf, he was met by none other than Governor William Smallwood, who invited Barney to be his guest at the governor's mansion and treated him to a round of teas, parties, and balls. The docked *Federalist* drew admiring crowds. Barney accepted Smallwood's hospitality for three days, then continued south, hugging the western shore of the Chesapeake. When he reached the broad mouth of the Potomac, he sailed up the river to Mount Vernon. Barney, like almost all Americans, revered George Washington, and he wanted to present the *Federalist* to the general as a gift from the shipmasters of Baltimore.

The unusual gift charmed General Washington. He knew of Barney's accomplishments, remembered meeting him briefly at Valley Forge, and admired his wartime exploits. Barney delighted Washington's stepson, George Washington Parke Custis, by taking him for a brief sail in the tiny ship. Washington made note of Barney's visit in his diary entry for Monday, 9 July 1788: "Captn. Barney in the Miniature Ship *Federalist*, as a present from the Merchants of Baltimore to me, arrived before Breakfast, with her and stayed all day and Night."[3] He expressed his gratitude in a letter of thanks to William Smith and the members of the shipwrights' guild in Baltimore for the "beautiful curiosity [the *Federalist*, that they had sent] as a present."[4] This visit to Mount Vernon was undoubtedly one of the social highlights of Barney's life, though, oddly, there is no description of it among his papers.

Another Mount Vernon visitor recorded a vividly graphic vignette of the scene Barney likely encountered there:

The General came in with his hair neatly powdered, a clean shirt on, a plain drab coat, white waistcoat and white silk stockings. At three dinner was on the table, and we were shown by the General into another room where everything was set off with particular taste and at the same time neat and plain. The General sent the bottle about pretty freely after dinner and gave "success to the navigation of the Potomac!" as his toast, which he has very much at heart. . . . After tea General Washington retired to his study and left us with the rest of the company. If he had not been anxious to hear the news of the Congress from Mr. Lee, most probably he would not have returned for supper, but gone to bed at 9 o'clock, for he seldom makes any ceremony. We had a very elegant supper about that time. The General with a few glasses of champagne got quite merry, and being with his intimate friends, laughed and talked a great deal. Before strangers he is very reserved and seldom says a word. I was fortunate in being in his company with particular acquaintances. . . . At 12 I had the honor of being lighted up to my bedroom by the General himself.[5]

After presenting the *Federalist* to Washington, Barney went on to Alexandria for several days. A thank-you note from the general to the merchants of Baltimore caught up with Barney while he was there. Washington was one of the more skilled and thoughtful politicians of his day, and the note reflects the political adroitness and acumen of America's first president:

Captain Barney has just arrived here in a miniature ship called the Fed-eralist, and has done me the honor to offer that beautiful curiosity as a present to me on your part. I pray you gentlemen, to accept the warmest expressions of my sensibility for this specimen of American ingenuity, in which the exactitude of the proportions, neatness of the workmanship and the elegance of the decorations, make your present fit to be pre-served in a cabinet of curiosities. . . . The unanimity of the agriculture State of Maryland . . . expressed in their recent decision on the subject of a general government, will not, I persuade myself, be without its due efficacy on the minds of their neighbors. . . . I cannot entertain an idea that the voice of the Convention of this State, which is now in session, will be dissonant from that of her nearly allied sister, who is only sepa-rated by the Potomac. . . .

I am with respect, &,
Geo. Washington[6]

Unfortunately, the *Federalist* had a short life. A fierce 1788 summer storm, described by Washington as a hurricane, lashed the eastern sea-board, delivering a glancing blow to the Chesapeake Bay and Potomac River. During the storm the *Federalist* was driven from its mooring and sank in the river.[7]

By the summer of 1788, eleven of the thirteen states had ratified the Constitution. Congress confirmed the vote and in September ordered a national presidential election. The first selection of presidential electors took place in January 1789, and the Electoral College convened for its vote in New York City, the temporary capital, on 6 April 1789. After the results were tallied, a messenger was sent to Mount Vernon with a for-mal certificate of election to the presidency of the United States of America for General Washington. The president was asked to set out as soon as possible to New York to assume office.

Capt. Joshua Barney was part of a committee appointed to greet the new president as he traveled through Baltimore on his way north. The committee members met Washington at the city limits and delivered a letter signed by Barney, among others, that wished him "successive elec-tions to the first station of human honor." The committee of honor then conducted the president-elect into the city.[8] The sharp reports of cannon salutes marked their progress to Grant's tavern, where Washington

replied to welcoming speeches, ate a hearty supper, and retired early
before resuming his journey to the inauguration. A month later Martha
Washington traveled northward on the same route to join her husband in
New York. As she approached Baltimore a similar committee met her at
Hammond's Ferry and led her into the city. After a boisterous parade fea-
turing fifes and drums, the citizens of Baltimore put on a fireworks display before supper and followed it with a sumptuous reception at the
home of Dr. James McHenry, a former aide-de-camp to General Washington, where Mrs. Washington was entertained by a local band. According to a newspaper account, the party at the McHenry home went on
until two o'clock in the morning. Martha Washington captivated all present with her dignity, elegance, and clothing, which was manufactured
"of our country in which her native goodness and patriotism appeared to
best advantage."[9]

Barney, with his simple honesty and good looks, had become a special
favorite of the first lady, who invited him to be her escort, bodyguard,
and traveling companion for the rest of her trip to New York. This was a
great honor for the young sea captain/merchant, and it provided a holiday from a business he had grown to dislike. Unfortunately, it also meant
leaving Anne Barney at home with their five children.

Travel in the late eighteenth century could be dangerous. Long unin-
habited expanses separated stagecoach stops and towns. Roads were often
in poor repair, causing breakdowns, and highwaymen occasionally waited
in ambush in the nearby woods. Martha Washington, her two grandchildren, her stepson George Washington Parke Custis and his sister Eleanor,
plus a maid rode in the Washington coach. Martha's nephew Robert
Lewis rode on horseback alongside Captain Barney. Two or three other
outriders rode on ahead to ensure the safety of the entourage. The welcome in Philadelphia started ten miles before the city limits with a greeting from Governor Thomas Mifflin and two companies of his Pennsylvania cavalry troops. Many of the Revolutionary War veterans who lined
the road into the city were visibly moved as the fifty-seven-year-old
matron passed by. Along the row of immaculately uniformed men there
rose a subdued but heartfelt cheer, "God bless Lady Washington."

As the Washington party came within sight of the city, carriages filled
with the ladies of Philadelphia society joined the entourage. The growing procession crossed the Schuylkill River at Gray's Ferry and was met
by Mary White Morris, the wife of Robert Morris and an acquaintance

of both Martha Washington and Captain Barney, and saluted by thirteen rounds fired from cannons in a nearby park. That evening Martha Washington delivered a brief public speech of thank-you to the cavalry and people of Philadelphia from the steps of the Morris home.

After a few days' rest, the party, now joined by Mary White Morris, crossed the Delaware River to New Jersey. Governor William Livingston entertained the group at his mansion near Elizabethtown as the common people lined the roads to cheer on the growing assemblage. At Elizabethtown Point, President Washington and Senator Morris met their wives, and the party of dignitaries boarded the splendid barge that had been built for the presidential inauguration the previous month and crossed the Hudson River to New York. The presidential inaugural crew of "thirteen eminent pilots in handsome white dress" rowed them in grand style to the foot of Manhattan.[10] The first family set up housekeeping at 1 Cherry Street, and Captain Barney was one of their early guests. Barney remained in the capital for an undisclosed period and renewed old acquaintances, including that of Vice President John Adams, who had befriended him early in his career.

One of Washington's most influential cabinet members was Secretary of the Treasury Alexander Hamilton, among whose tasks in that position was the organization of a revenue service. On 19 August 1790 Hamilton's deputy, Tench Coxe, asked Barney to "furnish [the] names of some proper persons to command and officer" the cutters assigned to the Revenue Service.[11] Barney sent a thoughtful reply suggesting several men who might be appropriate for the new service. On 25 August, after his return to Baltimore, Barney wrote to Hamilton advising him of the best way to enforce revenue laws on the Chesapeake Bay. Merchant ships, he said, should be met at the mouth of the bay, and revenue inspectors should examine their manifests and cargo there, before the ships entered the bay and had the opportunity to "disappear" into one of its many inlets and harbors.[12] Hamilton replied that "the ideas contained in your letter appear to me solid and judicious," and invited Barney "to continue to furnish me with whatever hints may occur to you relating to the security of the Revenue."[13] Washington suggested that Hamilton offer Barney a commission in the newly established Revenue Cutter Service, but the president added that he was uncertain if Barney really desired the appointment. On 15 September Barney wrote to President Washington declining a commission in the Revenue Service: "Inspectors which are the lowest Officers in the Customs have larger Salary, and are not confined to such severe duty, as they can attend their families and business, both of which these officers are deprived. I hope your Excellency will believe me sincere, when I declare my every Ambition is to render service to my Country, but my family require my consideration, and unless I leave them suffer, I can not accept the Commission offered me, upon the present establishment."[14] In a letter to Washington, Hamilton noted, "Mr. Gross [Simon Gross of Baltimore] is submitted on the recommendation of Captain Barney, who mentions favourably both him and a Mr. Daniel Porter, naming Gross first, but without expressing a preference for either."[15] Barney gave Coxe advice for operating the new service. Many of Barney's recommendations to Hamilton and Coxe were adopted, including the commissioning of Simon Gross (as master of the revenue cutter *Active*) and David Porter, who went on to have a distinguished career in the U.S. Navy, as did his progeny. Thus Joshua Barney influenced the structure and personnel of the Revenue Service, one of the original components of the U.S. Coast Guard.

It is not clear when or if Barney actually met Alexander Hamilton. Baltimore's James McHenry wrote a letter of introduction for Barney on 3 January 1791, three months after his correspondence about the Revenue Service and the offer of a commission. In his letter McHenry described Barney as "a man of many valuable qualities, and well-known for his distinguished services during the war. As yet however he is to receive his reward. I believe he goes up to Congress with the intention to petition for commutation, on the expenses incurred in his captivity."[16]

Barney's rejection of a commission in the Revenue Cutter Service did not mean that he was not interested in any government position. As a veteran of the Revolution, an avowed Federalist, and an acquaintance of Washington, Barney was named to the appointive post of first clerk of the United States District Court of the State of Maryland.[17] He tried the job for a short time but found it both unchallenging and unprofitable.

In the early months of 1790, seeing an opportunity in the auction business, Barney had entered into a partnership with John Hollins. Through Barney's political influence the firm won a commission to act as "vendue master" (a tax collector and supervisor) for the sale of state property auctioned by the state of Maryland.[18] Business thrived in the port of Baltimore, whose population had more than doubled since the Revolution to approximately 13,500. The Barney-Hollins partnership also thrived, providing Barney and his family with a steady and substantial income.

Eager to expand the business, Barney convinced his partner to invest with him in the purchase of a brig for trading with the Spanish in the Caribbean and South America. Barney would command the vessel on voyages to places where he had good contacts. Certainly, after six years ashore, the prospect of being on the deck of a sailing vessel once again was exciting. To initiate the new venture he bought the antiquated, relatively modest brig *Liberty*. In Baltimore he took on a profitable cargo that included slaves, then set a course for Cartagena on the northern coast of South America, where the human cargo was certain to bring a large profit. This particular venture would come back to haunt him, and the ugly epithet "nigger-trader" became a heavy liability when he later ran for Congress.

Slave trading, a highly profitable business, flourished in the northeastern states, particularly Rhode Island. American slave ships, which presumably resembled Barney's vessel, were sturdy and unusually swift because they carried a "perishable cargo." The slavers also wanted to be able to land their cargoes at the slave-trading ports at the optimal time of planting or harvest, when the strong demand would bring them the most favorable prices for their slaves. The slave trade was by far the most dangerous of maritime occupations. Contagious disease, relatively inexperienced or poorly trained crews, despotic captains, and the possibility of mutinies were constant threats. In addition, pirates, privateers, and others hunted slave ships for various levels of profit. Abolitionists offered a bounty for anyone who captured a slave ship and set the slaves free. The bounty varied but generally approximated sixty pounds for a male slave, thirty pounds for a woman, and ten pounds for a child. There was good profit in capturing a ship with a cargo of five hundred slaves, 70 percent of whom were likely to be men. Thus trading in slaves paid well, and the abolitionist trade paid about equally well to free them. The abolitionists obviously held the moral high ground, but neither occupation was particularly popular in maritime commerce.

The first thing an observer was likely to notice about a slaver was that the galley seemed to be overflowing in every direction. Usually a small

ship carried enough food, water, and utensils for the crew and a few passengers, perhaps about thirty people altogether. A slave ship had to carry
enough provisions to keep four to five hundred slaves alive for approximately six weeks to three months during a sea passage of four to five
thousand miles. The number of slaves carried varied with the size of the
ship and the "packing density" of the human cargo. Some captains and
owners felt that the more slaves they carried, the greater the number
they could deliver. Others felt that looser packing of slaves reduced their
losses along the way. The number of slaves who could be crammed into
a ship was calculated by a rough formula—three slaves for every ton the
ship displaced. Therefore, a 170-ton ship could carry about five hundred
slaves in the densely packed configuration.

Next the observer would notice the deck, which on slavers had a peculiar configuration that became known as a slave deck. It had no planking,
only a grating open to the air and elements that allowed for much-needed
ventilation and gave the crew the ability to keep close watch on the
"cargo" below. Each slave was allowed about two and a half feet under
this grating in which to sit, squat, or lie; usually they were kept in chained
pairs that formed rows. The sexes were segregated, with the men usually
forward and the women aft. The slaves were let up on deck only if no land
was in sight. Otherwise some might try to jump overboard and swim to
safety. They might be whipped to make them run for exercise or force-fed
the unappetizing food that was provided. At times their naked bodies were
hosed down with cold seawater and vinegar to clean them. There were no
sanitary facilities for the slaves. When they were seasick, which was
often, they vomited where they sat, and for their normal bodily functions
they used a necessary bucket, when one was available. These were hosed
out with a vinegar and water solution periodically. Slaves who were seriously ill or who died chained to others might not be discovered for many
days, particularly if there was a storm at sea. The slaves were essentially
exposed to the elements during these storms, with only the grating of the
slave deck to protect them. The foul stench generated by the heat and
lack of sanitation belowdecks made it easy to detect a slave ship more
than a mile away at sea if one was to windward.[19]

In 1783, abolitionists actively campaigned to prohibit the importation
of slaves into the United States. Members of the Constitutional Convention debated banning the international slave trade before compromising
on a provision that allowed the importation of slaves to continue for

twenty years, after which the government could ban the practice. In 1808 Congress enacted such a prohibition, although it remained legal to buy and sell slaves within the United States.

Like many businessmen of his day, Joshua Barney did not spend much time reflecting on the moral implications of his commercial ventures. The slave trade was obviously not popular, but slaves were considered necessary to develop the new colonies of South America and for the agrarian economy of the southern United States. In an ironic blend of career parallelism, Silas Talbot also dabbled in the slave trade for a short time. He bought a half interest in the slaver *Industry*, which in late 1785 transported a cargo of slaves from the Cormantyne coast of Africa to America. Nearly half perished en route.

Maryland was a slave state, and the Barney family owned slaves. Because his family owned a farm, it is reasonable to assume that Joshua Barney also employed slaves in domestic and agricultural work. Barney went out of his way, however, to say that the slaves chosen for his household were servants who had suffered personal misfortune or had been imprisoned and needed employment. He appeared to develop sensitivity about the moral issue of slavery and was very reluctant to discuss his slave-trading venture on the *Liberty* in his later years.

When Barney reached Cartagena, he sold the slaves he was carrying but was unable to get the price he wanted for his nonhuman cargo. Before visiting Cartagena he had a romantic vision of the Spanish colony; the reality, with its poverty and general air of misery, was a great disappointment. The city had the atmosphere of a cloister with its long, dark galleries lined with columns and its narrow streets. The houses and the natives were filthy, the air was heavy with smoke from burning refuse, and a gaseous stench permeated everything. Barney left in disgust to sail to Havana, where his goods sold at the projected profit. This Spanish colonial town was far more hospitable, and he found that by extending his stay he could avoid the severe Chesapeake winter.

The trip to the Spanish colonies turned only a small profit at a time when Barney's family had increased to five children and his financial obligations were growing. On 11 August 1790 the former lieutenant wrote to President Washington requesting an appointment as surveyor for the port of Baltimore on the death of the incumbent, Robert Ballard. In his letter Barney noted that his previous position as a court clerk had not paid him enough to support his family. The surveyor's position was not available, but, not to be discouraged, Barney wrote to the president again, this time asking if "something may [be] offer[ed] in which I may once more be called into public life so as to render services to my Country and a comfortable subsistence to a large family."[20] Nothing came of this request, but Barney was not a man easily turned aside. On 21 February 1791 the frustrated Barney appealed again to President Washington, complaining that Congress had rejected his petition for the $896 he believed was owed for nine years of naval service and for the expenses he had incurred during his escape and return to America to rejoin the navy. As compensation he asked for appointment to the Excise Service (collector of revenue on distilled spirits for the District of Maryland), but his request was not granted.[21] Fearing, perhaps, that Washington considered him unappreciative of his last appointed position, in this letter Barney again stated that while his commission as "vendue master" did bring in some income, it was insufficient for his needs. Apparently, some local merchants had formed an association to avoid going through his auction office, which reduced his revenues. His "only motive" in applying to Washington, he said, was "to support my wife and children."[22] He sent another letter to Washington dated later in 1791 asking for an appointment as U.S. marshal for Maryland. None of the letters produced a government job. There is no evidence that he had fallen out of favor with Washington. More likely Barney's petition was lost among those of the many veterans of the Revolution who were pressing the government for federal employment.

The auction business was making a modest profit, but Barney, whose mother had just passed away, became restless. His partner did most of the day-to-day running of the company. There was not much for him to do, and Barney yearned to return to the sea. Although his previous venture with the *Liberty* had made only a small financial gain, he was confident that a similar (but nonslave) excursion on a larger ship would yield a far greater return. He persuaded his firm to buy the *Sampson,* a fine copper-bottomed ship of three hundred tons, and over the next three years Barney made several voyages in that vessel.

His first cargo was hard currency in an unidentified form, processed flour, and finished dry goods. He sailed from Baltimore in the autumn of 1792 bound for Le Cap Français, Saint-Domingue (Haiti), on the island of Hispaniola. It was an extremely volatile time to be trading on the island.

The French Revolution was now in its third year and the colonies under French domain were in disarray. The black slaves who made up the majority of the island's population had suffered terrible brutality under their French masters and excitedly hailed the revolution in France as an opportunity for their own freedom. The government in Paris, however, did not immediately set them free. The first mandate to initiate the emancipation process came from the Constituent Assembly in May 1792, but the white overlords in Saint-Domingue refused to obey the order. This led the slaves to revolt.

The uprising was most widespread in eastern Saint-Domingue, where the black slaves almost succeeded in capturing Le Cap Français before French settlers struck back. In reprisal for the carnage, the white settlers set up three scaffolds for executing the blacks they had captured. The white Frenchmen beat, mutilated, or killed up to thirty blacks per day, then placed the heads of the corpses on pikes along the roads to scare the others. Rather than intimidating the blacks, the reprisals led to expanded uprisings. When Barney innocently sailed into Le Cap Français on the *Sampson,* the number of blacks in the rebellion had swollen to one hundred thousand. It was the worst possible time and place to try to engage in peaceful trade. There certainly was a market for flour and dry goods, but delivering the cargo was extremely dangerous. Barney managed to get away unscathed and sold his cargo at St. Marc, a town on the west coast of the island that had not yet been touched by the revolt. He purchased some coffee with his cash and sailed for nearby Guadeloupe, then turned to Martinique to sell his coffee at a profit and purchase wine. He continued on to various Caribbean ports that could be safely entered, buying and selling whatever he could find like a seagoing peddler. In his trading he followed a basic rule of commerce: shortages arise during wartime; by furnishing whatever the belligerents need, there are likely profits to be made. But this trading strategy can be both difficult and dangerous.

At one point Barney chartered a small sloop that could navigate in shallow water. He loaded it with wine and sold it in the little seaside villages still relatively untouched by the revolt. Profits ran as high as 250 percent and boosted Barney's confidence at a time when he may have begun to lose faith in his business abilities. With these profits in hand, he ran before the trade winds to Havana, loaded the *Sampson* with sugar and molasses, and sailed for home in March 1793 with a substantial return on his investment.

This way of doing business excited Barney. He offloaded his cargo quickly, left the resale of the goods to his partner in Baltimore, and returned to Le Cap Français in early May. When he arrived, the town was under siege, hidden in a haze of smoke from the fires of recent destruction, and the inhabitants were eager to purchase the provisions Barney carried. Since these were the only supplies to reach the port in two months, another large profit was guaranteed.

The rebellion had grown worse in Barney's absence, and the population was now split into four factions: the French bureaucrats who did the day-to-day business and the governing; the wealthy white landowners; the mulattos, who were in a racial purgatory; and the black slaves. The two middle groups constantly realigned themselves with whomever they thought might ultimately win. This led to mistrust, betrayal, and chaos. The rebel leader Toussaint-Louverture tried to discourage reprisals and end the revolt as peacefully as possible. A brief meeting with Toussaint left Barney unimpressed by the man who would become a legend in Haitian history.

The French government sent agents to establish some semblance of order, liberal-minded men who sought compromise among the passionate factions, but their attempts infuriated the white royalists, most of whom were army or navy officers who protected the colonists. These men had escaped being caught up in the French Revolution in Paris and were firmly established in the right wing. The white population was clearly polarized between the liberal government agents and the conservative white royalists. The latter group further polarized the population by favoring the mulattos over the black former slaves. In response, the blacks allied themselves with the liberal government agents. The *Sampson* lay offshore while the people of Le Cap Français abandoned all vestiges of civility and fought openly in the streets.

After the first battle the bureaucrats and the blacks appeared to have the upper hand. The losers took to small boats, abandoned the burning town, and sought refuge in the ships that dotted the harbor. Barney did not commit himself to a side, but stood as a merchant protecting his goods. He had a consignment of coffee stored in a warehouse ashore, as well as some cash. Under cover of darkness he took a small boat with a few men to the warehouse to recover the money, but they were viciously attacked and barely escaped with their lives.

A few days later, when the fighting subsided, Barney took two boats to the shore with the intent of recovering his cargo. The captain and the much larger crew landed at the dock with sailcloth sacks over their shoulders, cutlasses stuck in their belts, and muskets in hand like pirates going on a raid. They made their way unmolested to the warehouse, where they found the money intact. Barney distributed the money and other small articles of value among his men for carrying to the ship. As the men returned to the harbor, however, they were discovered by the two opposing mobs. When the prospect of gaining cash made temporary allies of the enemy groups, Barney and his men found themselves under attack from two sides at once. In defense of their lives, the Americans fired into both converging masses.

During the ensuing battle Barney came face-to-face with a huge mulatto wearing a hat with imposing plumes. Barney assumed the man was a leader or chief. The two men aimed their muskets at each other, but Barney shot first, killing his opponent. The ball penetrated at the point where two belts crossed each other at his breast. Before Barney could reload his weapon, a group of rebels rapidly moved toward him. He rallied his men to their boats, stopping to fire in order to keep the advancing insurgents at bay. The Americans all made it back with their lives, but Barney estimated that he left about two thousand dollars worth of goods behind.

The vessels anchored in the harbor were now crowded with distressed, frightened white settlers, mostly women and children. The *Sampson* alone took sixty of these refugees onboard. The mob of blacks, having gained control of the town, took to small boats to attack the ships. The pleading passengers convinced the ship captains to put to sea. Barney sailed a mere six miles to the village of Limbé, where he anchored to wait until the hostilities onshore moderated. Always a businessman, even in the face of adversity, he used the opportunity to negotiate for a load of sugar. Barney knew that he had the business advantage because there was hardly any local market for their produce, and he purchased the sugar at a very attractive price.

When the massacre at Le Cap Français ended in a few days, Barney sailed back into the harbor, now ringed with smoking, burned-out buildings. His first task was to try to recover the cargo of coffee and sugar that was owed to him in exchange for the flour and other provisions he had brought from the United States. The fire and carnage at the port made it impossible for the Haitians to keep their end of the bargain, and they made an alternative arrangement for the balance to be paid at St. Marc.

Now that his business side was satisfied, Barney let his humanitarian side emerge. The women and children sheltering on his ship were obviously frantic over the fate of their loved ones. Although fearful about what they might find, Barney took many of the refugees ashore, then waited at anchor to offer passage to America for those who wished to leave their terrible memories behind. When Barney returned to Baltimore, he carried seventeen French men, women, and children with him.

The Western world was in turmoil during this era. The storming of the Bastille on 14 July 1789 set off a quarter century of unrest and war. France's February 1793 declaration of war against Great Britain, Spain, and Holland had grave consequences for the young United States. Shortly after renewing its war against Britain, France threw open its West Indian ports to international trade. American merchants flocked there, Joshua Barney among them. The British government responded with a series of Orders in Council (1793 and 1794) that invoked the Rule of 1756, under which trade considered illegal in time of peace continued to be illegal in time of war. Thus, Americans who had been barred from trading with French islands before the outbreak of war could not begin trading with them even though the United States was neutral in the war between France and Britain. Royal Navy ships and privateers commissioned by Britain began to search and seize American vessels they suspected of carrying French goods.

Barney, who planned another voyage to Saint-Domingue, would soon feel the effects of the Rule of 1756. In Europe, the French Revolution had degenerated into the Reign of Terror. King Louis, after whom Barney had named his second son, and Marie Antoinette had been guillotined. France's American colonies were in chaos. Mulattos at Saint-Domingue allied themselves with the whites against the blacks, who continued their revolt with greater resolve.

As Barney cleared the Capes of the Chesapeake aboard the *Sampson*, a British privateer, the *Flying Fish*, ordered him to stop. The British captain rowed across to the Barney's ship, examined its cargo, papers, and money, and then, seeing that all was in order, allowed the *Sampson* to proceed. Barney resented the interference with his right to trade and a week later became even more vexed when he suffered the additional indignity of being stopped again, this time by three British privateers: the *Curlew* and the *Mary* out of Jamaica and the *Henrietta* from New Providence. The search went quickly and without incident under the watchful eyes of the captains of the *Curlew* and the *Mary*. The captain of the *Henrietta*, however, decided that an iron strongbox that Barney kept in his cabin was likely French property as well as being the receptacle for any cash onboard. He offered Barney freedom in exchange for the money contained in the heavy padlocked chest. If Barney refused, the captain would take the *Sampson* back to New Providence as his prize. Barney's rejection of this demand led to a dispute among the British captains, who were not about to let one privateer take a prize that all three might share. In the end, each of the three captains sent a prize company aboard the *Sampson*. They split up the *Sampson*'s crew among their ships, leaving only Barney, the boatswain, the carpenter, and the cook onboard. The convoy of three privateers and the *Sampson* then set sail for New Providence.

The privateers had taken into custody an ex–naval commander who had suffered at the hands of the British for three years. Adding to his humiliation, he was a prisoner on his own ship. Joshua Barney's patience was severely tried, but he knew from experience that the only way to beat the British was with composure and intelligence. His British captors threatened to shoot him or throw him overboard if he did not meet their demands. Barney was not easily intimidated, and the privateers soon realized that they might be in for a difficult time if they laid a hand on him. Instead they showered him with verbal abuse, calling him "Yankee traitor" and "rebel rascal." These epithets seem only mildly disparaging today, but they evidently insulted the proud American.

It was common practice to hide spare arms aboard a ship in case of mutiny or capture. Since the ship was Barney's command, he knew where a blunderbuss and broadsword were hidden. On the fifth day of their incarceration, he exchanged a few surreptitious words with the boatswain and the carpenter, evidently leaving out the cook. (Cooks were often disabled mariners who had lost a limb from an accident or battle during previous sea duty. Therefore, the cook may not have been of much use to them in a fight.) The two able American crewmen also knew where to lay their hands on a pistol and a bayonet. The three agreed to wait for an opportunity to recapture the ship.

That opportunity came during a squall the very next day. The prize crew was tired and wet from tending to the vessel during the storm. Most opted to take dinner in the forecastle, leaving only three guards and a helmsman on deck to watch Barney and his men. Barney gave his men the signal to wander aimlessly into the ship's galley, called the caboose, and fetch their hidden weapons. Once armed, the three Americans rushed the unsuspecting privateers. During the fight, one man was wounded in the arm from the accidental discharge of a firearm. A second was knocked to the deck by a blow from the flat of the sword. The third escaped to the forecastle to warn and rally the rest of the prize crew. The boatswain and carpenter were right on his heels, however, and fastened the scuttle shut behind him, locking the men below. Barney took care of the helmsman, and the ship was now back under his command. Three men had overcome fourteen by stealth and courage.

The three prize crewmen left on deck were placed in irons, and they shouted to the rest of the crewmen below that a blunderbuss trained on the hatchway of the forecastle would be fired if they attempted to retake the vessel. The British privateers decided to surrender and, one by one, appeared on deck to give up their weapons. Barney had the confiscated firearms thrown overboard. After that, he resumed the posture of a naval commander, lining up the men on deck and giving them a lecture. He pointed out that their officers had taken his vessel without legal reason and that the British prize crew had both insulted him and damaged his property. Under their principles of the rule of the strongest, Barney had the right to put them to death, but he professed no inclination to punish the crew. If they worked as responsible crewmen until the ship reached Baltimore, Barney promised pay them a fair wage for their service and discharge them without legal redress. He did not say what he might do to the officers. If there were any who felt they could not do this in conscience, Barney said that as an American patriot he understood their feeling. The men who did not choose to work the vessel would be given a small boat, food, and water and cast adrift in the Caribbean. The first alternative was the most attractive, and the entire crew changed allegiance. The sailors apologized, thanked the captain for his humane position, and begged to be treated as loyal seamen. Just in case any changed their minds, Barney armed himself with a pistol and placed an armchair on deck to watch the men. He rarely slept. When he did, an American crewman, also armed with a pistol, had orders to shoot anyone speaking to the prize crew officer who was kept in irons on deck. No British seaman was allowed abaft of the mainmast unless under an order. The privateers were either men of their word or sufficiently frightened by the forceful eye of Captain Barney, and the voyage to Baltimore was completed by the beginning of August with no untoward incident.

Barney kept his word about paying the impressed crew and discharging them. He was still infuriated, however, about his treatment at the hands of the British privateer captains. His only legal recourse was to complain to the British vice consul in Baltimore. He asked that the privateer officers be placed on parole in the vice consul's custody with a guarantee to be available for trial if necessary. The vice consul declined the responsibility. Incensed by the refusal, Barney then had the men taken to a revenue cutter for safekeeping because he was determined to make an example of them. He adamantly believed that they should be tried as pirates rather than privateers.

The next day, the vice consul won their release. He told Barney that the officers had produced copies of their letters of marque, thus establishing their right to take the *Sampson*. Barney did not believe this; while they were his prisoners they had not been able to demonstrate the existence of such orders for him. He was extremely angry about their release but legally powerless to act further. The incident evidently received a great deal of publicity, and public opinion was sharply divided. There were still a large number of British sympathizers in the United States, and some of them took Barney to task in the newspapers for his persecution of the privateer captains. Barney took the matter to the federal government, but by this time it was a moot point; the privateers were already on their way home. Barney was a patriot and a man of almost excessive pride, particularly when it came to maritime protocol; in his mind these attributes may have been considered the same thing. This affair produced contempt for his old enemy, the British, that would become loathing in time.

In September 1793 the political and economic problems in Saint-Domingue continued unabated. Barney believed he was owed about thirty thousand dollars from his last trip to that tortured land and feared that if he did not return there to press his claim, it would soon be uncollectable. Determined not to be intimidated by privateers again, Barney refitted the *Sampson* with fourteen guns and increased the crew to thirty. He also took a group of thirty Frenchmen as passengers to help defray the cost of the return voyage.

Barney made landfall at Le Cap Français on 1 October 1793. Fighting in the town and countryside continued. French officials thought peace could be established by freeing the slaves on the island, but they miscalculated. The newly freed blacks took advantage of their freedom to attack the mulattos who had previously sided with the whites. At the same time colonists and royalists felt betrayed and refused to grant the blacks their freedom. Adding to the confusion, the British landed a force at Jérémie to restore the old order of slavery in the French colony.

As Barney soon discovered, proper timing in business can generate bountiful profits. French commissioner Léger Félicité Sonthonax was about to abandon his post at Le Cap Français just as the *Sampson* arrived in the harbor. Sonthonax had dealt with Barney on his previous trips and they had become friends. Therefore, he asked Barney to help evacuate the French officials and take them safely to Port Républicain (now called Port-au-Prince). Barney complied, and on arriving at Port Républicain sold his cargo for the highest of prices, satisfying shortages of just about everything. In return for saving the commissioners, Sonthonax arranged for Barney to receive payment of the bills from his last voyage from the French consul in Philadelphia. The primary purpose for the voyage now fulfilled, Barney headed north with a cargo of cotton, coffee, sugar, and indigo worth fifty-five thousand dollars that would bring a handsome return in Baltimore.

Three days out of Port Républicain, the *Sampson,* sailing in the company of a French privateer, *Le Reparateur,* was spotted by a British frigate. The American and French ships separated, hoping the frigate would choose one victim and allow the other to escape. Since the French were at war with England, the frigate should have gone after the French warship, but the British captain evidently thought the merchantman was the easier prey. Barney now had a Hobson's choice of engaging a frigate by himself or submitting. There was really no option, and when he followed the order to heave to, the ship identified itself as the thirty-two-gun frigate HMS *Penelope,* commanded by Capt. Bartholomew Thomas Rowley. After he boarded the captured ship and scanned the *Sampson*'s papers, Rowley realized that this ship was the one recaptured from British privateers by the brazen Barney the previous July. Rowley became verbally abusive, using language that infuriated the proud Barney. The short-tempered Barney returned insult for insult. Rowley had earned his reputation for arrogance, and he was particularly condescending toward those he still considered rebels against the Crown. The master of the *Penelope* had Barney shackled between two guns and ordered his guards to "blow the rascal's brains out if he opened his mouth again." A prize crew was placed aboard the *Sampson* with orders to sail it to Jamaica. The frigate then turned to give chase to *Le Reparateur,* which was also captured and taken as a prize.

Shortly after the *Sampson* made port at Port Royal, the *Penelope* dropped anchor not far away in deeper water. Barney's ship was now under the cannons of a British fort on one side and the guns of the frigate on the other. He was roused in the early morning hours the next day, rowed ashore, charged with violating British maritime laws before the clerk of the Admiralty, and placed under arrest at the residence of Don Fraser, deputy marshal of the Vice-Admiralty Court. Fraser turned out to be a reasonable and kind man. He advised Barney that he might gain his release if he sued for a writ of *habeas corpus.* Fraser also felt that Barney stood a better chance of fair treatment if his trial could be moved to Kingston, the seat of the chief justice. The deputy marshal helped arrange for Barney's bail through a local mercantile firm. Meanwhile, the *Sampson* was brought to a wharf so that its cargo could be unloaded and secured by an agent for the *Penelope.*

Barney was forced to remain in Kingston for two months because the court that dealt with matters on the high sea did not meet until February. During his forced stay in the city Barney made many friends among the other American captains and seamen who were also awaiting trial for maritime offenses. On 13 February 1794, Barney was brought before the bar of the British Admiralty Court charged with "piratically and feloniously rescuing and bearing off a ship and cargo that had been seized at sea while under his command in July last." According to Admiralty law, once a ship was under the command of a British captain, even if it had been taken as a privateer's prize, it became subject to the king's law. Technically, retaking one's own ship by force of arms was an act of piracy. One possible defense might be to prove that the ship was illegally seized in the first instance. Alternatively, one might attempt to discredit the testimony of the accuser. A second charge was entered "for firing upon with intent to kill and wounding" one of the prize masters. The penalty for piracy was death. Conviction of attempted murder carried a punishment of a long prison term, only marginally better to contemplate.

The trial became an important local event. American seamen held in the port for litigation attended the proceedings to see what they might expect at their own court appearances. In addition, many Jamaicans were drawn to the court because they disliked Bartholomew Thomas Rowley and hoped to see him humbled. Barney was at a disadvantage because he was unable to call as witnesses the Americans who had been aboard the *Sampson* during its seizure and detention. The attorney general was eloquent in framing the complaint against Barney. Opening his case with a lengthy speech, he stated the severity of the accusations of piracy along with attempted murder of a British subject in cold blood. He made the point that Barney was fortunate to have been captured by such a gallant representative of His Majesty's navy. Another captain might have saved the jury the trouble of a trial by summarily executing the upstart. A second government advocate tried to excite the passions of the jury by referring to Barney as a "blood thirsty Jacobin" who committed "daring insolence" on one of His Majesty's officers. He then went on to present a distorted description of Barney's treatment after his capture by the *Penelope*.[23]

The prosecutor told the story of Barney's retaking of the *Sampson* with relative accuracy, except that the number of Americans who overwhelmed the prize crew was elevated to twenty. That distortion of truth was probably to save face. It was obvious that the defeated prize crew did not want it known that they had capitulated to a mere three men. Several witnesses testified for the prosecution, but the principal witness to the piracy charge was the prize master, the man Barney was accused of shooting. In fact, the man had received buckshot wounds from the accidental discharge of the blunderbuss and had acted like a thug while Barney was his prisoner. Barney was again a prisoner of the Crown, so the prize master reverted to his bullying mode. In addition, he bragged about how they had captured the *Sampson*. In doing so, the British sailor exposed his true character. It became obvious to the jury that the man was untrustworthy. The foreman interrupted to say that the jury need not waste the court's time; they felt that Barney was not guilty of the charge of piracy. The judge agreed, and the charge was dropped. The second charge of wounding with the intent to kill was also declared moot. A greatly relieved Barney and his friends retired to a nearby tavern to celebrate his victory. Members of the jury joined them for an evening of "convivial festivity." Rowley and Barney never crossed paths again, but Barney continued to have altercations with crewmen from British naval vessels as long as he was in Kingston. Barney felt that the captain, the officers, or the crew of the *Penelope* might have been behind the conflicts, but he treated them as inconsequential; they were more of an annoyance than a threat, and not worthy of retribution.

The court's confiscation of his ship and cargo put Barney in financial straits. After a long delay, the hearing for the release of the *Sampson* was finally adjudicated. Evidence was presented to show that Barney was deeply involved with the French government of Saint-Domingue and was a friend of Commissioner Sonthonax. Barney admitted to helping French refugees escape from the island during the recent rebellion but claimed that he was motivated by humanitarianism. The most damaging evidence was some French property found on the *Sampson*. According to British maritime law, the ship and entire cargo could thus be condemned and sold as a prize. Barney petitioned for a full evaluation of the cargo. His barrister argued that the Crown lawfully was entitled only to the portion deemed belonging to their enemy. The judge gratuitously granted him the privilege of applying for the valuation—for a fee of fifty pounds. Once the fee was collected, the judge immediately ruled that application of the Admiralty law was consistent and the petition was denied.

Until this episode Barney had simply disliked British justice; now he absolutely despised British officials and their laws. He knew that he had been cheated, and yet he was at their mercy. They had taken him for approximately six thousand dollars in legal fees that fattened the wallets of the bureaucratic agencies and barristers. Some years later, a joint commission under Article 7 of the Jay Treaty would award him and his partner, John Hollins, restitution for the loss of the *Sampson* and its cargo.

While the American ship captains awaited their economic fate on the lovely tropical island, James Madison delivered a speech in the House of Representatives urging the passage of an embargo against the British. Barney drafted a letter of support that is now part of the Madison papers and had it signed by twenty-one of his fellow detainees awaiting trial in Jamaica.[24] He wrote a second, more personal, letter to Edmund Randolph, the secretary of state, two weeks later in which he stated that "the expenses [of the Americans for keeping their ships and cargo at anchor] are enormous and ruinous. Several Americans have been obliged to abandon their vessels and return home owing to the willful delay and heavy expense of Admiralty trials. During the last twelve days not less than 20 American cargoes and several American vessels have been condemned."[25] In addition, Barney complained about the abuse and humiliation heaped on Americans by the British, citing as an example an episode in which the British kept the captured American ship *James* at anchor in the harbor with the Union Jack flying over the American flag, an unforgivable insult even in time of war.[26]

The formal diplomatic protest about the embargo of American ships in Jamaica was delivered to George Hammond, the British minister (ambassador) in America. Hammond, in turn, was asked to forward the dispatch to Lord Greville, the governor of Jamaica, with a request for immediate action. This involved President Washington himself, who wrote in a journal note: "Colo Smith [of Maryland] put into my hands sundry letters written by Capt. Joshua Barney, and others [sic] papers relating to his being captured by a British frigate & carried into Kingston, Jamaica & treated in a most shameful manner. Sent papers to Sec. of State . . . to take the case into consideration."[27] Matters were complicated by the rumor that Joshua Barney was being tried for piracy in Jamaica. News of Barney's acquittal had not yet reached Philadelphia, and the description of his danger caused grave concern in Congress, particularly among the representatives from Maryland. Under the flag of America's only organized naval service at the time, the Revenue Service, President Washington sent a Charleston pilot schooner lying in Philadelphia to Jamaica with letters of complaint from Secretary of State Edmond Randolph through Minister Hammond to Governor Greville.[28] The ship, which bore the bizarre name *Slavery* and sailed under the command of William Story, was in poor repair but evidently was the only one available to make the voyage. The *Slavery* left Philadelphia on 1 April, racing southward because the captain was under the impression that Barney was still to be tried for piracy. The vessel encountered a terrible storm in the Gulf Stream that cost it both masts. The ship's company was convinced that they were on a mission of mercy, so they proceeded toward Jamaica using jury-rigged sails hoisted on sweeps (long oars). On the way they encountered an American sloop that gave them some additional provisions and water but refused them a spar. As they neared Kingston harbor, the crew took down their jury-rigged sails, used their sweeps to make headway against the outgoing tide, and rowed the *Slavery* into port on 18 April. The men were exhausted but pleased to find that Joshua Barney was still alive and well.

Barney was deeply moved when he learned of the travail the crew of the *Slavery* had experienced in attempting to influence the outcome of his trial. He arranged to have the revenue cutter repaired, new masts stepped onto the keel, and the sails replaced. He took special care to ensure that the American Revenue Service crew was well treated. When Lieutenant Governor Adam Williamson, who was in charge of the colony in Governor Greville's absence, received the letters from the American president and Congress, he realized that they had detained no ordinary merchant captain but a man of influence. Williamson had no jurisdiction over the Admiralty courts, but as the chief officer of Jamaica he could invite Barney to dinner and extend the hospitality of the mansion. This was hardly compensation for the loss of a ship and its cargo, but it was the single act of civility that Barney received from British officials during his time in Jamaica.

Barney set out for Baltimore aboard the *Slavery* together with most of his *Sampson* crew. About halfway home they encountered another American ship, which appeared to be running cargo to Jamaica against the embargo order. The revenue cutter boarded the ship and found it full of flour and corn. Barney was furious that an American ship was about to engage in trade against the government's embargo order, and even more angry that they would be feeding the British as well. Of course, he had profited from political tensions himself only months before, but this specific business activity might help the British. He was in no mood to tolerate this particular lack of patriotism. Although Barney had no official authority to do so, he ordered the arrest of the captain and his schooner, put a prize crew aboard the captured vessel, and had them follow the *Slavery* to Baltimore. This put him once again at risk of being tried as a pirate, but this time the matter was between Americans in an American court.

When the two vessels arrived in Baltimore on 17 May, Barney traveled to Philadelphia to report his actions to Secretary of State Randolph, who personally approved of his taking the ship into custody.[29] The captain was tried before the American admiralty court for violating the embargo and found guilty. As punishment the seized schooner and cargo were to be sold as a prize. The trial was highly publicized, and its outcome infuriated Americans who sympathized with Great Britain. Many of them, particularly those in the Maryland tidewater countryside, turned against Barney for his part in the affair.

The embargo was due to expire on 25 May, but Barney lobbied Congress to extend it indefinitely. Believing the United States should remain neutral between the warring powers, he vigorously campaigned by handbill and speech. He also felt that America should withdraw from all trade with both belligerents. Barney was convinced that only by strictly observing the laws of neutrality while carrying on trade would the United States be spared from the degrading insults American seamen received at the hands of British cruisers. Therefore, he led the cause of no trade within the policy of neutrality and gave an account of his own recent experiences at the hands of the British navy. British sympathizers in America were further antagonized by Barney's campaign.

In Baltimore, his audience was largely composed of seamen and fellow merchant captains, and most agreed to keep operating under the embargo for at least another ten days. The majority would remain in port, hoisting the American colors at dawn over their ships as a symbol of solidarity in their belief. The local pilots were approached to enlist their cooperation in the embargo extension. Finally, the captains and pilots drafted a petition to Congress with 104 officers signing the document. The effort proved futile. Congress ignored their petition, and the embargo expired. When it did, Barney moved quickly to take financial advantage of the situation by capitalizing on the repealed embargo. Succumbing to the annoying quirk of opportunism in his character, he spoke to the French minister, his friend M. Fauchet, and contracted to deliver large quantities of flour to France.

The political price for his actions against the British and his support of the embargo would be great. Barney was unjustly branded a pirate in some influential circles and a reactionary in others. In politics, the voters remember a bad reputation, no matter how unjustified.

7

FRANCE

Capitaine de Vaisseau du Premier

hen America was a part of the British Empire, the most powerful navy in the world protected its citizens and its trade. Now, with the United States independent and Britain and France once again at war, both sides began seizing American ships suspected of trading with the enemy. The belligerents hunted down each other's vessels wherever they were found—frequently, off the coast of North America. As the United States grew into a prominent commercial nation its ships were increasingly detained by English and French vessels; in addition, British naval commanders short of sailors occasionally impressed American seamen and forced them to serve in the Royal Navy. Nor were England and France the only nations preying on American shipping. At virtually the same time, Portugal and Algiers signed a peace treaty. Algiers, like the other Barbary States, had a policy of always being at war with at least one nation, giving it an excuse to seize the ships of its "enemy" and to extract tribute from the enemy nation, a common national extortion scheme at the time. Now that Portugal was no longer the designated enemy, the Barbary corsairs stepped up their attacks on American ships.

In April 1793 President Washington recommended the construction of six frigates to defend American ships from attack by the Algerians. For more than a year Congress ignored his advice. In March 1794 Secretary of State Thomas Jefferson delivered a message to President Washington stating that seizures by the British, the French, and the Barbary States had reached such alarming heights that they posed a serious threat to America's international trade. The U.S. government had four possible courses of action: do nothing, pay blackmail to obtain the release of American sailors, hire a stronger European navy to provide protection for U.S. shipping, or build an American navy. The Federalists, led by Washington and Hamilton, together with the commercial interests of the Northeast favored establishing a navy. In opposition were the agrarian southerners, who believed that a navy would be very expensive to build and maintain. The cheapest way to maintain foreign trade, southerners believed, was through the use of economic coercion such as embargoes against nations that would not respect U.S. rights. Congress debated the alternatives before passing compromise legislation by a margin of only two votes. The Navy Act of 1794 gave birth to the U.S. Navy by authorizing the purchase or construction of six frigates. The inclusion of a clause providing that all work on the ships would cease should peace be made with Algiers reflects the fact that the act was primarily aimed at that African state rather than at Britain and France.

Joshua Barney became caught up in these events in a most unusual way. On 5 June 1794 he received a letter from Secretary of War Henry Knox appointing him one of the first six captains in the new U.S. Navy. He was honored until he read further and noted that the six new captains were listed in order of their seniority: John Barry, Samuel Nicholson, Silas Talbot, Joshua Barney, Richard Dale, and Thomas Truxtun. Barney was furious at being listed after Silas Talbot. He contended that Talbot had served as a Continental army lieutenant colonel, but never as a naval officer, let alone as a captain. He was convinced that the appointment was political. Talbot was then serving as a congressman from New York, having just beaten Judge William Cooper of Cooperstown, the father of James Fenimore Cooper, in a hotly contested election. His belief that the appointment was politically motivated may have had some validity, but Barney's statement about Talbot's military service was incorrect, and he must have known it.[1]

Wounded six times in a series of land and sea battles, Talbot was a much greater hero of the Revolutionary War than Barney was. Talbot had enlisted in the Rhode Island militia at the very beginning of the Revolution. He commanded a fire ship that damaged the sixty-four-gun *Asia* in New York harbor and, as mentioned earlier, served as an artillery officer in the defense of Fort Mifflin while Barney was serving on the *Andrea Doria* only a few hundred yards away. Talbot and his men captured the floating battery *Pigot* in 1778. Like Barney, he became the captain of a privateer, the *Argo*, which took twelve prizes along the southern coast of New England. Talbot also fought with the bureaucracy over compensation for the prizes he had captured. Talbot was the captain of the *General Washington* when it was captured by the British and renamed the *General Monk*. Since its recapture was his proudest victory, Barney must have known this fact. (One might speculate that Barney lost respect for Talbot because he surrendered his ship to the British, but Barney had done the same during his naval career.) The two officers were fellow prisoners in the *Jersey* and were sent together in the infamous *Yarmouth* to Plymouth for internment at Old Mill Prison. Shortly thereafter, Talbot was exchanged for a British prisoner and released. On his return to the United States he was commissioned a captain in the Continental navy, a rank Barney never achieved during the Revolutionary War. Because of the paucity of available ships at the time Talbot never had his own naval vessel to command, and so, technically, Barney was correct about this minor point, but it is difficult to explain how he could complain about the seniority ranking.

When Barney's strong objection reached the War Department, Secretary Knox responded: "Since the nominations to the Senate have been known, it has been said that you would not accept the appointment on the ground that Capt Talbot was junior in rank to you during the late war. That the reverse of this is the case, will fully appear by the enclosed resolve of Congress creating Col Talbot a captain in the navy on 19 September 1779; whereas it appears from the list that you continued as lieutenant to the end of the war. Respect to the justice of the President of the United States requires that this circumstance should be mentioned."[2] The letter's reference to President Washington, the man Barney respected most in the nation, was particularly painful. Barney had brilliantly commanded a twenty-gun ship for more than two years with the title of captain, but because of the ship's size and armament, naval regulations stated that his official rank must remain lieutenant. Barney did not reply to Knox; nor would he accept a commission in the newly formed navy. Thus the services of one of the most capable naval officers in the nation were lost over pride. The lives of Barney and Talbot criss-crossed again and again, and they were strikingly alike in character and accomplishments. Barney's place in American naval history might have been much higher had he not quarreled with Knox about his seniority to Talbot.

By a strange twist of fate, a dispute over seniority in rank would later mark Talbot's career as well. Captain Talbot was assigned to superintend the construction of the frigate *President* in New York. When peace was reached with Algiers, work on the navy's frigates was suspended and Talbot was inactivated without pay. Although the date of Talbot's original commission was 1794, work on the *President* stopped before that on the *Constellation,* the *Constitution,* and the *United States.* A simmering conflict with France led Congress to order work resumed on all the ships. When this occurred, Talbot found himself junior to Thomas Truxtun on the navy's seniority list. According to the rules of hierarchy, length of continuous service counted more than date of rank. This placed Truxtun in line for the command of a frigate before Talbot. Enraged because Truxtun had been junior to him all through the Revolutionary War, Talbot openly refused to serve under him and appealed to his longtime friend and supporter John Adams for help. Talbot regained his place on the seniority list and ultimately became the second captain of the frigate *Constitution.*

Barney's rejection of a commission may have had a more practical motive than seniority of rank. He was thirty-three thousand dollars in debt from the *Sampson* incident, and the French consul general in Philadelphia had refused to honor the note Barney presented from the government officials of Saint-Domingue. Barney could not live on the pay of a naval captain and meet his family's financial obligations. Thus he may have opted to remain in private enterprise, which offered prospects of better income.

The merchant firm of Barney and Hollins, in which Barney was the senior partner, desperately needed a flour-shipping contract to earn a profit. Barney spoke passable French and had a number of contacts in the French army and navy, so he decided to go to Paris to try to collect on the note and secure contracts from the new French government. Barney crossed the Atlantic as the commander of the packet ship *Cincinnatus.* Among the passengers on the voyage were James Monroe, who had just been appointed minister to France, and his family, plus Fulwar Smith, the American consul general in Paris. Monroe and Smith might be able to help him recover his money and arrange contracts, and Barney was thus immensely pleased to have them as passengers. He sailed from Baltimore on 28 June 1794 and landed at Le Havre on 30 July. There they heard the news of the death of Robespierre and renewed turmoil in Paris. Anarchy seemed to be a real threat, so the Americans stayed onboard their vessel until the violence appeared to ebb and the diplomats could safely take up their posts.

After ten days spent adjusting to his new home in Paris and establishing preliminary relations with the new government, Monroe, in the company of Barney, was to be introduced to the National Convention of the Republic of France. This body, roughly equivalent to the American Constitutional Convention combined with the early Continental Congress, was convened at the Tuileries, a former palace of Louis XVI and Marie Antoinette, who had been guillotined in January 1793. Barney had last entered the palace as a guest of the royal couple, and the changed circumstances caused him some moments of reflection. James Monroe, the first envoy representing a sovereign nation to address the convention, delivered his speech in English. As it was translated, the assembled delegates applauded and shouted, "Vive la Republique! Vivent les Republiques!" The president of the convention kissed Monroe's cheeks in the traditional French fraternal salutation and ordered "that the colors of both nations should be suspended at the vault of the hall as a sign of perpetual alliance and union." Monroe seized the moment and ordered an American flag to be made by the finest flag maker in Paris. It was completed on 25 September 1794, and Barney was given the singular honor of delivering it to the convention hall. The following are segments of the proceedings of the convention:

26th Fructidor [12 September] 1794
Bernard of Saints, President.

The President: A letter . . . announces that the Minister Plenipotentiary of the United States of America sends a stand of colors. . . . It is brought by an officer of the United States.

The Convention orders him admitted. The American officer enters the bar amidst universal shouts of applause; he carries a standard, the colors of which are those of our standard of liberty, with the only difference that the blue field is interspersed with stars.

Along with the flag Barney brought a letter from James Monroe, translated below.

> The Convention having decreed that the colors of the American and French republics should be united and stream together in the place of its sittings as a testimony of the union and friendship, which ought to subsist forever between the two nations, I thought that I could not better manifest the deep impression which this decree has made upon me, and express the thankful sensations of my constituents, than by procuring their colors to be carefully executed, and in offering them in the name of the American people to the Representatives of the French Nation.
>
> I have had them made in the form lately decreed by Congress, and have trusted them to Captain Barney, an officer of distinguished merit, who has rendered us great services by sea, in the cause of our Revolution. . . . Accept, Citizen President, this standard as a pledge of sensibility with which the American people always receive the interest and friendship which their good and brave allies give them.

Joshua Barney then made a short speech to the assembly.

> Citizen President: Having been directed by the minister . . . to present to the National Convention the flag demanded [asked] of him, the flag, under the auspices of which I have had the honor to fight against our common enemy during the war which has assured liberty and independence, I discharge the duty with the most satisfaction and deliver it to you. Henceforth, suspended beside that of the French Republic, it will become the symbol of the union which subsists between the two nations, and will last, I hope, as long as the freedom, which they have so bravely won and wisely consolidated.

The assembly's response to Barney's speech would prove to be prophetic:

> The citizen who has just spoken at the bar is one of the most distinguished sea-officers of America. He has rendered great service to the liberty of his country, and could render the same to the liberty of France. I demand that . . . the fraternal embrace be given to this brave officer.[3]

The flag was graciously received by the president, who embraced Captain Barney amid applause from the audience. A member of the convention rendering homage to Barney's talents and services as an officer told him that the republic could usefully employ him.

Joshua Barney had once again been involved in a historic incident involving the American flag, and the impressionable naval warrior was moved by his reception. The implication that Barney was worthy of a commission in the French navy was flattering. The French were at war with the British, for whom Barney had developed great contempt. Further, he felt that America had insulted him by placing him below Silas Talbot on the seniority list of naval captains and dishonored him when it offered no reasonable alternative to his commission. Nevertheless, the acceptance of a commission in the French navy was far from the business mission he had in mind when he took his ship to France. Barney turned his energy toward obtaining the cargo that would make his journey profitable. Now that he had the respect of the National Convention and its Committee of Public Safety, the bureau that controlled matters of international commerce, Barney was able to settle the payments owed him from the convoluted *Sampson* incident. That had been one of Barney's most frustrating business ventures, but the final settlement proved extremely profitable.

The French minister of marine was determined to enlist the American seaman into the naval service of France. Most French naval officers were royalists, and thus no longer willing to serve France. Many had gone into exile and others had been executed. France was rebuilding its navy and needed experienced naval commanders. Thus, the minister tried to entice Barney into service by offering him a prestigious command, that of the seventy-four-gun ship *Alexander* recently captured from the British. It was far larger than any ship in the American fleet and would be one of the most formidable ships of the line in the French navy. Barney reluctantly but courteously declined the honor because such a vessel would be an integral part of a fleet commanded by an admiral. He preferred the independence of being the captain of a frigate. Command of a smaller ship offered both the chance of prize money and, more important to Barney at the moment, the opportunity to militarily repay the British for their transgressions against him. On the other hand, Barney was on the verge of a profitable business undertaking. Ego satisfaction, the desire for revenge, and the possibilities of financial gains pulled Barney in opposing directions. In the end, he decided that he needed firm financial security before he could seek personal satisfaction and revenge by accepting a French naval commission.

One evening Barney returned to his quarters in Paris to discover that someone had entered his bedroom through a secret door that was hidden by an armoire. The thief had taken all his money, but of far greater importance, the culprit had taken Barney's golden eagle badge of the Society of Cincinnati and the fine sword presented to him by the state of Pennsylvania. The theft of the sword was Barney's most devastating personal loss because it was the memento of his most gratifying naval victory. None of these possessions would ever be recovered, nor would the thief be caught.

The next few months were very difficult for Barney. First he contracted to carry wines and brandies from Bordeaux to America, but there was a long delay in obtaining the cargo. This meant that he had an idle ship with ongoing expenses. Although Barney was not truly wealthy, he was relatively insulated from the poverty the French were suffering in the postrevolutionary economic depression. Many Frenchmen were convinced that all Americans had money, and Barney became the victim of a series of petty robbery attempts. On top of this, the winter in Paris that year was one of the coldest in memory. Food and fuel were in short supply, and his funds were being drained by the spiraling cost of necessities. The rationing of bread particularly frustrated Barney. At first, individuals were limited to half a kilo per day. Before long this was reduced to one hundred grams. When he dined in his favorite restaurant Barney had to bring bread in his pocket if he wanted some with his meal. But money and guile, as always, tended to solve rationing problems. Barney's baker showed him a way to elude the letter of the law. "*Citoyen le Capitaine,*" the man said, "as the regulation confines its restriction to bread, if you will allow me to put *tant soit peu* of butter or lard in the flour, it may then be called pastry!"[4]

The war on land was going well for France in spite of the fact that its soldiers were fighting in rags and on starvation rations. French forces had overrun Holland, France's leaders had signed an alliance with Spain, and only Austria and England continued as foes. The French people adopted a very liberal constitution, and order was slowly being restored. Convinced that the French navy needed to be bolstered, the minister of marine once again offered Barney a commission, this time with the title of capitaine de vaisseau, a rank equivalent to post captain in the British navy. The title and authority were right. A delighted Barney courteously accepted. Through shrewd dealings Barney had managed to keep his vessel working while he waited for his cargo of wine to be readied. With relative financial security achieved, he could now prudently accept a commission in the French navy and still support his family in America.

He was soon to realize that the timing of his acceptance was terrible. France and the United States were sister republics, as the recent color ceremonies in which he participated showed. The two republics shared a deep love of liberty and a hatred of Britain. Unfortunately, the American diplomat John Jay was in England negotiating a treaty just as Barney became a capitaine de vaisseau. France's leaders believed that the signing of the treaty, in which America accepted British maritime rules concerning contracts and neutral trading rights, made the United States a virtual economic ally of Britain. James Monroe attempted to allay their anger by negotiating a new treaty with France, but the French government refused to cooperate and instead ordered the seizure of American ships caught trading with Britain or its colonies. This drove a wedge between the two former allies and moved them close to war.

His loathing of the British led Barney to agree with the French on this issue. Britain was the enemy of both nations. If his fellow Americans did not have the stomach or courage to fight the British, he certainly did. The fact that the French were now harassing American shipping did not seem to be a factor in Barney's mental equation. Although he was considered a hero in America for his Revolutionary War service, Barney's foreign service would become an issue in later years when he tried to embark on a political career in the United States.

Barney's life as an officer in the French navy was one of paradox and perplexity. Although he accepted his appointment as capitaine de vaisseau in late January 1795, Barney did not receive orders until April, when he was directed to take possession of some previously captured Dutch warships in poor repair and return with them to France. Before the ships could be readied for sea, France and Holland reached a peace agreement and the ships were returned to their Dutch owners. Thus, in October, Barney returned to Dunkirk with little to show for his months away from home.

Barney decided that Paris would offer more exciting things to occupy his time and energies while he awaited new orders. When he reached the capital city, the name Napoléon Bonaparte was on everyone's lips. Former royalists had marched on the convention as part of an insurrection.

The chief of defense of the convention, Citizen Barras, felt powerless against them; recent history had taught him the capabilities of such mobs. Napoléon, a pallid Corsican who had asked Barras repeatedly for employment, inquired once again if he might be of service. In desperation, Barras gave the diminutive young man the task of putting down the rebellion. Within hours Bonaparte organized a nine-thousand-man army with thirty cannons at its disposal. As an estimated thirty thousand people converged on the grounds of the Tuileries Palace from multiple directions, Bonaparte ordered his artillery to fire into the mob. When the insurgents dispersed and his men had saved the Paris convention, the twenty-six-year-old Corsican was rewarded with an appointment as commander in chief of the Army of the Interior, the French army stationed within the borders of France.

A few month earlier, on 26 October 1794, the central government of France had changed from the convention to the Directory of Five, assisted by the Council of the Ancients (the cabinet) and the Five Hundred (the assembly). The new directory ordered Barney to remain in Paris to assist in the reorganization of the Armées Navales. The capitaine de vaisseau had few alternatives, so he accepted. While serving in that role Barney saw an opportunity to both earn some money and take revenge on the English for the indecencies they had inflicted on him, particularly in Jamaica. Since he enjoyed relative wealth in a country suffering economic hardships, Barney was able to purchase a fine cutter at a good price and fit it out as a privateer. The ship was appropriately named *La Vengeance*. Barney sent it to sea with fourteen guns and a crew of 104 men commanded by a French naval lieutenant. Barney ordered *La Vengeance* to stop any British ship and take it as a prize, but never to interfere with a vessel flying the American flag. *La Vengeance* should, in fact, offer American ships aid and protection. The privateer venture proved successful. During its first cruise *La Vengeance* took fourteen British merchant ships as prizes. In the next six weeks, the privateer captured nine others while sailing off the Norwegian coast. In addition to bringing him money, this venture did much to satisfy Barney's desire for revenge.

Unfortunately, Barney found himself caught in a web woven by article 21 of the Jay Treaty. The article states that if a subject or citizen of Great Britain or the United States "shall accept any Foreign Commission or Letters of Marque for arming any Vessel to act as a Privateer against the other party, it is hereby declared to be lawful for the said party to treat and punish the said Subject or Citizen, having Such Commission or Letter of Marque as a Pirate."[5] Alexander Hamilton, in a letter to Phineas Bond, noted that the British transport ship *Eliza* had been captured by a French privateer outfitted and owned by Joshua Barney, a member of the French navy but a citizen of the United States. Hamilton commented, "If Mr. Barney comes within the 21st Article of our treaty with Great Britain, it would make him liable, if taken by Great Britain to be punished as a Pirate. But it will be observed that the stipulation would not oblige the United States to treat him as such." Hamilton went on to recommend against such a prosecution of the American patriot.[6] As Barney averted capture by the British while under service to France, this provision of the Jay Treaty was never tested.

The naval officers holding the title capitaine de vaisseau were divided into three classes of seniority. The highest class was a captain with three or more years in command of a post ship, a sixth-rate ship of at least twenty-four guns; his title was post captain, and he was eligible for promotion to the rank of rear admiral. At the middle level was a captain in command of a post ship for less than three years, and at the lowest level was a captain of a smaller vessel, in rank roughly equivalent to master and commander in Britain's Royal Navy or, later, master commandant in the U.S. Navy. Obviously, French officers had seniority of service on their ships as well as influence in the maritime department. Therefore, bureaucracy being bureaucratic, Capitaine de Vaisseau Barney was assigned to the third category, a position similar in seniority to his American naval rank. This wounded Barney's fragile ego, and he resigned his commission. The minister of marine asked him to reconsider, promising that once the new assignments had been made and "shaken down," a better opportunity would likely become available, but Barney remained firm in his decision.

He left Paris and traveled overland to Flushing, where *La Vengeance* was docked. Taking personal control of his share of the money from the ship's prizes, he used a portion of it to form a partnership with two Americans to buy two additional vessels. The first, the lugger *Le Vengeur,* was refitted as an armed cruiser; the second was a brig called *Revenge.* Barney now had his own privateer fleet with which to harass the British.

In March 1795 French politics were becoming more and more complex. A third insurrection, this time supported by the British, had been recently put down. Napoléon had established himself as the head of France's underfed, underclothed, and underpaid army and was beginning his campaign in Italy. When France stepped up its seizure of U.S. ships in the West Indies and began maltreating many of their crews, the American minister to France, James Monroe, found himself in an untenable position and asked to be recalled. His status at home was in jeopardy because many ordinary citizens thought Monroe had bungled matters and destroyed America's close relationship with France. The political sensitivity of the new government of France was not clearly understood by the president and Congress of the United States, any more than the French leaders understood American views.

Fortunately for Barney, the French naval hierarchy respected him as a naval officer, and his citizenship was of no apparent concern. As the war with Britain expanded, France was ever more in need of experienced naval leaders. The minister of marine persuaded the directory to promote Barney to the rank of capitaine de vaisseau du premier, or commodore. Barney was flattered and accepted. He now held a rank that exceeded any he could hope to obtain in the United States.

After officially accepting his new commission, according to the new calendar of the Republique de France on 22 Floreal 1796 (12 May), Barney's first assignment was to take the forty-four-gun *La Harmonie* and the thirty-six-gun *La Railleuse* to Saint-Domingue. On 28 May the newly appointed commodore was ceremoniously rowed to his flagship. Even when funds were scarce, the French navy, with a long and proud history, reveled in nautical splendor. A now stately Joshua Barney was ushered aboard his ship amid the shriek of silver boatswain's pipes and walked between rows of saluting uniformed side boys. Most likely the French sailors were wearing short blue jackets, crimson sashes at their waists, duck trousers with a stripe in the tricolor of France on the seams, and broad-brimmed tarpaulin hats covering an occasional greased pigtail.[7] At the age of thirty-six, Capitaine de Vaisseau du Premier Barney commanded a fleet consisting of two large men-of-war plus thirteen frigates, which, after crossing the Atlantic, would disperse to other French Caribbean ports. During the voyage the French fleet captured a number of small ships. One carried a welcome cargo of much-needed spare clothing. Barney's men helped themselves to this booty and saved selected pieces for their families. Another prize proved to be a disabled ship whose crew had mutinied against an American captain, and Barney found himself in a position to administer maritime justice.[8]

When *La Railleuse* made landfall at Saint-Domingue, Barney set out to assemble a fleet of French warships to intercept British shipping from Jamaica. Once he put to sea there were occasional encounters with elements of the British fleet, but no conclusive engagements ensued. The variable wind direction and velocity, unexpected currents, and cover from islands and coral reefs, coupled with dark nights followed by blinding dawns, frequently "reshuffled the deck for the draw" of advantage and disadvantage between the British and French. An unexplained sickness that broke out aboard Barney's vessels disabled ninety of his men and took the lives of a few. Morale started to plummet, so Barney sought shelter in the familiar waters of the Chesapeake Bay. Just as the light marking Cape Henry came into view, a group of five British ships was spotted sailing between the French ships and the mouth of the bay. Barney signaled to his two consorts to follow him eastward back out to sea.

The following dawn, with the sun at their backs and only one enemy sail visible on the horizon, Barney's ships attempted to venture into the bay. Before long, however, the other four British ships appeared on the scene and formed a battle line. The slowest and most ungainly of Barney's fleet swiftly fell away from the others toward the enemy. The largest British ship of the line then turned to engage the two remaining French ships. Barney ordered the *Railleuse* to stand close by in case of a firefight. The British ship altered its short-hauled course and was joined by a frigate. The French and the British vessels parried at a distance for the remainder of the day. At nightfall, the ships lost visual contact. Barney ordered his carpenter to build a makeshift raft with a small sail. He then had a barrel of tar placed on it and set alight. The British, fooled into thinking they were following a ship's lantern, chased after the decoy for much of the night. Meanwhile, Barney and his men escaped to the southeastward toward Bermuda.

Barney's satisfaction at the success of this simple ruse soon faded as he and his men found themselves in even greater peril. On 1 September a fierce North Atlantic hurricane with mountainous waves and unrelenting winds blew in on them. There was so much water in the air and so much air mixed into the ocean that it was difficult to demarcate the surface of the sea. The *Harmonie* and the *Railleuse* were badly battered, and Barney broke his thigh when he was washed under one of the quarterdeck cannons. The two ships survived the forty-eight-hour ordeal, but they emerged as barely navigable hulks. Fortunately, the backside of the hurricane brought fair weather, allowing them to reach the safety of Le Cap Français on 14 September. The ships were in terrible shape, but repairable given enough time. Barney decided not to wait for the repairs and found private transportation back to France. When he reached Europe, he sought a financial accounting of his privateer fleet. To his pleasure, the profit from the privateer enterprise together with a series of complex business dealings left him with net earnings of sixty-five thousand dollars, a sizable fortune in the 1790s. Barney forwarded the money to his family in Baltimore.

When news of the generous remittance became public knowledge, many at home deemed the cash to be blood money. The policy of the French government to capture any U.S. vessel entering or leaving any British port was well known, as were the facts that Barney was a ranking officer in the French navy and that he owned privateers sailing under letters of marque from that newly perceived enemy. What the general pubic did not know was that the commander of Barney's privateer ships had obeyed the commodore's strict instructions to leave American vessels alone. While searching the high seas for prey, *La Vengeance* intercepted and boarded twenty-nine American vessels and released all of them unharmed. Stories were fabricated alleging Barney's savagery at sea. Gossip and rumor overwhelmed the truth. Compounding Barney's problems, some members of the French Ministry of Marine resented his sparing American ships. The government of France was issuing his orders, and citizens of the Republic of France were paying his salary and furnishing him with naval ships, men, and arms that were in short supply. What right had he to decide unilaterally to spare an enemy of France?

Barney's next assignment was command of the port of Le Cap Français in Saint-Domingue. During his stint there he became involved in the politics of this nation in transition. The Spanish had abandoned their half of Hispaniola, leaving a population comprised largely of freed slaves. Of the island's population of 556,000, about 90 percent were former slaves. There were rebellions in a number of locations, and the British supported the insurgents with money and arms. The French government managed to keep things under control by applying republican principles of liberty, equality, and fraternity. It could be argued that the republicanism practiced in Saint-Domingue during this time was closer to the ideal than that seen in France itself. Barney was a total convert to this form of government and somewhat of an acolyte. Unfortunately, not every French government official felt the same way. In particular, a secretary to Commissioner Sonthonax was using his power to take advantage of the privileges of rank. The commodore argued with the man, lost his temper, and assaulted him. This was the age when pistol duels were considered an honorable method of defending injured honor. The opponents met, exchanged shots that missed their respective marks, and were luckily interrupted by French soldiers. Neither man was hurt, and politeness, if not warmth, characterized their future encounters. Although dueling was the moral practice of the day, the fact that Barney would place his life in danger by dueling reflects his continuing immaturity and lack of self-control.

Forever the businessman, Barney noted that sugar was the currency of the island. He invested in a sugarcane plantation thinking that it would ensure his wealth while he was away at sea. Agricultural operations often require the presence of the owner to oversee operations, however; in the owner's absence, the property can rapidly deteriorate. So it was with Barney's sugar plantation. To make matters worse, the world price of sugar fell, and the people of the island, for whom Barney had developed a strong affection, were in terrible economic trouble. France, their protector, had its own problems, and open starvation threatened Saint-Domingue. In an act of altruism, Barney drew up a contract to supply a monthly shipment of food to the island. Now he had to find a source of supply. The obvious place to obtain the provisions was America. This also presented a chance for Barney to be reunited with his family, whom he had not seen for two years! Barney appointed a young man from Baltimore to look after his business interests in Le Cap Français and, turning over his command of the area to another officer, sailed for America with two frigates, the *Medusa* and *L'Insurgente*, in early December 1796.

On 7 December 1796 President Washington delivered a speech to Congress that recommended the creation of a permanent navy:

> To an active external commerce, the protection of a naval force is indispensable. . . . This is manifest of wars to which a state itself is a party. But besides this, it is in our own experience, that the most sincere neutrality is not a sufficient guard against the depredations of nations at war. To secure respect to a neutral flag requires a naval force organized and ready to vindicate it from insult or aggression.

This may even prevent the necessity of going to war, by discouraging belligerents from committing such violations of the rights of neutral party. . . . It would seem as if our trade to the Mediterranean, without a protective force, will always be insecure, and our citizens exposed to the calamities from which numbers of them have but just been relieved. These considerations invite the United States to look to the means, and to set about the gradual creation of a navy. Will it not then be advisable to begin without delay to provide and lay up the materials for building and equipping of ships-of-war, and to proceed in the work by degrees, in proportion as our resources shall render it practicable without inconvenience, so that a future war of Europe may not find our commerce in the same unprotected state in which it is found by the present?[9]

Congress listened with respect but took no immediate action.

By the time Barney arrived at Norfolk, it was evident that his ships would need extensive repairs before they could return to sea. As a flag officer in the French navy, Barney negotiated with a shipyard to have them overhauled, then left for home. It was just a few days before Christmas, and Commodore Joshua Barney's arrival in Baltimore came as a surprise to his family. Barney's eldest son, William, had lived with the commodore in France for a short time before going home on an American packet ship with instructions to persuade his mother, Anne, to join Joshua in France. Mrs. Barney had resisted his pleas and stayed in Maryland, however, because she disliked long ocean voyages.

Barney's first priority on reaching Baltimore was a pleasant family reunion. His second order of business was contracting for the cargo of food he had promised to obtain for Saint-Domingue. It was now early January and Baltimore's harbor was almost entirely frozen. Some sturdy vessels managed to get out to sea to deliver a trickle of the much-needed supplies. As Barney went about his venture he became acutely aware of the depth of the political hostility that was dividing his country, particularly in Baltimore and Philadelphia. Both the English and the French were infringing on America's rights as a neutral nation. In the dispute over who was the lesser villain, the Federalists favored the English and the Republicans leaned toward the French. Barney, whom many Federalists considered a traitor, was disparaged in a political cartoon as the devil incarnate. Influential Federalist newspapers carried a story about Barney's return to America, saying that on his arrival for the first time as a French naval officer he had the American flag run up to the yard of the *Medusa* upside down, an egregious insult. Barney explained to friends that indeed the American flag had been ordered aloft, and that an inexperienced hand had hoisted it "capsized" by accident. The error was immediately corrected when noticed by an officer on deck. If any American took pride in his association with his nation's flag it was Joshua Barney, and this charge particularly distressed him. The hostile newspapers did not print Barney's account of what had happened, and many Americans continued to believe the story.[10] This episode added to the weight of evidence that convicted Barney of disloyalty in the court of public opinion.

When the commodore wrote to the French consul general in Philadelphia describing the repairs that were necessary on the two frigates in Norfolk, he was surprised to learn that the consul had been recalled and that his successor said that the Republic of France would not pay. Barney then had a draft drawn on the Bank of France through the chargé d'affaires for the French minister to America to pay for the repairs. With the threat of war between the United States and France becoming greater each day, however, no American bank would honor the draft. Barney's only hope for obtaining cash for the repairs and for the supplies purchased for Saint-Domingue was to return to Paris. Meanwhile, the commodore had to finance both debts from his own modest estate.

Barney's ships were now ready at Norfolk, but the British had heard that the two French frigates were being repaired and had stationed two frigates of their own in Hampton Roads to intercept them when they put to sea. Another half dozen British ships lay in wait closer to the Capes. According to traditional rules of naval combat, ships of belligerent nations leaving the same neutral port were to allow a twenty-four-hour grace period before engaging each other in combat. Barney asked for assurance that the British would honor these rules. Their response was that *they* would never violate these civilized regulations, but they were not sure that the French would be as fair. Barney, who knew his foe, did not believe them. He decided to offer a challenge. Barney and his two ships would meet any two of the British ships in battle off Hampton Roads if the British would pledge that no other vessels would interfere in the contest. The offer of a fair contest received no reply, but on a hot, humid August morning the British fleet, unannounced and seemingly without purpose, weighed anchor and put to sea, thus voiding the genteel rules of engagement. Ships under way at sea were permitted to attack immediately when they encountered enemy vessels.

Barney feared that he was trapped, but having the advantage of an intimate knowledge of these waters, he decided to take a chance and leave the safety of the inshore anchorage. The two ships slipped into the midstream at half ebb tide and a breeze carried them forward into the bay. When Barney reached Cape Henry, he anchored in the shelter of the bayside. The American had taken part in many a sea chase as both hunter and quarry, and he knew that they tended to be long and tedious affairs. The capitaine de vaisseau du premier had no desire to set out on such a contest at a disadvantage.

It was now an hour before dusk, so Barney sent a pilot boat out to lead the way in view of a British man-of-war. The small boat sounded the depth of the water in the relative shallows and raised a small lantern to guide Barney's two ships past the cape. A moonless darkness descended, and Barney silently reversed course and headed back up into the bay out of sight of the British and his pilot boat. The next morning the British could not find the pilot boat or the two French ships and assumed that Barney had slid by them in the night and put to sea. The simplest of ruses had worked. When the British sailed away, Barney returned down the bay and entered the Atlantic unmolested.

Barney's ships eluded the British until they reached the waters off Saint-Domingue. There they made a number of insignificant contacts with British vessels. The ships sparred with each other, firing occasional shots and inflicting insignificant damage, but neither side gained an advantage. Finally, the naval chess match appeared to have Barney boxed in. Checkmate was a strong possibility. At any moment the commodore's ships might strike the soundings and find the bottom; they had to change course or risk running aground. Barney was now forced to sail on a bearing that would take him near the guns of the ships of the line. He ordered all hands beat to quarters, decks cleared for action, and a course set to close with the enemy. Barney put *L'Insurgente* in the lead and ordered it to fire on the British ship with its bow guns. He followed with shots from the quarterdeck and the stern gun of the *Medusa*. The nearest British frigate tacked away, and Barney's flagship found itself in position to deliver a broadside together with heavy carronade fire. The big English vessel, trying to come about, backed its topsails, lost forward momentum, and almost hove to. Barney took advantage of the enemy's loss of maneuverability and continued on his course, racing to safety in nearby Port de Paix.

When the British gave up their chase and bore away, Barney made his way back to Le Cap Français, where he was saddened to learn that his friend Commissioner Sonthonax had been recalled to Paris. This was a grave loss to the people of Saint-Domingue. Sonthonax had worked hard to restore housing, arrange for provisions, and bring a level of French culture to the beleaguered colony. Sonthonax's recall was also a financial blow to Barney because he had always honored Barney's claims against the French government. Barney was further distressed by a message that awaited him from the minister of marine. It was an official order to seize all American vessels bound for or from British ports, an order Barney knew he could not obey.

A third piece of misfortune descended when Commodore Barney was stricken with a tropical illness that almost took his life. In the end, this proved to be a blessing because Barney's two frigates had to return to France without him, and he thus avoided a test of his divided loyalty. During his recuperation he wrote a detailed account of all his personal expenditures on behalf of the republic for the new commissioner. There is no record of a response from Paris. The new government of Saint-Domingue had enough trouble providing for the island's current needs without being concerned with paying for food already consumed.

In his first message to Congress, on 16 May 1798, newly inaugurated President John Adams reaffirmed the wisdom of Washington's earlier statement about the intolerable situation that had developed in Franco-American relationships. He quoted from a report commissioned by President Washington stating that between three and four hundred American vessels had been captured by French cruisers. During that session of Congress, the order came to fit out and employ the new frigates being built—the *United States*, the *Constitution*, and the *Constellation*—and also to complete three other frigates then in the early stages of construction in various shipyards.[11]

The Jay Treaty had largely ended the problems between Britain and America, but the agreement had clearly alienated France. Relations had become so strained between the two republics that America could no longer even trade with the West Indies in safety. On 28 May 1798 the

U.S. government authorized the capture of French vessels in retaliation for France's seizure of American ships. On 7 July 1798 the treaties between the United States and France were declared null and void because French cruisers continued to harass the maritime commerce of the United States.

On 9 April 1798, prior to the beginning of the Quasi-War, the secretary of war submitted a formal plan to the House of Representatives for the protection of commerce. In what became known as the XYZ affair, President Adams sent three ministers to France to negotiate a treaty to protect American shipping interests. Three French intermediaries, later diplomatically referred to as X, Y, and Z, approached the American ministers. The French diplomats suggested that the Americans pay a bribe of $250,000 to Charles-Maurice de Talleyrand-Périgord, the French foreign minister, and that Congress offer a loan of ten million dollars to the French government before negotiations began. When this matter was made public in the United States there was a great national outcry. American citizens, until now split over the Jay Treaty and relations with Britain, quickly focused their enmity on France. The XYZ affair tipped the balance, and Congress issued a decree of belligerence against France, the rough equivalent of an informal declaration of war in 1798. The result was a political rupture between America and its oldest European ally.

On 9 April 1798, at about the same time that the XYZ affair became common knowledge, the secretary of war, who also headed the infant navy, submitted a formal plan to the House of Representatives for the protection of commerce. Among the plan's recommendations was the creation of an independent Department of the Navy. Congress enacted legislation on 30 April 1798 based on those recommendations, and Benjamin Stoddert took office as the first secretary of the navy. Six post captains, full captains just below flag rank, were appointed contemporaneously, and the new navy was formally organized.

On 15 May 1799 John Adams offered Capt. Silas Talbot the command of the frigate *Constitution*. He assumed formal command on 5 June 1799 and two months later sailed southward to protect American interests in the West Indies, particularly in Saint-Domingue on the island of Hispaniola. Fortunately, Barney had returned to France by this time, and a historic naval clash between Joshua Barney and Silas Talbot was averted. The two men worked for opposing governments among the same West

Indian islands but never came into direct contact because their times in the islands did not overlap.

In the summer of 1798, when Barney had recovered enough to take command of a frigate, he set sail for France to present his case for remuneration in person. In yet another piece of misfortune, he found the British blockading Le Cap Français and was forced to return to port. But he did not sit quietly on Saint-Domingue. Because it was early summer and the weather and seas in the Caribbean were favorable, Barney decided to charter a small pilot boat of fifty tons, load it with a cargo of coffee, and sail to France. A ship from the British blockade gave brief chase but, assuming that such a small vessel would have nobody of importance onboard, did not continue the pursuit. Again Barney had outsmarted the British.

The commodore and his small vessel were almost swamped in heavy seas and ran very low on food and water. At one point a British ship of the line, a frigate, and a cutter gave chase, firing ineffectively over the great expanse of ocean. Barney escaped once again, but by now the ship's food and water were in extremely short supply. When another ship appeared on the horizon, Barney, in desperation, decided to intercept it. The ship turned out to be a Portuguese merchantman hauling salt, and the captain generously gave Barney enough provisions to reach Portugal. Eventually, after an arduous forty-three-day trip, the tiny ship reached safe harbor in Bordeaux. Barney, always seeking a business opportunity, sold his cargo of coffee for a 400 percent profit. It was the last voyage Barney would make under the French flag.

In Bordeaux, Barney purchased an elegant carriage for his trip to Paris and his use in the capital city. Once there, he met frustration attempting to obtain the monies that were owed to him for his prizes and his service. Bribery and corruption were common. Barney might have had a settlement for a substantial kickback, but his pride would not permit him to allow prize agents (deskbound clerks) to gain from the danger he had endured.

Meanwhile, back in Baltimore, Anne Barney endured trials of her own. On 16 January 1798 the *Baltimore American* reported that "Mrs. Commodore Barney's home, Nr. 11 Charles Street, was robbed at night of a travel toilet, containing two large round miniature pictures with glass backs encircled in gold, one small oval miniature set in gold, one gold and garnet rosary, a number of rings and bracelets and sundry papers; also a yellow satin bonnet with crape trim." This report contains the only historical reference to the religion of the Barney family. The notation about the theft of the rosary is evidence that the Barneys were Roman Catholic. Ever since its inception as a colony governed by Lord Baltimore, Maryland had had a large Catholic population. Perhaps Barney's religion, the same as the majority of the French people, contributed to making him a Francophile.

The Quasi-War with France, largely fought between ships at sea, had inflamed American opinion against the French. The undeclared conflict, which lasted from the summer of 1798 to the fall of 1800, ended in the last days of the Adams presidency; it was of little lasting significance and of short duration. The population of the United States had risen to about five million just before the turn of the century, and U.S. shipping had passed eight hundred thousand tons. This meant that the young nation's resources were about twice what they had been at the beginning of the American Revolution. With the federal government on a firmer financial footing, Congress felt able to provide for a navy to defend American shipping. By the end of the Quasi-War it had authorized the construction of thirty cruisers, twelve of which were to be swift frigates of from thirty-two to forty-four guns. The U.S. Navy did not realize this size for many years. When Napoléon Bonaparte became the new first consul of France, John Adams saw an opportunity to obtain a peace treaty and sent William Vans Murray to Paris. The resulting Convention of 1800 brought peace between the United States and France. Only weeks later, Thomas Jefferson, a Republican, was elected president. Jefferson did not believe a large navy was needed any longer. Rather than complete work on the fleet authorized by the Federalists, he reduced the number of ships in commission.

The conclusion of the Quasi-War did not end anti-French feeling in the United States. To many Americans Barney appeared to be serving the enemy; the general public had no way of knowing that Barney had refused orders to attack American ships. On 2 September 1798 a gentleman from New York wrote a letter in which he described his capture and internment by the French privateer *Flower of the Sea.* The vessel was recaptured by the British ship *Aquilon,* and the passenger released. In his letter the man mentioned that "in passing Cape Français, I saw Barney's squadron, afraid to come out, there being three English 74's and several other ships off there."[12]

The blockade of Barney's fleet appeared to be to America's benefit because rumors had reached the United States that Paris had ordered

Barney to attack ports of the southern states. Secretary of the Navy Benjamin Stoddert's information in this matter was outdated, but he wrote Capt. Thomas Truxtun that "a frigate . . . I understand, was launched about the Time of the Western Insurrection first broke out, and in Honor to those Scoundrels, it is said she is called *La' Insurgente,* and afterward put under the Command of Commodore Barney. If this be the case, she should be the first taken."[13] When the *Constellation* captured Barney's former ship *L'Insurgente,* a Federalist newspaper wrote that "it is to be regretted that the renegade Barney who behaved so insolently in Chesapeake Bay in '97 was not in command."[14] His American political enemies had again tainted Barney's public image.

Napoléon returned from his campaign in Egypt in late August 1799, and shortly thereafter Barney asked the emperor to personally intervene in the matter of his compensation. He received no satisfactory answer, but evidently he had become a favorite of Empress Josephine because the capitaine de vaisseau du premier was invited to her soirées. Barney seems to have had a way with women, particularly those in high places. His best-known portrait, painted circa 1784–85 by Charles Wilson Peale, depicts a man with deep-set eyes, thick brows, and a pleasant appearance. Barney was also invited to the many French military parades, which he attended in the uniform of *chef de division,* or general officer. Despite the many honors he received, Barney soon tired of French society. He offered to resign his commission but instead received additional titles. He was now a *ci-devant* French citizen and chef de division des Armées Navales. These honors fed Barney's ego while costing the French government nothing. Both the commodore and the Marquis de Lafayette apparently felt that political disaster was about to befall France under the Jacobin tyranny. According to their correspondence, Barney offered to take Lafayette and his family to America, but nothing came of his plan.

Barney reluctantly stayed on in Paris, but after almost two years he resigned a second time. The French minister of marine wrote him a complimentary letter and assigned him a pension of fifteen hundred pounds per annum during his life. Barney always seemed to be in pursuit of what he considered his financial rewards. Uncharacteristically, in this instance he thanked the minister for his kind letter but declined the money. He left his business interests in the hands of a friend and booked passage to the United States on 1 July 1802, a civilian once more.

~*8*~

REBIRTH OF A PATRIOT

arney's return voyage to the United States should have been a pleasant one. He was returning to the family and country he loved, and his thoughts must have preceded him with eager enthusiasm. The commodore elected to take passage onboard an ancient French vessel, the *Neptune,* which left for Norfolk, Virginia, in July 1802. At first the venerable ship sailed reasonably well in a moderate sea, but before long the winds of the Atlantic blew and the waves rose. With a great cracking sound the *Neptune* started to come open at the seams. The captain wisely steered toward the nearest port, the island of Fayal. There was no sophisticated ship repair facility on that remote speck of land, so the crew made what repairs they could, and the *Neptune* headed back out to sea. The repairs were insufficient; waves of even moderate heights caused serious leaks, and it became evident that the ancient *Neptune* might not survive the transatlantic journey. The only prospect the captain saw for completing the voyage was to head toward the southern trade winds and lighter seas. This would add to the length of the trip, but it would increase the odds that the passengers and crew would see land again. The captain appeared indecisive, unsure of his navigation, and reluctant to take Barney's advice—which, one can be sure, was generously offered.

During the last week of September the ship finally entered the Gulf Stream off the Carolina coast just south of Cape Hatteras. There the wind picked up and the waves increased in frequency and loftiness, and seawater began to rise in the bilge. The crew bent their backs at the pumps, but the battle against the sea was being lost. In an attempt to lighten the load, the captain ordered much of the cargo and personal belongings of the passengers and crew thrown overboard. This helped keep the *Neptune* afloat, but it was now very low in the water and difficult to steer, particularly with the strong offshore breeze and current. Soon it became impossible for the ship to make headway. The captain, crew, and passengers could see the surf breaking on shoals, a foaming arm beckoning the *Neptune* to its grave. All hands, including the able-bodied passengers, pumped furiously for almost two days trying to save the ship. But by the morning of 29 September 1802 the water had reached the level of the lower deck. There seemed little hope of survival when a small schooner suddenly appeared out of the gloom, apparently on a course that would take it within hailing distance of the *Neptune*. As the schooner bore down, the French captain shouted through his speaking trumpet that the *Neptune* was sinking and he was about to order "abandon ship." The schooner, which was also foundering, was in a poor position to take more people onboard; nor was it clear that the transfer could be made. The sea raged, the visibility worsened, and it seemed impossible that a small boat could make passage between the two vessels. Barney, with the aid of two sailors, launched one of the *Neptune*'s boats into the tempest. The men scrambled into the pitching craft and pulled toward the schooner. The anxious schooner's crew dragged them aboard as huge waves struck the vessel abeam. One of the waves threw Barney against a weather chain plate, causing bruises and lacerations. Ignoring his wounds, he advised the captain of the schooner of a method of reaching the sinking ship. The *Neptune*'s longboat was hoisted over the side and a frantic transfer of humanity began. After a harrowing few hours, all the passengers and crew were saved. The *Neptune* was swallowed by a wave and disappeared entirely except for the top of its foremast, which stood as a grave marker.

The captain of the American schooner was not above turning the misfortunes of others into personal profit. He charged the rescued assemblage five hundred dollars to put them ashore at their destination, only a few days' sail away. The schooner did not have accommodations for the additional twenty-eight people, so most had to find what shelter they could on deck. There were no medicines onboard and Barney suffered greatly from his wounds. When the schooner finally made port on 2 October, he was taken to a doctor, then hospitalized for a number of days. It took several more weeks for him to recover fully after he returned home to Baltimore.

Shortly after his return Joshua Barney inadvertently became a central figure in a strange love story. Napoléon had three brothers and three sisters, all of whom became gatecrashers in the world of European royalty. The youngest of his brothers, Jérôme (Girolamo) Bonaparte, was known as "Fifi" in the French court because of his love of the good life, women, and wastrel ways. Although the boy was only nineteen years old and had little knowledge of ships, Napoléon commissioned Jérôme a capitaine de vaisseau in 1802 and sent him to sea. After a cruise to the relatively safe West Indies, Jérôme was ordered back to France. Instead he opted to visit the United States, first stopping at Norfolk on 20 July 1802 and later at Washington, where he was received by President Jefferson and the French consul general. The consul lent the young Bonaparte and his retinue—a general, a lieutenant, a secretary, and other attendants—some money and suggested that they stop in Baltimore. The only man Jérôme knew in that city was Commodore Barney, and so the Barneys played host to Capitaine Bonaparte. The assemblage remained in Baltimore for several weeks being entertained by the social elite. Among that group was the prominent local shipbuilder William Patterson, who had made a personal fortune importing guns and munitions during the War for Independence. At the time, Patterson, a businessman and property owner, was considered the second-wealthiest man in America (behind Charles Carroll of Carrollton, Maryland). Through his wife he was the brother-in-law of the influential Senator Samuel Smith. The Patterson family had a nineteen-year-old daughter, Betsy, who was described as stunningly beautiful with a svelte figure, creamy complexion, and wonderfully expressive brown eyes. Gilbert Stuart captured her radiant beauty in one of his portraits, which resides today in the National Portrait Gallery. Her high spirits and liveliness earned her the title "the Belle of Baltimore" among her friends. It was inevitable that the two young people should meet. Betsy spoke some French, but Jérôme spoke no English.

Betsy Patterson was young, but she was also very bright and well aware of the world outside Maryland. She wanted to leave what she perceived to be the stifling Baltimore society and later said that she would have married the devil himself to break out. Jérôme fell madly in love with her. Betsy apparently was aware of her suitor's shallowness but saw him as both the key to her escape and, as the brother of the most powerful man in Europe, an investment in the future. The French consul general warned the couple that according to French law, the young Bonaparte, being underage, could not marry without this elder brother's permission.

In an attempt to take his mind off Betsy, the amorous young Bonaparte purchased a handsome carriage and team for nine hundred dollars and asked Barney to accompany him to Philadelphia. Barney had many connections in the former capital city, and Jérôme Bonaparte became the center of adulation and attention there. Fearing the temptations of the city, Barney took his companion to the Pennsylvania resort communities of York, Lancaster, and the Springs, finally ending at Havre de Grace, Maryland, on the Susquehanna River. Jérôme enjoyed his travels, but before long his funds began to dwindle. He ordered the French consul to advance him approximately eleven thousand dollars for his expenses—a goodly sum, particularly from a consul of relatively humble means representing a country that was engaged in a costly war and had other financial difficulties as well. With the money in hand, Jérôme went on to New York to further forget his sorrow.

When he returned to Baltimore, Jérôme saw Betsy Patterson once again at Govane's racecourse. The flame of passion was rekindled, and he asked Barney to aid him in obtaining her hand. Barney was reluctant to help him and told Jérôme that the marriage would be ill advised. Bonaparte needed the approval of Napoléon, and it was not likely that the emperor would allow his brother to marry an untitled American Protestant. Barney also cautioned the Patterson family, including Betsy, that the union was unwise. Ignoring his brother, his personal future prospects, and everything but the fascinating young woman before him, Jérôme proposed and pressed the marriage. William Patterson was a careful and astute father. The marriage contract of his daughter contained a clause stating that if the marriage were annulled, no matter by whom, Betsy would have the right to a third of her future husband's fortune. Unfortunately, this contract would not have the force of law in the newly emerging French Empire.

Joshua Barney's efforts to emphasize the problems associated with the union likely postponed the marriage, but on Christmas Eve 1803, Jérôme and Betsy were married in a ceremony at the Patterson mansion with the Catholic archbishop of Maryland, John Carroll, officiating. All of Baltimore society attended. As further evidence of his Catholic religion, Joshua Barney signed the registration book as a witness. Unintentionally, Commodore Barney may have angered the Bonaparte family with these acts of courtesy.

When the news of the wedding reached France, Napoléon was enraged. The emperor ordered the chargé d'affaires in Washington to cease loaning Jérôme money and demanded his brother's immediate return to France. He also denied passage to "Miss Patterson" on a French ship, thus assuring that she could not accompany her husband. If she attempted to land in territory controlled by France, which at that time included much of Europe, she was to be deported. During this time Napoléon appointed himself emperor but left Jérôme's name off the list of new princes. On 11 March 1805, Napoléon had Jérôme's marriage to Betsy Patterson annulled, and on 9 April a despondent Jérôme Bonaparte finally returned to his homeland. Meanwhile, the pregnant Betsy went to England to give birth to their child, who entered the world on 7 July 1805. She called the baby Jerome Napoleon Bonaparte. Her estranged husband initially corresponded with her, professing his love, but he was never allowed to see their child. The state of Maryland granted Betsy Patterson Bonaparte a divorce in 1815. She subsequently added the name Patterson to her son's name for social and legal reasons. Emperor Napoléon paid Betsy a pension of sixty thousand francs a year. Jérôme Bonaparte was given a command in the French army. He distinguished himself by capturing several Prussian fortresses in the campaign of 1806–7; married Princess Catherine, daughter of the king of Württemberg; and became the king of Westphalia.

The American Jerome Bonaparte was not allowed a claim to the Bonaparte family fortune, but his mother, Betsy, did continue to receive financial assistance from Napoléon. The Bonaparte-Patterson union ultimately contributed to American history. Jerome Bonaparte Patterson's grandson, Charles Joseph Bonaparte Patterson, served as secretary of the navy in the administration of Theodore Roosevelt, and later as Roosevelt's "trust-busting" attorney general. The last American Bonaparte, Jerome Napoleon Charles Bonaparte Patterson, died in 1945 after

a freak accident that occurred while walking his dog in Central Park in
New York City.

The first decade of the new century marked a transition in the life of
Joshua Barney. For the first time in a quarter of a century he spent little
time at sea. Instead he concentrated on business, suffering some failures
because of his naiveté but generally prospering enough to provide a comfortable living for his family. On 18 August and 22 September 1804 James
Madison wrote to Thomas Jefferson concerning Barney's claim for compensation for the captured *Sampson*.[1] The claim was first rejected on a
convoluted interpretation of the Jay Treaty, but then the joint commission, reinterpreting the treaty in an unexpected reversal, gave a settlement of forty-five thousand dollars to the partnership of Barney and
Hollins for the seizure of the *Sampson* and brought the painful decade-
old incident to closure.

Barney's relative financial success and stellar military record brought
him back to prominence in Baltimore society once people learned the
truth about his service in France. In the fall of 1806 Joshua Barney was
persuaded by friends to run for Congress. The decision proved to be a
poor one because all the old false stories about Barney's perfidy during
the Quasi-War resurfaced during the campaign. Barney's opponent,
William M'Creery, described him as a Frenchman, deserter, and pirate.
Barney did find a number of ardent supporters, particularly in his home-
town, but not enough for him to win the election. The congressional district included both the city and the county of the same name. There
were four candidates, two of whom would be elected. Barney carried the
city of Baltimore, but two other candidates won the rural county by such
a margin that they were elected. The rural county was more conservative
and more Federalist than the city. Barney protested the election on the
grounds that he had won the vast majority of the votes from the city
while the candidate who finished in second place had won only in the
county. The House of Representatives rejected his contention that the
city and county should be tallied separately and ruled that the election
was based on the combined vote total regardless of the origin of the
votes. Thus a disillusioned Barney, who finished third in the overall bal-
lot, accepted his first electoral defeat.[2]

Though disappointed in politics, Joshua Barney appears to have had a
happy marriage. Substantial evidence exists that women found him

attractive, and although he exploited this attraction when it was to his advantage, no sexual scandal was ever attached to his name. His many political enemies would almost certainly have capitalized on even a hint of gossip, although possibly the mores of the time precluded its public use. Little is known about the details of his relationship with his wife, but they had five children: William, Louis, John, Caroline, and Henry. Anne Bedford Barney, a charming woman four years older than Joshua, developed arthritis and became worn and old before her time. Her premature aging may have been at least partly the result of repeated childbirth, and certainly bearing and raising five children virtually alone must have been difficult for her. Barney's occupations kept him at sea much of the time. Having a large family was a form of life insurance and old age security for a couple at that time—or for a woman whose husband's vocation could suddenly leave her a widow. One day while Anne was trying to rise from bed she fell and fractured a hip. This traumatic injury was slow to heal and shortened her life. Anne Barney died on 25 July 1808. On 24 April 1809, after only nine months of mourning, Captain Barney, perhaps in need of a mate to rear his five children, remarried. His second wife was Harriet Coale of Anne Arundel County, Maryland. Harriet's previous marriage to Charles Tunis had been annulled, a rarity in the conservative Roman Catholic society of the day.[3] Together, Harriet and Joshua would add three more children to the Barney family: Adelee, Elizabeth, and Joshua Jr.

On 22 June 1807, two years before Barney's second marriage took place, the U.S. frigate *Chesapeake* under Capt. Samuel Barron put to sea from Hampton Roads. The ship had been out of service since sailing against the Barbary corsairs and had just been refitted out of "ordinary" (mothballs). The fifty-gun HMS *Leopard* followed the *Chesapeake* out to sea and ordered it to "heave to" and allow a search for deserters from the British navy. When a boarding party led by Lt. John Mead asked Barron to muster his crew for inspection, the American refused. After Mead returned to his ship, the *Leopard* fired several warning shots across the *Chesapeake*'s bow. When Barron did not respond to the warning shots the *Leopard* fired four broadsides at point-blank range. The unexpected barrage staggered the American frigate. The *Chesapeake* was not prepared for the assault; stores still littered the deck from the recent refitting. When the smoke cleared, three Americans lay dead and another eighteen had been wounded, including Captain Barron. To avoid further carnage the *Chesapeake* struck its colors. The British boarded the American vessel and took off four alleged deserters, three of whom were naturalized American citizens who had at one time served in the British navy. The fourth had always been an American citizen. Afterward, the badly damaged *Chesapeake* returned home. This incident led to tremendous anti-British feelings in the United States. Barney was so incensed that he wrote to President Jefferson, "beg[ing] leave to make to you the tender of my personal services. I shall be happy to be employed by you, in any manner which may be thought conducive to the good of my country and the support of the administration."[4] If war had been declared at that moment, the entire country would likely have been united against Britain. Jefferson and the Congress felt that the nation was at a military disadvantage, however, and instead of ordering military action imposed an embargo on American shipping, hoping that economic coercion would force Britain to come to terms with the United States and begin respecting American maritime rights. The policy was a failure, and Britain and France continued to impose indignities on American vessels for another five years.

Barney's frustration mounted during this time. Convinced that his voice should be heard in Washington, he ran for Congress once again in 1810, this time against one man, the incumbent, Alexander McKim. Barney ran as an independent. The law had now changed so that one seat was to be from the city of Baltimore and one was to be from the county. The problem was that the votes were combined at the polls. Only the place of residence of the candidate determined the seat to which he would be elected. Barney was a firebrand, pleading for stronger measures to protect neutral America's rights and honor. One of his speeches printed in the *Baltimore Whig* gives the flavor of his homey style: "We are kickt by England, we are kickt by France, and by Lord Harry we are Kickt by that black fellow Christophe in the West Indies! . . . We have a population of 7 millions; we could receive and repel the greatest force of any nation on earth at the point of a bayonet or cannon's mouth. Yet our Congress, knowing the facts, has sat shivering or sleeping in the capitol at edicts and orders issued 3,000 miles off!"[5]

Of Congressman McKim, who had spoken before him, Barney said: "If gentlemen are once elected and imagine that they ought not to be opposed, they will fancy by and by that their seats in Congress belong to them. I don't know but they might go so far as to bequeath them to their oldest son in their will. . . . This puts me in mind of the sow that was dragged to the swill tub; they had to pull off her ears to fetch her there, and pull off her tail to take her away."[6]

Though Joshua Barney spoke with greater humor and effect, Alexander McKim had the edge in knowledge and eloquence. When the polls closed, McKim had been reelected. Barney had received a small majority of the city vote but lost badly in the county for a second time. He thought there was evidence of some irregularity in the voting procedure but did not to press the issue. This second loss appears to have ended Barney's aspirations for elected office.

In one more attempt to gain a public service appointment, Barney wrote to his acquaintance James Monroe, who had just become the secretary of state under President James Madison. Barney's long letter recalled his loyal service to the United States and the general officer rank he had achieved while serving under the French tricolor. He told Monroe: "Fortune [has] not smiled on me for some years. I have brought up a large family honorably and wish to see them do well." Barney concluded the letter with a request for "something . . . congenial to my Abilities such as Intendant at the Navy Yard or actual service in the Navy."[7] There is no evidence that Monroe ever responded to the letter.

By 1810 France had a policy of apprehending all neutral ships that stopped at British ports, and Britain had a policy of seizing all neutral ships that did not stop over at British ports before going on to the Continent. In the preceding year, about 900 American ships had been stopped by the British and approximately 550 had been seized by the French. The maritime situation was intolerable. Joshua Barney had definite ideas about who was the biggest offender, but somewhat cynically, he was also convinced that the United States could not defeat or make an effective stand against the Royal Navy. Perhaps in part because of his rejection by the Baltimore voters, Barney sold his house in the city and, in the spring of 1812, moved his family to Elkridge in Anne Arundel County, the former home county of his second wife. His oldest child, William, was now married and living in the area.

In Washington, Henry Clay of Kentucky, Speaker of the House of Representatives, led the "War Hawks," a vocal group of southern and western congressmen who believed that honor required the United States to declare war on Great Britain. On 18 June 1812 Congress followed their lead and, over the objections of the largely Federalist north-eastern congressmen, passed a formal declaration of war.

The declaration was far from popular among the Federalists. On 20 June 1812 the *Federal Republican* of Baltimore published an article saying that the United States was unprepared for war and appeared to be rushing toward its own destruction. By declaring war on Britain at this time, the newspaper argued, the United States was siding with Napoléon, whom many Americans disliked as much as, if not more than, King George IV, who had recently assumed power in Britain. Public opinion was so inflamed by the article that on 22 June a mob destroyed the newspaper office while, it was said, the mayor and local law enforcement officers looked the other way. There is no evidence that Barney took part in this event, but his sympathies were clearly on the side of military intervention.

With regular commerce at a virtual standstill, many shipowners in Baltimore turned to privateering after war was declared. Privateering had developed into a major enterprise in Baltimore, but British block-aders kept the privateers from bringing their prizes into port, which in turn discouraged seamen from seeking positions on the American vessels. Baltimore's merchants and shipowners needed an inducement to offer to potential crewmen. Financial incentives were an option, but they decreased the return on the shipowner's investment. Countering this was the strong emotional and patriotic argument that the destruction of British commerce served public as well as private interests. Baltimore business agent Christopher Deshon noted that "private profit and public service were not necessarily contradictory or mutually exclusive motives. Every British vessel taken was a loss to the enemy and a service to the national interest of the United States. . . . If profit-making were but one aspect of the entrepreneur's need for achievement, then his actions serving both private and public interests contributed to the attainment of that goal."[8]

Joshua Barney was very much a businessman, but he was a patriot above all else. Relishing the excitement and challenge of naval combat, he wasted no time getting involved in privateering. Although many of the Baltimore privateers during the War of 1812 were driven by desire for profit, Barney seized the opportunity to punish the British one more time. He felt there was little chance of obtaining a federal commission because he had turned down service in the navy some years before, the only former naval officer to do so. Therefore, he accepted command of a private armed vessel, the 206-ton, ninety-eight-foot schooner *Rossie,* originally built as a merchantman in 1807 by the noted naval architect Thomas Kemp. A consortium of eleven Baltimore merchants raised the funds to outfit the ship as a privateer. The rakishly built vessel carried one hundred men, eleven 12-pound carriage guns, and one long 9-pounder. To his pleasure, the president and Congress gave Barney their indirect blessing. On 12 July 1812, only twenty-three days after war was declared, a letter of marque, commission number 1, was issued to Barney and the *Rossie.*[9] On this same date, Deshon, the agent for the owners, met Barney at the Baltimore harbor pier where the *Rossie* was tied up and admonished him to avoid travel to European waters because of the difficulty of getting the prizes home. Beyond that admonition, he wisely allowed Barney to choose his own cruising ground.[10]

A day before the *Rossie* was to sail, a deputy sheriff came onboard and detained Barney on "suspicion of debt." It seemed that the captain owed approximately one thousand dollars and it was "necessary for him to do away with" the debt before he would be allowed to leave Baltimore. Barney gave himself up to the police officer "according to the law," but was released on his own recognizance so that he might raise the money. Barney sauntered up South Street to the mercantile house of a friend, Isaac McKim. Surprised at Barney's visit, McKim said that he assumed Barney would be halfway to the Capes by now. Somewhat embarrassed, Barney explained that he had been "nabbed" and must appear in court the next day. McKim dismissed the thousand dollars as a trifle and loaned him the money. Barney redeemed his parole, paid his debt, and returned to his ship a free man.[11]

Captain Barney ordered the crew to make the schooner ready for departure. The *Rossie*'s lines were taken onboard and the privateer moved into the channel and caught the outgoing tide. The surging flood in the bay carried the schooner toward an anchorage off Fort McHenry for the night. The following extracts from the log of the first cruise of the *Rossie* under the command of Joshua Barney give the flavor of both the voyage and the commander:

Sunday [July] 12th: . . . Appointed Mr. Christopher Deshon Agent for Prizes, at 2 P.M. got under way, at 7 P.M. anchored below North Point, near Man of War Shoals, saw coming down the River, the Privateers *Nonsuch, Comet, High-flyer,* & *Eagle* who anchored to the N. West of us.

Monday 13th: At 5 a.m. got underway, the above Privateers & several other sail in company, . . .

Tuesday 14th, July: [A]t Day light abreast of Point Look out, the *Nonsuch* near us, & the *High flyer* about six miles ahead. . . . Ran four of our Guns forward, where we immediately left the *Nonsuch* & in three hours was 1½ miles to windward of her at 7 P.M. weathered the *High flyer* at 10 P.M. anchored under New Point Comfort.

Wednesday 15th: [A]t 5 A.M. got under way. . . . considerable distance ahead of the *Nonsuch,* no other Privateer in sight—at 9 abreast of Cape Henry. . . .

Wednesday 22d: At 2 P.M. came up with the chase a Brig from Martinique bound for Newbury Port the *Nymph Capt Patch* being loaded with *molasses.* finding the *Governers Pass* from Martinique, loaded with *produce* from the Island, I made a Seizure, under the *Non Importation* Law, mann'd her and sent her for a port in the U.S. gave chase to a Brig & a Ship. at 5 came up with the Brig (American) from (St Ubes) for New London continued in chase of the Ship. . . . [D]ischarged them, the Ship called the *Reserve* belongs to Mr King of Bath. . . .

Thursday July 23rd 1812: . . . [A]t 9 perceived [a ship] was in chase of us. . . . [A]t 10 tacked to N.E. and discovered her to be a Frigate of the first rate, on passing to the windward of her, she began firing at us. without shewing any colours, she tack'd. as she tack'd we tack'd also on the contrary way, She then hoisted the *American Colours* & continued to fire at us . . . she continued her Fire untill she had fired 25 Guns I then made several private signals. . . .

Friday 24th: The Frigate continued in chase, but dropping to Leeward. at 3 P.M. the Frigate fired a Gun to Leeward & gave over chase, having carried away her flying Gibb Boom, we then tacked to the Easwd. . . .

Thursday 30th: . . . [G]ot Bottom on the Grand Bank in 47 Fathom water, at 5 a.m. discovered a Sail to the S.E. gave chase. . . . She was a Frigate we made private signal & fired 2 Guns, she hoisted a signal, fired a Gun to the Leeward & Shew American Colours. We bore down to the windward of her. She did not answer the signal. . . .

Friday July 31st: . . . [A]t 5 spoke her, an English Ship from Belfast to St Andrews. in *Ballast* sent on board her & took possession, found her of little value, took Sundry articles for use of the Schooner & set her on fire, at 7 saw a sail to the Eastwd after firing the ship. . . . [A]t 6 perceived she had painted sides & a *Tier* of *Ports* (20) got everything ready for action & stood down on her quarters. at 7 came alongside, she hoisted English colours, we hoisted American flag & ordered her to strike her colours which she instantly did. was Greenock to St Andrews in Ballast, being a fine ship, I mann'd her, sending on board Mr. Jas Stubbs & 6 hands leaving 4 hands of the ship on board, & sent 1 hand from the Ship I had burnt, & ordered her into the first Port in the United States. she is called the *Kitty* of 305 Tons, Daniel Thompson Master[.] The Ship burnt was called the *Princess Royal* 189 Ton Saml Heath Master at 9 left Prize & stood to the N.N.E. No Observation.

Saturday 1st August 1812: . . . [A]t meridian came up with the Chase, a brig out of St Johns Newfoundland loaded with Cod Fish 18,000, having a number of Prisoners was anxious to get rid of them, sent the two Mates of the Ship *Kitty* & *Princess Royal,* on board with 6 of their hands with orders to follow us & to send the Capt of the Brig on board, which they did. we then gave chase to the two others found her to be the Brig *Brothers* of St Johns Richd Penny Master & 9 men, cargo as above Latt Obv 45.20 Nth. . . .

Sunday 2d Augt: A fine breeze from the Southward, at 3 P.M. came up with the Chase another brig with Cod Fish. put on board her the Capt of the Prize Ship *Princess Royal* & 4 of his men, with orders to follow us & to send the Capt on board, which was done. she is the Brig *Fame* of Exeter England, Wm Standard Master, with 18,000 Cod fish—

Monday Aug 3d 1812: [A]t 2 p.m. came up with a Schooner, sent the boat on board & ran down to the Leeward to a Brig, our Boat took possession of the Schr and brought her down to us. she was a Fisherman with Fish called the *Race Horse,* Capt. John Mudge, 8,000 fish. the Brig was the *Henry,* Capt. Wm. Halling, both from St Johns. we took out the Crews & scuttled them & gave chase to the other which were to the E.N.E. . . . At 7 P.M. sent out our boat on board another Schooner & took possession of her, loaded with fish called the *Brothers,* Capt *John Mathison,* having then *Forty* Prisoners on board. I ordered the Schr Hallifax to be burnt & put all the Prisoners on board the *Brothers,* taking a Receipt & sent them to St. Johns to be exchanged for americans; during the last two days we have taken, burnt & destroy'd *nine sail,* and 156 *Prisoners.*[12]

The *Rossie's* cruise continued in much the same way for the remainder of August. Toward the end of the month Barney sailed for southern

New England. On the morning of 30 August, according to his log, he entered the harbor of Newport, Rhode Island, with a prize ship in his company: "At 10 came to anchor at New Port, & fired a *Salute* of 11 Guns—we have been *Forty Five days Effective* on this part of our Cruize, there remains *Forty Four days* to complete the Cruize, according to the articles. . . . Joshua Barney." A legend that has grown up about Barney's salute claims that one live cannonball was accidentally fired in the volley, wounding a woman onshore.[13] There is no mention of this in the *Newport Mercury* edition for 5 September 1812. Some local people also claim that Barney Street in the old port city was named for this incident, but Barney is also the name of one of the oldest Quaker families of Newport. Since there is no mention of the incident in Barney's log entry for that day, or in the local newspaper, the story seems to be no more than a compelling myth. In all, Barney and his crew had taken eighteen vessels with hardly a defensive shot being fired.

Barney spent a certain amount of time dealing with administrative details as well. On 2 September he made a formal accusation against John Nerbon of the *Rossie* for "cowardice and flying from his Quarters in time of action," and had him remanded for court-martial.[14] This action was permissible under article 15 of the U.S. law governing offences committed onboard private armed vessels. On another occasion Barney ordered the court-martial of John Marr, a gunner on the *Rossie,* for disobeying orders.[15] Finally, Barney sent a letter to Oliver Hazard Perry from Newport on 2 September 1812 saying, "I have sent on board your Vessel, a man by the name of Thomas Holden, he was taken by the private armed schooner *Rossie,* under my command, when Chief Mate of the British Ship *Jeanie* which ship engaged me. I find by his papers that he is a Citizen of the U.S. and that he has been employed onboard of one of the public vessels, having taken him In Arms against his Country, I have thought proper to deliver him over to the Authority of the County, & in consequence have sent him on board your Vessel and with him, the papers found in his possession proving his Citizenship, to be dealt with according to the Law."[16] These anecdotes are further evidence that in battle or in matters of patriotism, Barney was both a consistent disciplinarian and profoundly anti-British.

After a minor refitting and some changes to his crew, Barney departed for Caribbean waters. On the evening of 16 September 1812 the *Rossie* began its famous encounter with the British schooner *Princess Amelia.*

The schooner *Rossie,* the hunter, mounted each swell and raced down its backside as nightfall approached. A full moon rose, sending enough light to allow Captain Barney to make out a blur of white to windward. The image resolved into topsails, courses, and a hull studded with a row of gun ports. The *Rossie*'s sailing qualities were extraordinary because it was able to sail without losing much of its course toward the lee; as sailors say, the ship was almost innocent of leeway. The packet, by contrast, was much slower and less maneuverable. Sensing the disparity between his ship's capabilities and those of the ship approaching him, the British captain ordered defensive boarding nets set in place and prepared the crew for action. The *Rossie,* sailing on the weather gauge, changed from a vague darkened ship to a miniature man-of-war with gun ports opened, hammocks in netting, and guns run out. Every man was at his appointed station, ready for battle. The British captain signaled the small schooner to identify itself. Barney first ordered a Spanish flag aloft, a standard *ruse de guerre.* Then, maneuvering closer to a position of tactical advantage, he quickly displayed the American colors and sent aloft a signal ordering the other ship to surrender. Thus began the memorable hour-long battle by moonlight between the American schooner *Rossie* and the British packet *Princess Amelia.*

Barney's log describes the ensuing engagement:

When at 7 P.M. being very close I bore up across his stern, when I ordered him to strike to the flag of the United States, at the same time hauling down the Spanish flag & hoisting the American ensign at the Poop. We commenced a severe fire from cannon & small arms & run under his lee quarter. Our fire was returned with spirit for some time (we had fine moon light); in about ½ an hour I found the fire had ceased; I hailed him to know if he had struck his colours; was answered they had not, we again began our fire. I could see that every discharge cut him to pieces; we were always either on his quarter bow or abreast of him at a distance of 20 Yds. At about 5 minutes before 8 they hailed me to let me know that they had struck their colours.

We hoisted our boats, & sent on board; the small boat retd. with the mate who was wounded. he informed [me] the ship was his Majesty's Packet the *Princess Amelia* of 8 nine pounders and 30 men on bd. that capt. Moorsom was killed as was the master & 1 man, himself & 6 men wounded, that the ship & her boats were cut to pieces, all her rigging gone & sails torn from the yards, the fore yard cut in two. We sent a number of our officers & men to refit & send the prisoners on bd.

Having obtained information that they had left that morning a sloop of war Brig & a 16 gun schooner, with 3 armed ships & an armed Brig, which were then astern standing the same course she came—I ordered my officer on bd. the ship to get the Prize before the wind & to steer N.W. so as to be out of sight of the named squadron before daylight. (after the engagement I found that Mr. Long my 1st Lieut. & 5 men had been wounded. Mr. Long has his thigh bone fractured by a musket ball) We continued standing to the N.W. until 4 A.M. when we hove to. at daylight I went on bd. the Prize & found her in a dreadful situation, torn to pieces by our shot; 2 guns dismounted—

Finding she had new sails below, and the Carpenters fitting the Fore Yard &c., was determined to man her in. Accordingly put Mr. Jenkins & 6 men on bd., leaving her Doctor & wounded under his charge, with a Gentleman & his Lady, & sevl. who were passengers— we were all the morning fitting & repairing our own damage, fine weather, the prize left us at 10 A.M.

Latt. obsd 23.23 North (Tropic of Cancer). 6 wounded including J. Dougherty, blown up by powder.[17]

The engagement between the *Rossie* and the *Princess Amelia* became the subject of a marine painting depicting the "romance" of naval warfare fought under sail in moonlight. This was before photography, of course, so maritime battles were depicted in a heroic and not entirely factual way. The painting shows a powerful privateer defeating a vulnerable merchant ship. This is not quite true. The *Rossie's* relatively flush deck gave little protection for its crew, while the *Princess Amelia* provided a strong wooden bulwark as cover for its seamen. The protection afforded the crew of the *Rossie* consisted of nets strung along the rails forming narrow catwalks that held tightly rolled and folded hammocks. Nevertheless, it was a decided mismatch, the *Rossie* having twelve cannons to the *Princess Amelia's* eight. The British packet was 180 tons, five years old, and had a strong newly coppered hull that made it relatively swift. History has accorded a great deal of credit to the captain of the *Princess Amelia,* who fiercely fought "to the death" attempting to preserve his coveted mandate as a "Crown Ship" carrying the Royal Mail.

The day after the battle, Captain Barney secured the valuable *Amelia*, completed its repairs, and noted in his log: "The Man of War & small cruisers were all out in pursuit of the Americans." When he assessed the integrity of his own ship Barney realized that the damaged *Rossie* was vulnerable. During the next week Barney opted to join with the *Globe*, a fellow Baltimore privateer under the command of John Murphy, for a joint cruise in which each ship could support the other. Their partnership lasted for several weeks but proved unsuccessful. The *Rossie* ultimately limped home for a rest and refitting.

The excerpts from the log of the schooner *Rossie* portray Joshua Barney as a bold yet methodical man. His conduct as a captain on the eve of the War of 1812 differed from that during the Revolutionary War. Barney was not as intent on capturing prizes as before, and seemed more determined to destroy enemy shipping and gather prisoners as "commodities" for exchange.

The interdiction and destruction of small merchantmen and fishing boats by ships like the *Rossie* were not a major threat to Britain. Privateering was designed to harass commerce and increase operating costs of maritime trade by driving up the cost of insurance and forcing owners to replace ships, crew, and cargo captured by the enemy. The American strategy enjoyed limited success. Of the approximately five hundred privateers recorded by the Department of the Navy during the War of 1812, only about two hundred took a prize. The *Rossie* was one of the more successful privateer vessels, having destroyed or captured 3,698 tons of shipping worth an estimated $1.5 million and captured 217 prisoners. Barney profited greatly from these prizes and the seized goods. He received 16 shares of a total of 285 shares generated for the officers and crew. Barney was given 10 percent of the gains from the sale of the proceeds from the bounty plus 10 regular shares as captain of the vessel and 4 merit shares (reserve shares that he awarded to himself).[18] Although contracts varied, captains also usually received 10 percent of the aggregate share awarded to the crew. The owners and crew of the *Rossie* apparently were willing to forgo a bit of profit if doing so would attract a man of Barney's stature to serve as their captain. Their wisdom was indicated by his extraordinary productivity. Indeed, according to the financial records of the *Rossie*, Barney's portion amounted to $18,195, very good pay indeed for about ninety days at sea.

After assessing the damage suffered by the *Rossie* during its encounter with *Princess Amelia* a shipwright deemed the ship not worth repairing for privateer service. Barney agreed, saying, "I am only sorry my Cruise began so late, or I might have done much more injury to the Enemy—I find small vessels will no longer answer the purpose and have declined proceeding on another cruise indeed my Vessel has suffered so much that she is unfit for service being old and worn out."[19] The owners, however, were either more optimistic or more opportunistic, as the case may be. They put the *Rossie* up for auction on 28 October 1812 under an advertisement that read: "The elegant Privateer Schooner *Rossie,* as she arrived from sea, with her armament, Provisions, Water Casks, etc." The auctioneer described the ship as "not excelled in any point of beauty or sailing by any vessel belonging to the United States." The *Rossie* continued as a letter-of-marque trader for some months under the ownership of D'Arcy and Didier of Baltimore, but was captured off France in January 1813. A contemporary English report stated: "Came to Plymouth, England on 17 January 1813, the schooner *Rossie,* (J.D.) Daniel, from Baltimore to France with coffee, taken by the *Dryad,* a frigate of the Rochefort squadron. It is said that the above schooner had been a privateer and had committed depredations on our commerce having taken no less than twenty-six sail of vessels."[20] This small note served as the obituary for the *Rossie,* which then disappeared into maritime history.

⇜ 9 ⇝

DEFENSE OF
TIDEWATER MARYLAND

*A*s the War of 1812 proceeded, Adm. Sir George Cockburn and his fleet were ordered to harass American shipping on the Chesapeake, launch raids along its shore, and seize produce and goods from the coastal villages. Their objective was to destroy American morale and tie down U.S. forces so they could not be transferred to other theaters of operation. The results of this strategy were mixed. The raids turned some Americans against their government, but the depredations also aroused hatred of the British and heightened the patriotism of others.

By 1813 the port of Baltimore had become the third-largest city in the United States and a center for shipbuilding and maritime commerce. In addition, it was the home port of more privateers than any other American city. In fact, the British considered Baltimore a nest of pirates and a prime target for a British attack. In response to that threat the city's defenses were strengthened. Baltimore's primary protection from attack by sea was the garrison at Fort McHenry, and men drilled on its parade ground and fired its cannons in preparation for the anticipated British invasion. Under these circumstances a little morale boost for the American troops seemed necessary. In the early spring of 1813 Maj. George Armistead, the fort's commander, wrote to Gen. Samuel Smith, the commander of the defense of Baltimore: "We, Sir, are ready at Fort McHenry to defend Baltimore against invasion by the enemy. That is to say, we are ready except we have no suitable ensign to display over the Star[-shaped] Fort, and it is my desire to have a flag so large that the British will have no difficulty in seeing it from a distance."[1]

Shortly after Armistead wrote to Smith, a committee of three high-ranking officers—Capt. Joshua Barney, Brig. Gen. John Stricker, and Col. William McDonald of the 6th Maryland Militia Regiment—was convened to design a distinctive banner for Fort McHenry. The officers contracted with Mary Young Pickersgill, a local widow who specialized in making house and merchant ship flags, to make two flags: a thirteen-foot storm flag and a much larger banner with fifteen stars, each star measuring two feet across. Each of the banner's eight red stripes and seven white stripes was to be two feet wide. The finished dimensions of the larger flag would be thirty by forty-two feet. Mrs. Pickersgill estimated that this unusual banner would require four hundred yards of bunting. The flag had to be made in sections and was so long that it could not be made in one building. A brewer named Eli Clagget gave the hard-pressed seamstress permission to use his ale brewery's malt-room floor for the final stitching of the banner, an unusual birthing place for a national icon and the inspiration for the American national anthem. On 19 August 1813, with the help of her thirteen-year-old daughter, Mary Young Pickersgill completed the hand-sewn flag for Fort McHenry, charging the committee $405.90 for labor.[2]

While Barney participated in the design of the flag his thoughts quite naturally turned to maritime matters. On 4 July 1813 he sent Secretary of the Navy William Jones a detailed plan for the defense of the Chesapeake Bay. In the plan Barney noted that "the Enemy has on this station, 11 ships of the line, 33 frigates, 38 Sloops of war, and a number of schooners &c." These vessels carried approximately eight thousand men, giving the enemy sufficient manpower and armament to attack both Washington and Baltimore. Barney also wrote that Adm. John Borlase Warren had left Bermuda,

> where I conceive he is now gone to meet the *Marines and Royal Artillary from England* [and] there to organize and provide everything necessary for the Campaigne. . . .

I am therefore of the opinion the only defence we have in our power, is a Kind of *Barge* or *Row-galley,* so constructed, as to draw a small draft of water, to carry Oars, light sails, and *One heavy long gun,* these vessels may be built in a short time, (say 3 weeks) Men may be had, the City of Baltimore could furnish Officers & Men for *twenty Barges,* without difficulty. . . . [Each] boat ought to *carry 50 officers & Men,* and 25 soldiers; A Squadron of *twenty* Barges would require 1000 officers & men, and 500 Officers & Soldiers, which in a few hours could be transported to any given point. . . . let each boat have One 24 pounder, and small arms compleat. . . . The expence of the Barges would not be great, they would cost about 3000$ each, and after the service was performed might be sold to advantage for *Coasters,* having but a deck to put on them."[3]

Barney accompanied the letter with a pen-and-ink sketch of his barge design. Since the middle of the Jefferson administration, the bulk of the American navy had consisted of small gunboats, most carrying one long 32-pounder plus perhaps a swivel gun or two. These small vessels were intended to provide coastal defense, and Barney's proposal was consistent with this strategy. Each of his proposed gunboats would be one hundred feet long and fifteen feet wide, and would have three feet of freeboard above the openings for the oars. The boats would have twenty seats and twenty oars per side. In addition, there would be a fifteen-foot flush deck forward to support a cannon, and a similar deck at the stern.

Secretary Jones needed both a plan of action for the defense of tidewater Maryland and a leader capable of executing the scheme. Joshua Barney was his man. The Revolutionary War veteran had the reputation of being aggressive, resourceful, and valiant in battle. He was admired by nearly all who had served with him. Jones admired Barney's record of accomplishments, and now that the seaman was a mature fifty-four, the secretary felt that his many military assets far outweighed his main flaw, a tendency to disregard orders that he considered unwise.

A disquieting incident occurred during the formal appointment hearings of this new command. An old enemy, the Baltimore merchant Lemuel Taylor, sent a letter to Secretary Jones in which he accused Barney of being "a most abandoned rascal both as to politics and morals." He went on to say that "if Barney is appointed to any command most of the usefull men will be obliged to retire."[4] This insult to Barney required redress, and Barney challenged Taylor to a duel to be fought with pistols in the neighboring state of Virginia. Barney's luck or marksmanship prevailed once again. Taylor was wounded with a ball in the chest, but he recovered and later fought in the defense of Baltimore.

On 20 August 1813 Navy Secretary Jones made a reply to Barney:

Sir,

The nature of the force, necessary for the defence of the extensive Bays and rivers of the U. States, and the means of manning and employing that force, requiring an organization, in some degree different from that of the general Naval Establishment, The President of the U. States, . . . has determined to select, for special command of the Flotilla, on the upper part of [t]he Chesapeake, a Citizen, in whose fidelity, skill, local knowledge, and commanding influence with the Mariners of the District, reliance may be placed, in case of emergency.

I have, therefore, the pleasure to offer to you that Special Command, subject only to orders of this Department. . . .

It is not intended, because it would be incompatible with the rights of others, to appoint you, by Commission, to any regular and permanent rank in the Navy of the U. States; but, for the purpose and direction of your command, you will be considered as Acting Commandant, in the Navy of the U. States, respected, and obeyed as such [as] Master Commandant. . . .

The Officers immediately subordinate to you, as commander, will be Sailing masters in the Navy of the U. States, and such other subordinate and petty officers as this Department shall direct. . . .

They will moreover be shipped for twelve months, for special service of the Flotilla, and not be liable to be draughted for any other service.[5]

The plan calling for a shallow-draft flotilla and the barge design were clearly Barney's. The flotilla and its commander would be under the direct command of the secretary of the navy. The commandant's primary duty was to recruit officers and men, and Barney proceeded at once to do that. On 15 September 1813 he added Lt. Solomon Rutter of Baltimore to his roster. In the middle of December 1813 he persuaded a second Solomon, Maryland state senator Solomon Frazier, to accept an appointment as a lieutenant in the flotilla unit. On Christmas Day 1813 Baltimore's *American and Commercial Daily Advertiser* published the following advertisement:

CHESAPEAKE FLOTILLA

Where an honorable and comfortable situation offers to men out of employ during the Embargo; where Seamen and Landsmen, will receive two months pay advanced, and their wives to receive half-pay monthly, and single men can provide for aged parents, and widows for helpless children, in the same manner; with the advantage of being near their families, and not drafted into the militia, or turned over into any other service. Apply to the recruiting officer, or JOSHUA BARNEY Com'dt of U.S. Flotilla[6]

The construction of the initial eight barges had already begun in Baltimore when Barney officially assumed his post. The cutter *Scorpion* and the schooner *Asp* were to augment his force, along with three gunboats. The shipwrights and carpenters built additional barges through the winter of 1813 and into the spring of 1814. With the arrival of the warmer April weather, the British fleet started up the Chesapeake Bay. On 17 April Barney had sufficiently organized his flotilla to embark from Baltimore. His fleet consisted of ten barges, the five-gun cutter *Scorpion,* and a gunboat. It took him a day to make the trip to Annapolis, where he retired with the fleet to the safety of the Piankatank River. During this short familiarization cruise he noticed that some of the smaller second-class barges shipped too much water. Three of them were sent back to Baltimore.

On 26 April 1814 Secretary Jones advised Barney that he had been appointed to the rank of captain in the U.S. Navy: "Herewith you will receive a commission from the president as Captain in the Flotilla Service of the United States. You will be entitled to seventy five dollars per month and six rations per day, being the pay and subsistence of a Captain in the Navy commanding a ship of 20 and under 32 guns, and governed by the rules and regulations provided for the government of the Navy."[7] Barney's official reappointment had been long in coming. A similar letter appointing Frazier and Rutter to the rank of lieutenant was received the same day. It is important to note that these commissions were special ranks covering a new naval subset, the Flotilla Service. The new titles apparently did not apply to the regular blue-water navy.

Barney tried to test his armaments by challenging the British who were assembling not far from Annapolis, but they refused to give battle and he returned to Baltimore to oversee repairs and alterations to the smaller barges. Although the orders from Secretary Jones called for the barges to be fitted with 24-pound cannons, they were furnished with lighter 18-pounders. Even these proved too heavy and were replaced by more easily handled 12-pounders. Eight inches of additional bulwark was installed on each barge to prevent flooding in turbulent water or excessive spray from missed cannon shot. When the work was completed, Barney sailed his flotilla south down the bay in the hope of attacking a British outpost on Watts Island in Tangier Sound. The date was 24 May 1814. The American force consisted of thirteen barges, two gunboats, one galley, one lookout boat, and their flagship, the cutter *Scorpion*. The schooner *Asp* was not yet ready to join them.

On the morning of 1 June 1814 the small flotilla was anchored in the mouth of the Patuxent River. A lookout sounded the alert that a large British force was coming up the bay toward the river. After a brief exchange of shots, Barney took his force up the Patuxent River and into the shallow waters of St. Leonard's Creek. The menacing third-rate, seventy-four-gun HMS *Dragon* and a British schooner stationed themselves at the mouth of the river. On 7 June, a brig and a razee, a vessel with its center of gravity lowered by the removal of a deck, reinforced the formidable English blockade. The opponents also had fifteen barges to the Americans' thirteen, but Barney had an additional two gunboats and a galley at his disposal. He strategically retreated up the side creek where he would be safe from the sailing ships and could reasonably match the British gunboats in firepower.

Barney moored his barges in a line from one shore to the other about two miles up the creek. The barges were fixed in place with kedge anchors from their sterns, but when they rode forward on the outgoing tide their large bower anchors lay almost directly under them. In fact, if the tide fell sharply, there was a danger that the barges might be impaled on their own anchor flukes. Barney then divided his small fleet into three sections. The commodore took personal command of the red section and assigned the white to Rutter and the blue to Frazier; he put his eldest son, marine major William Barney, in command of the *Scorpion*. The British squadron cautiously rowed up the small creek in their fifteen formidable barges. At eight o'clock in the morning they started to fire Congreve rockets at the Americans. At long range these special munitions proved inaccurate, doing little damage to the American fleet. The rockets did, however, harry the sailors by churning up mud and spray. Barney responded by firing the bow guns mounted on his barges. The 12-pounders had insufficient range to reach the British, so he ordered his flotilla to get under way and attack, firing their cannons as rapidly as possible. The British barges quickly withdrew through the wall of smoke and flame to the protection of their mother ships. An hour or two before sunset the British regrouped and tried another rocket attack on the American barges lying in wait up the creek. Barney's men once again repulsed the British, but this time at a price. One rocket landed directly on a white-squadron barge, killing one man and wounding three others.

That incident and those of the following days are recounted in letters from Barney to the secretary of the navy:

St. Leonard's Creek, June 11, 1814
On the evening of the 9th, the enemy moved up with twenty barges, having received more force from the 74, at the mouth of the Patuxent. I met them, after a short action drove them until dark, and returned to my anchorage. Yesterday they made a bold attempt; at 2 P.M. they moved up with twenty-one barges, one rocket barge, and two schooners in tow. On making their appearance, we went down on them; kept up a smart fire for some time, and seemed determined to do something decisive. But they soon gave way and retreated; we pursued them down the creek. At the mouth lay the eighteen-gun schooner; she attempted to beat out, but our fire was so severe, she ran ashore at the entrance and was abandoned. We still pursued, until the razee and brig opened on us a brisk fire, which completely covered the schooner and the fleeing barges &c. We must have done them considerable damage.

St. Leonard's Creek, June 13, 1814
I had the honor of addressing you on the 11th giving a short detail of our action with the enemy on the 10th. By information, they suffered much. The large schooner was nearly destroyed, having several shots through her at the water's edge; her deck torn up, guns dismounted, and main-mast nearly cut off about half way up, and rendered unserviceable. She was otherwise much cut; they ran her ashore to prevent her sinking. The commodore's boat was cut in two; a shot went through the rocket boat; one of the small schooners carrying two 32 pounders had a shot which raked her from aft, forward; the boats generally suffered; but I have not ascertained what loss they sustained in men. . . . Saturday and yesterday the enemy were employed on the Patuxent River, in landing on the

banks to plunder stock, &c. . . . The frigate is the Acasta, *and the brig the* Jassear. *They left only 200 men & one small boat aboard the* Dragon *at the mouth of the Patuxent.*[8]

The British naval units now settled into a siege disposition. The sunken white-squadron barge was raised and put back into service. Barney noticed that the masts of the barges provided a mark for the British cannons and ordered the masts removed and stowed. This also made the barges easier to row. He then had stakes driven into the creek bed and erected a boom across the tributary in front of his fleet of barges as protection. He placed a 24-pound carronade in position to defend the branch of the creek that held the *Scorpion* and the gunboats. Reinforcements arrived on the scene by land. Six hundred Maryland militiamen were stationed along the high banks of the creek to harass the British if they tried to sneak up on the flotilla. Capt. Samuel Miller added one hundred marines and three 12-pounders to this troop concentration. For a time things remained quiet.

Barney was in Federalist country, and as far as the commodore was concerned, the area's inhabitants were simply old-fashioned Tories with a new name. Many of the people were siding with the British and passing along information about troop and ship dispositions. Barney became particularly angry at one local resident, a Mr. Parran, who claimed to have been held captive by the British. Parran gave Barney information about the overwhelming strength of the British force, but added that the British had vowed not to harm the Marylanders or destroy their property if they did not resist and stayed in their homes. Then he started to ask a series of pointed and detailed questions about Barney's flotilla. When Parran let slip that he planned to return to the British flagship, Barney became furious and tried to have him arrested as a spy.[9]

Because the local militia was also made up of Federalists, Barney questioned their loyalty and willingness to support the flotilla. He was right to do so. Among the militia units assigned to guard his men was the 36th Regiment under the command of Col. Henry Carberry. One morning Carberry and his troops simply marched away without notice, abandoning Barney and taking his provision wagons with them. As they left they spread word that Adm. John Borlase Warren and his troops from Bermuda were on their way, panicking the local inhabitants. This and similar moves by the Maryland militia certainly did much to confirm

Barney's negative view of Marylanders, particularly those from the tide-water region. The feeling was mutual; some citizens of Calvert County opined that the president and particularly Joshua Barney were the cause of "the mischief the British have done . . . enough to make you and every man abuse Jim Madison and old Barney in Hell."[10]

The Navy Department feared that Barney's barges were in danger of being captured and used by the British to attack Washington, so the secretary of the navy ordered Barney to destroy the flotilla and retire to the Washington Navy Yard. When the order reached them on 20 June, Barney's men were already suffering from declining morale. Their perception that they were fighting against an overwhelming force had made them edgy and downcast. The thought of dismantling their boats and carrying their guns ashore further disheartened them. The next day the order was rescinded. Barney wrote a letter to his second son, Louis, assessing the situation: "As they cannot or dare not trust themselves within the creek, I expect Commodore Barrie has gone down to the Admiral to consult what means they are to take for my destruction, but sooner then they shall do it, I will put fire to the flotilla and walk off by the light of the Blaze."[11]

Barney became impatient with the waiting game and took his force down the creek to attack the moored 38-gun frigate *Loire*, Thomas Brown commanding, and the 32-gun frigate *Narcissus* under the command of John Richard Lumly. The attack was to be supported by an artillery battery under the command of another militiaman, Col. Decius Wadsworth. In order to ensure proper coordination and provide the militia leaders with some professional military assistance, Barney sent marine captain Samuel Miller, twenty of his sailors, several light guns, and his veteran sailing master, John Geoghegan, to join the militiamen. Unfortunately, Col. Wadsworth ignored the advice offered by Miller and Geoghegan regarding the placement of the guns and positioned his cannons below the brow of a hill on sandy soil. The recoil of each shot sent the guns backward down the hill, and each round sailed high over the masts of the target ships. The British were able to return almost four rounds for every shot fired by the Americans. Captain Miller was positioned on the left of Wadsworth's battery, and Geoghegan occupied the right of the promontory at the western entrance to St. Leonard's Creek. The two leaders from Barney's flotilla received an intelligence report from Wadsworth that a British party was landing to their northwest.

Miller took his force to counter this invasion, and Geoghegan spread out his battery and continued to blast away at the British. In the next few minutes Geoghegan was wounded in the knee and one of his gunners was also hit. Barney's land-based naval artillery support was faltering.

The creek narrowed at the point where the American flotilla made contact with the British force some four hundred yards away. This meant that Barney could engage the British with only eight barges at a time, making his boats vulnerable to heavy cannon fire from the enemy. In spite of these advantages the two British vessels retreated, thus breaking off their siege for the moment. The gnatlike forays of Barney's flotilla merely served as an annoyance to the larger enemy force that would eventually overwhelm them. After the disengagement Barney wrote, "It would have been an act of madness in such a force, unassisted, to contend against two frigates, a brig[,] two schooners, and a number of barges, in themselves equal in force that could be brought into action from the flotilla."[12] The *Loire* took fifteen shots from 18-pounders through the hull and suffered considerable damage topside, but incurred no loss of life. The *Narcissus*, a name associated in mythology with beauty, was also scarred by the guns of Barney's flotilla. The Americans lost two barges with eleven men killed or wounded. Capt. Thomas Brown of the *Loire* wrote an embarrassingly short report of the battle, stating that only one person, the boatswain of the *Narcissus*, had been wounded. He did not mention that he had let an inferior American force, outgunned and outmanned, evade entrapment. His carelessness permitted practically the entire American flotilla to regroup to fight another day.[13]

At this juncture Barney left his position in the creek and moved his force up the Patuxent River. Lieutenant Rutter was ordered to transport excess materials overland. Rutter and his men were attacked by a British marauding force and lost much of the equipment while trying to escape. Fortunately, the lieutenant evaded capture and was able to rejoin Barney. After establishing a temporary headquarters in Benedict, Maryland, on 27 June, Barney wrote to Secretary Jones requesting additional orders. He was summoned to Washington, which was about twenty-five miles away. Jones told him to hold his present position and dispatch Lieutenant Rutter and five hundred men to Baltimore. Once there, Rutter would take command of fourteen barges newly built for the defense of the city. Commodore Barney would retain overall command of the Chesapeake flotilla units. It was agreed that the flotillamen defending Washington and Baltimore would come to the aid of each other if attacked.[14]

On 4 July Barney returned to the *Scorpion*. Four days later he received an intelligence report indicating that Admiral Cockburn's flagship had entered the mouth of the Patuxent River. This news implied that an attack was imminent. When Barney received a report on 11 July that enemy ships were advancing on Benedict, he readied his forces to meet them, but the British fled before a shot could be fired. A swift six-oared gig was outfitted to act as a scout to warn of more incursions. The Americans patrolled diligently, and for a month all was relatively quiet. Then, on 19 August, the British moved up the Patuxent with a squadron of twenty-three ships and landed troops near Benedict in an attempt to surround Barney's forces as a crucial first step in their march on Washington. Realizing that he was outflanked, the commodore put 400 men ashore and marched them to a better defensive position at Marlboro. Barney left Lt. Solomon Frazier in charge of the flotilla, now consisting of 120 men. The Navy Department once again feared that these vessels might be used against the American forces if captured and sent a firm and final order for the immediate destruction of the flotilla. As Admiral Cockburn's frigates and fleet of barges prepared to take possession of the American vessels, the boats blew up literally in their faces. Fifteen of the sixteen barges were completely destroyed as Frazier and his men escaped.

The American flotilla laid in ruins, sunk in the mud of the Patuxent, but Barney's men had managed to remove five of their cannons, which they mounted on carriage wheels and towed away. The British, under the command of Maj. Gen. Robert Ross, now had an estimated four to five thousand armed troops on the ground in the vicinity of Benedict. Their next objective was to march on Washington by way of Bladensburg, where the eastern tributary of the Potomac River was fordable.

The progression of the invading forces up the tidewater area toward America's mid-Atlantic population centers is the subject of a poem by Angus Umphraville. This short piece captures the feelings of those caught in the path of the advance:

She comes! the proud invader comes,
To waste our country, spoil our homes,
To lay our towns and cities low

And bid our mother's tears to flow,
Our wives lament, our orphans weep,
To seize the empire of the deep!

On 21 August Barney reassembled his "red" and "blue" squadrons at the village of Upper Marlboro. The sailors were exhausted, having just dragged two naval 18-pounders and three 12-pounders with them overland. Added to this, many of the men had lost their shoes in their haste to abandon and destroy the barges. Secretary Jones, accompanied by Captain Miller and seventy-eight marines, joined them the next day at nearby Wood-Yard in order to assess the situation. The band of American citizen-soldiers decided to retreat to a temporary billet at the Marine Barracks of the Washington Navy Yard.

On the twenty-fourth, Gen. William Winder, the brother of the governor of Maryland and a political appointee given command of the American forces in the capital area, ordered Barney and his men to perform as soldiers and guard the long bridge over the east branch of the Potomac (now called Anacostia Creek). Word was received in headquarters that the British troops were approaching Bladensburg. Winder directed his infantry to meet the advancing enemy there, leaving Barney and his men to defend the bridge. Barney was frustrated by this passive assignment. When President James Madison happened to ride up in a carriage to cross the bridge, Barney respectfully pointed out that the bridge could be denied the enemy by having it blown up by a couple of barges loaded with explosives that could be ignited by a small detachment of men. He felt that his flotillamen could be better used in the field of battle. The president concurred and ordered him to Bladensburg. Once again Barney had acted against orders from a superior, but this time by appealing directly to the commander in chief.

When Barney and his men reached Bladensburg, the Americans had already set up their defensive lines. General Winder ordered the new arrivals to join the third and last defensive position as a supportive artillery unit. Barney's guns were placed on a hill commanding the shallow valley overlooking a creek crossed by Turncliff's Bridge. The British resolutely, if somewhat exhaustedly, advanced to the attack. Almost immediately the American militiamen found their position outflanked. Their lines quickly crumbled before the numerically superior and more disciplined British regulars, but nature had given the Americans a small advantage.

This was August in steamy tidewater country, and the redcoats were wearing hot woolen uniforms and marching under heavy packs as they carried their arms up the dusty road from Benedict. The British were routing the American militia, but the heat and humidity were not conducive to zealous pursuit. The soldiers had left the stifling confinement of their transport vessels and rapidly marched overland with little time to acclimate to the terrain and weather; they were overcome by heat exhaustion and fatigue. The Maryland militiamen were defending their homes on very familiar ground. They should, by all measures, have had an important advantage. The British became temporarily and uncharacteristically disorganized as they advanced to a choke point at Turncliff's Bridge. As the British troops reassembled into their military units on the road beside the creek, they found themselves below Barney and his five naval cannons. The gun crews were supported by other flotillamen acting as a contingent of infantry guarding them to their "port" and "stern." The marines covered the "starboard" and part of the ground immediately to the front of their line so that the cannons could fire over them. The sailors delivered ball and grapeshot fire with deadly effect, sweeping the British off the road repeatedly. Three times the British advanced on Barney's position, trying to take it by assault; three times the Americans drove them back. Finally, a forth attempt succeeded in crossing the creek. By sheer force of numbers and bravery under fire the British advanced through the dense smoke and formed a strong battle line. This rank now threatened Barney's right flank, where Captain Miller and his marines were dug in on the side of the promontory. Barney ordered them to meet the army column head-on and turned his guns on the British advancing in support. Miller's seventy-eight-man marine unit charged screaming down the hill, crossed an open field, and leapt over a stone wall topped by a wooden fence where the British had taken cover to catch a temporary breath in the intense summer heat. The Americans drove the weary regulars back into a ravine, wounding many officers and men with musket fire and bayonet stabs. The wounded included Col. William Thornton, commander of the infantry regiment, plus his second- and third-ranking officers, Lt. Col. William Wood and Maj. George Brown. Commodore Barney's men, firing naval cannons turned into field artillery, and Miller's seventy-eight marines had repelled about six hundred of the king's soldiers.

A couple of American regular army regiments could have turned the tide of this battle—and, indeed, of the entire British invasion—with a counterattack. Unfortunately, no regular army troops were left on the battlefield to mount a counterattack, leading to one of the great tragedies of the War of 1812. As the smoke cleared and the bark of cannons ceased, Barney was appalled to see that his sailors and marines were the only American troops left on the battlefield except for two small Maryland militia detachments on his right. Their feeling of triumph disappeared as they realized that everyone else had retreated in haste toward safety. Even Barney's munitions wagons had joined the flight. Barney tried to rally his men, but the British were again advancing on the right and starting to surround him. The militia that was protecting his left flank had long since abandoned its ground. Victory was now impossible, but Barney thought that he still might be able to save his cannons from capture. He mounted his horse to lead an evacuation, but before he could assemble the gun crews a sharpshooter shot his horse out from under him. When he was able to regain his feet, a musket ball struck his thigh— the first significant wound Barney had suffered in his long career as a warrior. When word arrived that his guns were running out of ammunition, he had no choice but to abandon them and ordered his men to retreat. Like Silas Talbot at Fort Mercer on Mudd Island long before, Joshua Barney was now a defeated artillery officer.

Three of his officers made a litter to take him from the battlefield. Barney felt too weak from loss of blood to be moved, so he ordered them to leave him. Perhaps they might escape capture and rejoin the fight elsewhere. Two of the men complied, but Lt. Jesse Huffington insisted on staying at the side of his commander to face capture. At that point a fleeing American officer on horseback rode close by the wounded commodore and his junior officer. It was Barney's aide-de-camp, George Wilson. Huffington pleaded with him to stop and aid in the commodore's evacuation. Wilson refused, yelling that he too was wounded, and spurred his mount away from the battlefield. This incident later led to some nasty exchanges in print between Barney and Wilson. In the end, however, Barney thought the man too "contemptible to bring to Court-martial and . . . let the miscreant go unpunished."[15]

An account of the engagement written by a British observer gives Barney's men their due: "With the exception of a party of sailors, from the gun boats [barges] under the command of Commodore Barney, no troops could have behaved worse than they did. The skirmishers were driven in as soon as attacked, the first line giving way without offering the slightest resistance, and the left of the main body was broken in half an hour after serious engagement. Of the sailors, however, it would be injustice not to speak in the terms which their conduct merits. They were employed as gunners, and not only did they serve their guns with quickness and precision which astonished their assailants, but they stood till some of them were actually bayonetted, with fusees in their hands; nor was it till their leader was wounded, and they saw themselves deserted on all sides by the soldiers, that they quitted the field."[16]

There were 6,000 militia and 370 seamen at the start of the battle. Of Captain Miller's 114 marines, 11 were killed and 16 were wounded. The estimate of British losses compiled by Dr. Hanson Catlett, a U.S. surgeon, was 180 killed and 300 wounded, but the British commanders reported only 64 dead and 185 wounded. Catlett also estimated that the Americans suffered up to 12 killed and 30 wounded. General Winder believed this number to be higher, a loss of 30–40 killed and 50–60 wounded. In addition, the Americans lost ten valuable cannons, five of which were from Barney's flotilla.[17]

James Fenimore Cooper also paid homage to the Americans' courage: "The people of the flotilla, under the orders of Captain Barney, and the marines, were justly applauded for their excellent conduct on this occasion. No troops could have stood better; and the fire of both artillery and musketry has been described as to the last degree severe. Captain Barney himself, and Captain Miller, of the Marine corps, in particular, gained much additional reputation; and their conspicuous gallantry caused a deep and general regret, that their efforts could not have been sustained by the rest of the army."[18]

In a retrospective look at the Battle of Bladensburg, Margaret Smith (a descendant of William Smith) wrote: "Ah, their commanders, Armstrong and Winder. On their shoulders lies the blame of our disastrous flight and defeat. . . . More than 2000 had not fired their muskets when Armstrong and Winder gave the order for retreat, and to enforce that order added terror to authority! The English officers have told some of our citizens that they could not have stood more minutes longer, that they were exhausted with thirst, heat and fatigue."[19]

British soldiers expeditiously took Barney and Lieutenant Huffington prisoner. The commander of their unit was John Wainwright, the captain of Admiral Cockburn's flagship, HMS *Albion*. Captain Wainwright had great respect for the legendary Barney. He ordered his captive's wounds dressed by the *Albion*'s senior surgeon and informed the admiral and General Ross of the capture of the distinguished American. Ross, moved at meeting Barney, greeted him with respect, saying, "I am very glad to see you, Commodore." Captain Barney, who was now about to become a prisoner of the British for the sixth time, replied, "I am sorry I cannot return the compliment, General." The general then commented on the fact that it was the flotillamen who had engaged them, and Admiral Cockburn agreed, saying, "You were right, though I could not believe you. They have given us the only fighting we have had."[20] General Ross praised Barney as a brave officer who, with only a handful of men, had given his troops a very severe shock. Sorry at seeing that the commodore was grievously wounded, he granted Barney a parole, then had the stricken flotilla commander evacuated by litter to a Bladensburg inn. On arriving there, Barney found that Captain Miller had also been wounded and was a fellow prisoner. A sailor from Barney's flotilla lay on a cot nearby, horribly wounded with an arm nearly severed. Shreds of flesh hung in a bloody mass from what must have been a cannon injury. When the young man saw that he was in the presence of his commodore, incredibly, he found the strength to rise in his litter to grasp his commander's hand. The British attendants were extremely moved by this gesture of loyalty and affection. "Well damn my eyes!" they exclaimed. "If he wasn't a kind commander that chap wouldn't have done that."[21] Barney offered the guards and orderlies who had cared for him a fifty-dollar note for their kindness and trouble. All refused compensation except the sergeant of the guard, who said that he would keep it for his men. Barney discovered the next morning that the sergeant and his detail had deserted.

On 25 August, only one day after the Battle of Bladensburg, the British invasion force reached Washington. The riverbank town then evolving into the capital of the United States contained about eight thousand inhabitants and was practically defenseless. When a rumor circulated in Washington that the British were bringing a considerable force of ships up the Potomac, the panicked Americans set fire to the arms, ammunition, and ships at the Washington Navy Yard. Among the vessels destroyed were the forty-four-gun frigate *Columbia*, which was being repaired; the newly launched but incompletely fitted eighteen-gun *Argus*; and the twelve-gun *Lynx*. The latter ultimately escaped complete destruction at the hands of the fleeing Americans. Admiral Cockburn's sailors and General Ross's troops stormed into the capital. Ross's invasion force was unusual in consisting of a naval brigade; the Chasseurs Britanniques, a foreign legion of non-Britons without specific loyalties; a group of convicts; and some Spanish mercenaries. The British burned a good part of the capital, including the Senate, the Treasury Building, and the president's mansion. The invaders captured the mansion so rapidly that General Ross and his officers were able to enjoy part of a meal on a table set for forty guests hastily left behind by the Madison family. In the Potomac, the British frigates *Seahorse* and *Euryalus* led three bomb ships and a rocket ship in a bombardment of Alexandria, Virginia, a short distance south of Washington. On the twenty-sixth, General Ross feared that the British might have extended themselves too far from their supply lines and ordered a withdrawal. On the twenty-seventh, Barney's wife and son Louis arrived at Bladensburg with their doctor. General Ross wished Barney a swift recovery and farewell, and the Barney party departed by carriage for home at Elkridge, outside Baltimore.

The remaining flotillamen, about 250–300 men, had been moved to Washington but were without orders or a commander. General Winder did not consider them part of his command, and with Barney wounded and out of action they were considered a rogue unit. Because they were not part of Winder's Washington defense force, Barney's men ignored the general's order to retreat. As the exhausted sailors took cover from the marauding British, the tough old sailing master, John Geoghegan, stepped forward to rally and lead them. The sailors harassed the British with musket fire when the opportunity presented itself. Ultimately they straggled toward Baltimore, where they joined Lieutenant Rutter and his flotillamen in time to help in the defense of Baltimore.

The British knew the city would be difficult to capture because of its compact size and large population of forty thousand. As opposed to the militia on the Maryland peninsula, its citizens serving in the local militia were highly motivated to defend their homes. Good fortifications protected Baltimore from sea invasion, but only temporary earthen breastworks defended the land routes to the city. On 12 September British troops landed at North Point intending to mount a raid from the east. Their landing site, on a neck of land east-southeast of Baltimore, was only a mile or two from the boyhood home of Joshua Barney on Bear Creek. At the same time, a fleet of British frigates, sloops, and bomb ships entered the Patapsco River to bombard the garrisons that faced the sea. Troops fresh from the burning of Washington, led by General Ross, were also landed nearby to take advantage of any break in the defenses that resulted from the bombardment. After proceeding a scant five miles, the British forces were confronted by a local militia unit on patrol. The Americans formed a line, opened fire, and maneuvered to surround the British. The ensuing skirmish cost General Ross his life. The firing alerted the main force of American defenders and led to the major 1814 land battle around Baltimore. Thirteen thousand Americans challenged an invading force of six thousand. The human price of battle was 163 Americans dead and 50 captured. The British suffered three hundred casualties. After the death of General Ross and the ensuing carnage, the English forces abandoned their attack and retreated to the safety of their fleet.

The attack on Baltimore from the water was equally unsuccessful for the British. In the aftermath of that battle, Mary Young Pickersgill's impressive American flag, raised on 14 September 1814, would become the symbol of a small nation's defiance of the most powerful nation on earth. Fort McHenry, the main American garrison defending Baltimore from the sea, endured a constant bombardment for twenty-five hours from sixteen frigates and bomb ships, one of which fired Congreve rockets. Within the walls of the star-shaped fort were two companies of sea fencibles, a coastal guard militia mostly comprised of fishermen and boatmen under naval command, and a battery of guns from Barney's flotilla. Under the command of Master's Mate Solomon Rodman, the sixty men returned fire from the fort throughout the fusillade. The remainder of Barney's original flotilla, now under the command of Solomon Rutter, was moored at the Lazaretto, a point of land just east of Fort McHenry. A unit commanded by Sailing Master John A. Webster was particularly effective. When the British attempted to steal past the harbor defenses in the middle of the night in a fleet of barges, Webster set up a blockade of Ferry Branch, west of Fort McHenry, at a hastily made earthworks dubbed Fort Babcock. Also called City Battery, his four 18-pounders and two small brass cannons stopped the British from bringing the fort under a brutal crossfire delivered from the western part of the harbor.

A contemporary account of the battle from the American point of view gives an inspiring portrait of this battle and puts Barney's flotilla into the fray:

At the time, aided by the darkness of the night and screened by the flame they had kindled, one or two rocket or bomb vessels and many barges, manned with 1200 chosen men, passed Fort McHenry and proceeded up the Patapsco to assail the town and fort from the rear, and, perhaps, effect a landing. . . . [T]hey gave three cheers, and began to throw their missive weapons. But, alas! Their cheering was quickly turned to groaning and the cries and screams of their wounded and drowning people soon reached the shore; for forts McHenry and Covington, with the City Battery and the Lazaretto, plus the barges vomited an iron flame upon them, and a storm of heavy bullets flew upon them from the great semicircle of large guns and gallant hearts. The houses in the city were shaken to their foundations; for never perhaps, from the time of the invention of cannon to the present day, were the same number of pieces fired with so rapid succession. Barney's flotillamen, at the City Battery, maintained the high reputation they had before earned.[22]

The guns of the City Battery were commanded by Sailing Master Webster, and the Lazaretto was defended by Lieutenants Rutter and Frazier, all three of Barney's flotilla unit.

James Fenimore Cooper later described their part in the battle as follows: "The barges [of Rutter], in particular, though exposed for nearly a day and a night to the shells and rockets of the enemy, maintained their position with unflinching firmness, and when more closely attacked, repelled the attempt with ease. At a most critical moment, several vessels were sunk in the channel, which would have completely prevented the enemy from bringing up his ships, had he attempted it."[23] The sunken vessels were barges deliberately scuttled by Barney's men a half mile from Fort McHenry to present a navigational hazard to the British.

On 1 September 1814, almost two weeks before the battle, a poetically inclined Georgetown lawyer named Francis Scott Key had been asked to help negotiate the release of Dr. William Beanes, a sixty-five-year-old physician from Upper Marlborough, Maryland. Beanes had been taken from his bed and arrested for his part in jailing stragglers from Ross's retreat from Washington, and was being held prisoner on a British vessel off Baltimore. President Madison's concern about Beanes's fate was more than altruistic. Prisoner exchanges were a matter of human accounting, with each side maintaining a "credit" and "debit" ledger balance. If the doctor was considered just another prisoner of war, Madison feared the enemy might be induced to seize and carry off other unarmed citizens to exchange for British prisoners. Because of the political implications of Beanes's capture, Madison ordered a sloop of truce placed at Key's disposal. John S. Skinner, a government agent in charge of the exchange of prisoners, was sent to accompany Key to aid in the negotiation of Beanes's release.

Before engaging in the battle that would later take his life, General Ross received Key and Skinner. Ross was not well disposed toward Beanes, who was responsible for the capture of some of his troops, but he nevertheless decided that His Majesty's government would gain nothing by keeping the elderly doctor. Key and Skinner were transferred from the *Royal Oak,* the flagship of Admiral Cockburn, to the British frigate *Surprise.* There they met Dr. Beanes and were allowed to board their own American vessel, but under a guard of British sailors and marines. Rather then being released, the three men were held in British naval custody until after the attack on Baltimore. During the battle Key thus found himself a prisoner on a flag-of-truce ship at the mouth of the Patapsco River about eight miles southeast of Fort McHenry.[24] From this position, even with the aid of a telescope, Key probably could not see the small storm flag that flew over the fort. White gunpowder smoke from Fort McHenry's fifty-seven cannons clouded the distant ramparts. The Americans might have caught glimpses of the flag as the rockets and aerial bombshells meteorically illuminated the darkness. Presumably the "proof" that it was still there was the continual British rocket bombardment. Regardless, they anxiously watched for the distant banner during the entire day and into the night. The British fired approximately eighteen hundred shells and rockets during the twenty-five-hour bombardment. The American commander of the fort, Maj. George Armistead, and his militia, together with Joshua Barney's flotillamen, withstood the terrible artillery punishment. Only four Americans defending the fort were killed, but twenty-four were wounded.

Key started to pen a poem as he stood on the deck watching the bombardment. He was moved as he saw the British warships retreating. At daybreak, Armistead ordered the storm flag to be replaced with the fort's special huge banner. The flag caught a breeze aloft and was illuminated by the early morning sunlight. Key, watching through a telescope from his distant vantage point, was both exhilarated and inspired when he saw it. He wrote more lines and brief notes on the back of a letter as his boat

neared the Maryland shore. That evening he continued to write and edit
his piece in his hotel room in Baltimore. He set the poem to the meter
of a popular song sung by the English Anacreon Society written by John
Stafford Smith and titled "To Anacreon in Heaven." Robert Treat Paine
had used the same melody in a contemporary patriotic song called
"Adams and Liberty," and Key himself had used it once before in a composition honoring the heroes of the Battle of Tripoli.

The next morning Key shared his inspired work with Skinner and his
brother-law, Chief Judge of the Maryland Court of Appeals Joseph H.
Nicholson. The magistrate was so excited about Key's account of the battle that he had a local printer, Benjamin Edes, distribute it in handbill
form. Edes took the first copy off the press to his favorite tavern next to
the Holliday Street Theater, a meeting-place for local actors. Ferdinand
Durang, a talented singer, answered calls from the pub crowd to sing the
poem to the well-known tune. Thoroughly enjoying it, the boisterous
throng cheered wildly. Always looking for an addition to their repertoire,
Ferdinand and his brother Charles Durang decided to sing Key's song at
the Holliday Street Theater that evening. The approval of this more discerning audience was even greater than that at the tavern.

Although the song described a local event, Key's composition soon took
on national significance. On 21 September, eight days after the bombardment, the text of the poem was printed in the *Baltimore American* under
the title "Defense of Fort McHenry." The author's name was omitted. Some
weeks later it became known as "The Star-Spangled Banner." Because it
was inspired by a peculiar incident of war, "The Star Spangled Banner" did
not meet the dignified standards that a national anthem usually necessi-
tates. For many years, additional verses were added to the song to meet the
requirements of the North and South before and after the Civil War. Published versions of "The Star Spangled Banner" occasionally include them,
presenting an interesting anachronism or historical note. In 1916 the song
was adopted by the U.S. armed services and played at the morning and
evening "colors" ceremonies of the army and navy. It was not accepted as
the national anthem of the United States, however, until 1931. The familiar
first two stanzas of the national anthem of the United States quoted below
should be read as a poet's eyewitness report of the battle:

Oh! say, can you see by the dawn's early light,
What so proudly we hail'd at the twilight's last gleaming?

Whose broad stripes and bright stars thro' the perilous fight,
O'er the ramparts we watch'd were so gallantly streaming;
And the rockets red glare, the bombs bursting in air,
Gave proof through the night that our flag was still there?
Oh! say, does that star-spangled banner yet wave
O'er the land of the free, and the home of the brave?

On the shore dimly seen thro' the mists of the deep,
Where the foe's haughty host in dread silence reposes,
What is that which the breeze, o'er the tow'ring steep,
As it fitfully blows, half conceals, half discloses:
Now catches the gleam of the morning's first beam,
In full glory reflected now shines on the stream:
'Tis the star-spangled banner! oh, long may it wave
O'er the land of the free, and the home of the brave.

The enormous fifteen-star and fifteen-stripe flag that Joshua Barney and his committee had ordered a year earlier for Fort McHenry became a symbol of the battle and one of the most revered of all emblems of the United States. Currently undergoing restoration, the tattered flag is usually displayed at the entrance of the Smithsonian Institution's Museum of American History. The original draft of Key's poem is exhibited at Baltimore's Star Spangled Banner Museum.

James Fenimore Cooper put the assaults of Washington and Baltimore during the War of 1812 into perspective when, thirty years later, he wrote: "This warfare was generally beneficial to the American government; the excesses into which the enemy were led, whether intentionally or not, having the effect to disgust that portion of the population which had been seriously adverse to the conflict; and the administration was probably never stronger, than after wanton destruction of the public buildings at Washington."[25]

Barney's relationship with the early history of the American flag can be described with only one word: extraordinary. The teenaged Barney was the first to use the banner for naval recruitment in Maryland and probably in the colonies. He was master's mate on the *Hornet,* one of the first of a fleet of Continental navy ships to fly the American flag. He was second in command of the *Andrea Doria* when its flag received the first salute from a foreign nation. Barney was given the honor of carrying the American flag into the National Assembly of France as the new French republic received its first diplomatic recognition. Finally, he was part of the committee that ordered the fabrication of the Fort McHenry standard that became arguably the best-known national icon of the United States. Having participated in any one of these events would have been remarkable; to have been part of all five is indeed truly exceptional.

❧ IO ❧

TWILIGHT OF
THE COMMODORE

*T*he musket ball was so deeply embedded in Barney's leg that the surgeon could not extract it. The fifty-five-year-old veteran would have to live out his life with a souvenir of the Battle of Bladensburg. Barney did recover, but he was never the same physically. A limp took away his former agility, he suffered from intermittent pain, and the experience seemed to age him. On 28 September 1814, the Board of Alderman and the Council of the City of Washington passed a resolution to reward Joshua Barney with a presentation sword in recognition of his valor at Bladensburg:

> Resolved, by the Board of Alderman and board of Common council of the City of Washington, That the Mayor be, and he hereby is, authorized to present to Commodore Barney a sword, as a testimonial of the high sense which this Corporation entertains of his distinguished gallantry and good conduct at the battle of Bladensburg.
>
> Resolved, That the Mayor be and he hereby is, authorized to present through Commodore Barney, the thanks of the Corporation to the gallant officers and men, who served under his orders on the twenty-fourth of August last- and to assure them this Corporation entertains the most lively sense of their services on that day.[1]

The resolution was signed by R. C. Weightman, president of the Board of Common Council; Joseph Gales Jr., president pro tempore of the Board of Aldermen; and James Blake, mayor of Washington.

The sword, now on display at the Washington headquarters of the Daughters of the American Revolution, features on its blade a mythological emblem of a figure wearing a visored helmet. He is holding a fasces, indicating union, in his left hand. His right hand grasps an inverted spear erect on a globe. His left foot rests on the prow of a galley and his right foot is on land. The whole is symbolic of military valor on sea and land. Also on the burnished blade is an eagle clutching an anchor surrounded by eighteen stars. The hilt is a gilded eagle's head. The guard and scabbard are made of solid silver and also gilded.

By the first week in October, Barney felt sufficiently recovered to take command of an American schooner that was to carry British prisoners to Hampton Roads, exchange them for American prisoners, and return to Baltimore. The exchange took place onboard Adm. Sir Pulteney Malcomb's flagship, where the British received the released prisoners with naval pomp and ceremony. During this transfer Barney was granted freedom from his personal parole obligation.

Barney resumed command of the remnants of his flotilla in Baltimore on 10 October 1814. Morale among his men was very poor. They had faced extreme danger in combat, had lost friends, had been forced to abandon most of their personal belongings, and had not been paid in many months. One of Joshua Barney's greatest leadership attributes was his devotion to his men. He arranged for the introduction of a special act of Congress to appropriate funds to replace their lost articles. The compensatory sum requested was relatively small and obviously justifiable.

While the bill sat in Congress, Barney's men became more and more despondent. About 180 of them left the flotilla to sign on as privateers, readily attracted by the highest bidder. By 20 October the bill had passed the special committee, but after considerable discussion it was tabled by the House. Angered by the insensitivity of Congress toward veterans who had fought so valiantly, Barney wrote the House of Representatives a fervid letter in which he attempted to explain why his men deserved special treatment. The men, he said, had been ordered by their commanders in Washington to run their vessels aground and blow them up in order to deny them to the British. Before doing so, however, the men had salvaged the ships' guns for future use against the British. There had been no time to save their personal effects. The British had captured the few men who elected to stay behind and retrieve their own things. Barney tried to make the case that with winter approaching, the men needed clothing for their very survival. The proposed legislation for "two months pay exclusive of the common allowance for the petty officers and seamen attached to the flotilla under the command of captain Joshua Barney" narrowly passed the House on 2 November.[2] When the act reached the Senate, however, the legislators seemed insensitive to the desperate need of a select few and concentrated on the exclusion of officers who might also be eligible to receive compensation because "it would set a bad precedent for remuneration of officers in the other cases where they should lose baggage." The Senate voted to refuse the act, and Barney's men did not receive their pay. The only positive outcome of the Senate's debate was the confirmation of Barney's commission as "Captain of the Flotilla." Of course, he had *accepted* his first commission as captain in the U.S. Navy as of 6 February, but Congress waited an unreasonably long nine months to confirm it.

In mid-November Barney received orders to have the men who remained under his command help in fitting out a steam frigate that was in the shipyard in Baltimore. The mandate must have contained strong language because the proud Barney uncharacteristically acquiesced. On 1 December 1814 Gen. Samuel Smith suggested to Baltimore's Committee of Safety and Defense that the flotillamen be employed to raise ships that had been scuttled to avoid capture and use against the Americans. Not coincidentally, many of these vessels happened to belong to the general. Smith suggested that the men should be paid for their work as extra duty, in an attempt to "make a reasonable allowance to these distressed men . . . to do the work."[3] The committee rejected the supplemental allowance and rudely ordered the commander of the flotilla to begin raising the vessels immediately. Barney ignored the order. Appealing up the chain of command, General Smith wrote to the quartermaster general in Washington, asking him to inform Barney that the order was being written from the office of the secretary of war. Until that letter actually came from Washington, however, Barney still declined to act. Another naval captain in Baltimore ordered Lieutenant Rutter, Barney's second in command, to raise the ships. This time it was Rutter who declined, feeling that he could not obey an order from someone outside Captain Barney's command. When Barney heard of the attempt to go around him he threatened to resign. With an ego bruised yet again, he wrote that he conceived himself "superseded in my command. . . . [S]tung to the quick . . . [and] suffering severe and excruciating pain" from his wound, he opted to retire to his home at Elkridge. Two days after Christmas, Barney received an official order from Washington to use his flotillamen to raise the ships. In fury, he wrote a scathing letter to Congress.

A good military leader should have his mission and the interests of his men as his foremost concerns. Barney's natural and acquired leadership abilities and loyalty to his men were well known. In his passionate letter Barney described how his flotillamen set out to help defend Washington clothed for the heat of a tidewater August. They were forced to leave all their belongings behind because they lacked transportation. They had to manually tow their heavy naval guns and carry their ammunition on their backs. When the flotillamen finally were able to unite with the army at Bladensburg, they were fed only biscuit and water for three days. Their gallantry during the ensuing battle was clearly established, but during the retreat the army quartermasters and commissaries refused them assistance. With the fall of Washington, the remnants of the flotillamen were marched to Baltimore, then back to Washington, down the banks of the Potomac, and back to Baltimore once again. During all this time the sailors' clothing consisted of linen shirts and rough cotton pants. With the constant maneuvering they had little time to wash or repair their garments. When the survivors of the Bladensburg battle finally reassembled with the other flotilla unit positioned for the defense of Baltimore, the combined force beat the enemy and helped to save the city from capture and destruction. As the cool autumn set in, sickness and exhaustion took a heavier toll on 150 of these men than the muskets and cannons of the enemy had done. As the "reward for their bravery" they were given no wages and forced to wear summer rags to cover their emaciated backs. Barney castigated the Senate for defeating the bill that would have provided relief for his men. He countered the Senate's belief that assisting his men would set a bad precedent by saying, "But have they not set a precedent which may be more fatal to the Nation—if merit is not to be rewarded, who will strive for it?" Although he nowhere overtly stated it, Barney considered being asked to raise the sunken ships of civilian merchants, particularly in the harsh winter, an insult to himself and his men.[4]

This eloquent plea went unanswered. Barney's men were forced to sell what military warrants they had for fifty cents on the dollar to buy food and provisions for their families. The men became gaunt, sickly, and depressed. Their wives were reduced to begging for food and clothing in the streets. This was more than the commodore could tolerate as a naval officer. The flotillamen had given their allegiance to a cause. They might have continued that allegiance if they could see a purpose to their duty. Humiliation and death were both bearable for a cause, however foolish or false, good or damnable. Aimlessness, however, maimed and killed the spirit of warriors. Most of the flotillamen left when their enlistment expired; a few chose to desert. Barney wrote to Congress one last time describing his frustrations with the chain of command. The letter ended with his resignation from naval service and enclosed Barney's commission.[5]

History does not reveal whether it was Acting Secretary of the Navy Benjamin Homans or the new secretary of the navy, Benjamin Crowninshield, who prevailed on Barney to withdraw his resignation, but one of these gentlemen was persuasive. Barney put aside his bitterness at his inability to help his men. In accepting his reappointment he wrote, "I do most solemnly pledge myself not to quit the service or lay down my sword untill death or a peace such as our Country ought to obtain, External Enemies or Internall Traitors not withstanding."[6]

As Barney set about recruiting replacements for the many flotillamen who had left the service, the Treaty of Ghent was ratified on 17 February 1815, ending the conflict with Britain. The war ended without the feeling of triumph that had characterized the conclusion of the Revolution. The contest seemed to signify nothing, and the people had lost their passion for fighting for a common cause. The nation failed to comprehend that it had participated in the maturation process of a remarkable and novel political adventure.

With the war with Britain at an end, U.S. leaders could focus their attention on the dey of Algiers, who had taken advantage of the war to renew his seizures of American vessels. Commodore Barney volunteered his plans for a naval strategy and an operation in the region, but it is not clear if his suggestions were implemented.[7] Barney's last order as a naval officer was to form his command into a crew for the ship *Ontario*.[8] This turned out to be impossible. Many of his flotillamen had left the service and were now engaged in the merchant service at higher wages; the few who remained were no longer a viable unit, and the group was demobilized. Ironically, all the officers and men received a bonus of three months' pay at demobilization.

At this, Barney's *final* resignation from the navy, Secretary of the Navy Benjamin Crowninshield praised his "vigilant, active and brave (service) as commander, to whom your Government and your Country have unequivocally bestowed the mead of praise, and the well-earned tribute of thanks."[9] Joshua Barney's pension for his many years of service to a grateful nation was six hundred dollars per year. Barney spent the first few months of his retirement trying to settle past accounts with the navy. The commodore seemed obsessed with financial matters concerning the government. In the end, he enjoyed little success and came to believe that "Congress one and all ought to be hung, they have destroyed the Nation by delays and folly."[10]

Congress had indeed demonstrated folly in failing to build a strong navy before the war and substituting many small gunboats for the frigates that were needed, in effect sending a swarm of mosquitoes to confront the greatest navy in the world. Once the war began, Congress tried to construct an adequate navy. At first, Englishmen scoffed at the new American ships, but within months these ships had humbled the pride of Britain and its great navy. Up until that time the British had admitted to only five defeats in approximately two hundred single-ship engagements. In the two and one-half years during which they fought the ships of the United States they were defeated in fifteen of eighteen single-ship battles. Strangely, in the face of these losses, this second American war is little noticed in British history.

On 29 April 1815 Barney was asked by President Madison to carry some dispatches to the American peace commissioners still residing in Europe. Barney was always open to receive an honorable commission from his government, and he was pleased to have the opportunity to go to sea again, although this time only as a passenger. The commodore celebrated his fifty-sixth birthday in the now-familiar port of Plymouth, England. His wound from Bladensburg became painful, and he suffered from sickness throughout the tedious trip. This was Joshua Barney's last sea voyage. On his return to the United States on 13 October Barney retreated to his home, where he uncharacteristically became peevish, irritable, and a recluse.

Reaching the autumn of a career brings about retrospection, regret, and sometimes recrimination. Collecting awards and garnering tokens of reminiscence take on an importance that seemed trivial only a few years before. In those arduous days of physical pain and fading self-confidence Barney became concerned about his place in history. He petitioned the legislature of Pennsylvania for permission to have a replica of the presentation sword made to replace the one that had been stolen some years earlier in Paris. The resolution passed, but Barney was deeply hurt when he learned that there had been heated opposition to it during the debate.[11] The *Hyder-Ally* incident was Barney's fondest personal military achievement, but its significance had already been forgotten. He applied for a consul position, but his letters "met with disappointment" from the "cold neglect of those in power."[12] Barney started to show symptoms of clinical depression. He became convinced that the president no longer held him in high esteem. The mental pain acted in synergy with his physical discomfort.

The spring of 1816 brought warmer weather and a rise in the commodore's spirits. Although he was not a poor man, Barney felt the need to secure his financial future. He had earned and lost a number of small fortunes during his naval and business careers. The one holding that he had not benefited from was his land in Kentucky. Barney and his family planned a trip that would take them to this western commonwealth for the fall. When they reached Frankfort, the state capital, the day after Christmas, the whole family was feted with a grand banquet. Kentucky legislators and veterans of both wars against Great Britain made grandiose public speeches honoring the commodore. It was the perfect tonic for Barney's bruised ego. He was offered a particularly grand toast four days later in Louisville: "Commodore Barney, our gallant guest—Two wars, the land and the ocean, bear witness that he is a patriot and soldier!"[13] In response he enumerated the facts of his combat in seventeen battles during the Revolution and nine battles during the War of 1812. Although Barney had been captured six times, he maintained that he had been defeated only in his last battle. Barney went on to say that if he had had two thousand Kentuckians at his side rather than seven thousand Marylanders, the outcome would have been different and the city of Washington would have been spared. This statement made for good politics in Kentucky, but it must have generated some anger back in Maryland. It did not really matter; Joshua Barney always spoke his mind. He was at a point in life where a good insult was like a bracing sip of whiskey. He might lash out in frustration, but Barney was extremely proud to be called a Marylander.

The journey both buoyed him and compromised his health. He returned over the Appalachian Mountains to Baltimore during the spring of 1817. Barney's old friend James Monroe now occupied the White House and, as an act of political patronage, appointed Joshua Barney naval port officer of Baltimore. The job paid a handsome salary. It was also a "good anchor to windward" in case his investments in Kentucky did not turn out to be profitable. The commodore placed his son William Bedford Barney in charge of establishing the boundaries of his Kentucky land and developing the fifty thousand acres near what is now Fort Knox.

Barney held on to his appointed naval post as long as possible for its security and prestige, but by September 1818 he had become weary of administrative work. In late October he sold his estate at Elkridge and decided to retire with his family, servants, and slaves to Kentucky. As they headed west, Barney became ill on a river flatboat only a short distance from Pittsburgh. The practice of medicine was then more palliative than curative, so he was forced to fight for his life alone. Although he managed to hang on for about a week, fifty-nine-year-old Joshua Barney finally died, apparently from a thrombosis from his leg wound. On 1 December 1818 a British musket ball—and thus, symbolically, the hated British—caused Barney's death. The lead slug was removed at his autopsy and presented to William Barney. The bullet is now housed at the Museum of the Daughters of the American Revolution in Washington, D.C.

Joshua Barney did not die alone; most of his family and servants were by his side. Yet he died among strangers, people he fought for but never knew. The city of Baltimore commissioned Rembrandt Peale to paint a posthumous portrait of Barney that now hangs in the Maryland Historical Society in Baltimore. But the great city on the Chesapeake is not the resting place for its most distinguished maritime hero. Barney's grave is under a modest military monument in the Allegheny Cemetery in Pittsburgh, far from the sea he loved.

Some may describe Joshua Barney as having "more sail than ballast," to use a naval expression meaning "more dash than discretion." He was courageous, cunning, and creative, yet at times he was also vain, volatile, and vengeful, as well as opportunistic, arrogant, and petty; and sometimes he was an irresponsible "loose cannon." On the other hand, perhaps Barney's sail and ballast were in good balance, particularly for the times in which he lived. Those who write post-contemporaneous biographies assume that they have greater insight into the character of the subject than those who knew him. In truth, the best a biographer can do is recite facts and wonder why. A critical analysis of this man's extraordinary life, with its many complex facets, would be an exercise in sophistry.

Barney's portrait appears both in a commemorative garland of Revolutionary War naval heroes and in a similar one commissioned by N. Currier of naval heroes of the War of 1812—a sort of naval "all star team" of the time. He is the only person to have won dual recognition. Many of Barney's exploits were set into rhyme. It thus seems appropriate to close the commodore's biography with a verse written by Capt. James Hopwood that might serve to summarize his character.

> *On the strength of one link in the cable,*
> *Dependeth the might of the chain.*
> *Who knows when thou mayest be tested?*
> *So live that thou bearest the strain.*[14]

Joshua Barney's link to the anchor cable of life did indeed bear the strain.

❧ EPILOGUE ❧

Joshua Barney lived on in the four naval ships that were named for him. The first was the 143-foot, 512-ton steamer *Commodore Barney,* a Civil War wooden ironclad gunboat. Purchased at New York on 2 October 1861, the shallow-draft side-wheeler was a double-ended converted harbor ferry. On 8 August 1863 the *Commodore Barney* struck an electrically operated torpedo (mine) in the James River about six miles south of Fort Darling. The torpedo lifted the bow of the vessel about ten feet out of the water, disabling it and throwing forty of its crew into the river.[1] The damaged vessel was towed downriver, where it ran into a Confederate shore battery, and though hit by dozens of artillery shells and some small-arms fire, made it safely to Newport News. The ironclad was restored but did not engage in any further significant combat. The *Commodore Barney* was sold at action to the Fulton Ferry Company of New York on 20 July 1865 and continued service as a New York ferry under the name *Ethan Allen.* There is no clear record of when it was taken out of civilian service.

A second ship was the 175-ton torpedo boat *Barney* (TB 25). Laid down at the Bath Iron Works in Bath, Maine, on 3 January 1900 and launched 21 October 1901, the fast vessel was the first of three in the Barney class of small torpedo boats, each carrying three torpedo tubes.[2] The boat was used as a training ship from 1912 through 1917. Its last naval duty was at Norfolk, where it patrolled Hampton Roads and the outer Chesapeake Bay. The *Barney* was taken to Philadelphia on 17 January 1919, decommissioned 11 March 1919, and sold for scrap on 19 July 1920.

The third vessel to bear Barney's name was a World War I Wickes-class destroyer, the *Barney II* (DD-149), which displaced 1,154 tons and was 314 feet long. Classified as a flush deck "four stacker," the *Barney* mounted two fore and aft 4-inch guns. The keel was laid on 26 March

1918 and launched on 5 September 1918 by William Cramp and Sons
Ship and Engine Building Company of Philadelphia. Miss Nannie Dornin
Barney, a great-granddaughter of Commodore Barney, served as the
ship's sponsor at its commissioning on 14 March 1919. The USS *Barney*
reported to Division 19, Atlantic Fleet, and engaged in fleet exercises and
maneuvers along the East Coast until 30 June 1922, when it was taken
out of commission at Philadelphia. Recommissioned on 1 May 1930, the
Barney operated on the East Coast and in the Caribbean until it tran-
sited the Panama Canal in February 1932 to participate in fleet exercises
off San Francisco. It remained on the West Coast for some years and in
1935 cruised to Alaska, Hawaii, and Puget Sound. On returning to the
East Coast, the *Barney* was decommissioned in November 1936, only to
be recommissioned again on 4 October 1939 to serve on patrol duty.
Between December 1941 and November 1943 the *Barney* was assigned to
the Caribbean area, escorting convoys between Trinidad and Guantá-
namo Bay, Cuba. On 18 September 1942 the *Barney* collided with the
destroyer USS *Greer* (DD-145), resulting in severe damage. After extensive
repairs, the *Barney* served as an escort for two convoy crossings to North
Africa during the early spring of 1944. From May 1944 until February
1945 the destroyer returned to escort duty in the Caribbean. In March
1945 it was assigned to training exercises with submarines in Long Island
and Block Island Sounds. Decommissioned shortly after the war, it was
sold for scrap on 13 October 1946. The USS *Barney* received one battle
star for its escort of Convoy UGS 37 (11–12 April 1944).[3]

The most recent vessel to bear the name *Barney* is the Charles F.
Adams–class guided missile destroyer DDG-4. The 432-meter, 3,370-ton
ship was built at the New York Shipbuilding Company. The keel was laid
10 August 1959, and the ship was launched on 10 December 1960 and
commissioned on 11 August 1962. It was decommissioned in Philadelphia
on 17 December 1990 and subsequently scrapped.[4]

In an attempt to remember the commodore in a more historical context, a replica of the miniature ship *Federalist* that Barney sailed from
Baltimore to Mount Vernon and presented to George Washington was
constructed and is currently displayed in Baltimore-Washington International Airport. Recent interest in the 1814 Battle of Bladensburg has
included marine archaeological excavations of the scuttled gunboats
from Barney's flotilla under the auspices of Maryland's Calvert Marine
Museum; a study of the site by the author and historian Donald

Shomette; and the construction of a scaled-down replica of a row galley designed by William Doughty. The latter is on display at Waterfront Park in Prince George's County, Maryland. In addition, the Barney Family Historical Association, many of whose members are descendants of the commodore, has published a book called *Genealogy of the Barney Family in America* and produces a periodic newsletter.

❧ Notes ❧

Chapter 1. Molding a Mariner

1. Mary Barney, *Biographical Memoir of the Late Joshua Barney*, 4.
2. Ibid., 8; Hulbert Footner, *Sailor of Fortune: The Life and Adventures of Commodore Joshua Barney*, 3.
3. M. Barney, *Memoir*, 14.
4. From Joshua Barney, *Autobiography*, Daughters of the American Revolution (DAR) Library, Washington, D.C.
5. Ibid.
6. Joseph J. Ellis, *American Sphinx*, 75; Thomas Jefferson and John Adams to American Commissioners, 28 March 1786, in *The Papers of Thomas Jefferson*, ed. Julian P. Boyd, 10:357–9.
7. Charles Petrie, *King Charles III of Spain*, 157–60.
8. Footner, *Sailor of Fortune*, 11.

Chapter 2. The Continental Navy

1. Quoted in Peleg D. Harrison, *The Stars and Stripes and Other American Flags*, 43.
2. G. S. Graham, "Considerations on the War of American Independence," 23.
3. Edgar Stanton Maclay, *A History of the United States Navy from 1775 to 1898*, 1:44–45.
4. L. H. Butterfield, ed., *Diary and Autobiography of John Adams*, discourse of 7 October 1777, 2:198.
5. M. Barney, *Memoir*, 30; J. Thomas Scharf, *Chronicles of Baltimore*, 236.
6. William B. Clark et al., eds., *Naval Documents of the American Revolution*, 4:598 (henceforth *NDAR*).
7. Ibid., 5:18. The official inventory of captured arms was seventy-one cannons, fifteen cohorns (mortars), six thousand shells, ten thousand assorted shots, and 140 grenades. One of the cannons is currently located at Fort Phoenix in Fairhaven, Massachusetts.

8. Ibid., 17–18. The heavy iron matchstick ready for application to the touch-hole of a cannon mentioned in this sentence is a focal point in Mary Barney's *Memoir* (p. 33), which claims that Joshua Barney hurled this flaming spike at the captain's head. Captain Hallock ducked, and the point stuck into the frame of the after cabin door. This incident is not described in Barney's autobiography but is implied by the marginal entry: "note; the Match staff" (*NDAR*, 4:597). The story might be an embellishment making young Barney appear heroic.

9. Ibid., 4:924.

10. Ibid., 6:766, 782.

11. M. Barney, *Memoir*, 44.

12. Footner, *Sailor of Fortune*, 32.

13. *NDAR*, 6:1387.

14. Ibid., 7:525.

15. Ibid., 7:508.

16. Ibid., 7:601. The British Anglicized the Italian name "Andrea" to "Andrew."

17. Ibid., 7:586–88.

18. Ibid., 7:1018–19.

19. Samuel Flagg Bemis, *The Diplomacy of the American Revolution*, 123. Over the years this incident has grown in historical importance. In 1939 a plaque was presented to St. Eustatius bearing the signature of President Franklin D. Roosevelt, a descendant of Dutch settlers: "In commemoration of the salute of the flag of the United States fired at this fort November 16, 1776, by the order of Johannes de Graaff, Governor of St. Eustatius, in reply to the national gun salute fired by the Brig-of-War *Andrew* [*sic*] *Doria*. Here the sovereignty of the United States of America was first formally acknowledged to a national vessel by a foreign official." J. F. Jameson, in "St. Eustatius in the American Revolution," 691, presented evidence that the Grand Union flag was first saluted in St. Croix by the Danes in mid-October three weeks earlier, a view that has gained wide acceptance. Most histories state that the first naval salute to the American flag was by the French fleet at Quiberon Bay on 14 February 1778. The recipient was the ship *Ranger* commanded by Capt. John Paul Jones. This was the first *governmentally sanctioned salute* to an American flag, but the flag was not the same design as that flown by the *Andrea Doria*. On 14 June 1777 the Continental Congress adopted a "flag of thirteen stripes, alternate red and white [and ordered] that the union be thirteen stars, white in a blue field representing a new constellation." In a curious historical coincidence, during that same hour Congress also ordered John Paul Jones to command the ship *Ranger*. He later sentimentally wrote, "That flag and I were twins; born in the same hour from the same womb of destiny. We cannot be parted in life or death." On 14 June Americans still celebrate Flag Day in remembrance of Con-

gress's approval of the new official nation emblem, a variation of which Jones flew from the *Ranger.*

20. *NDAR,* 10:435.

21. Ibid., 10:568.

Chapter 3. Captive and Privateer

1. M. Barney, *Memoir,* 76.

2. Barney to the Continental Congress, 26 July 1780, *Records of the Continental Congress,* no. 41, 1:301.

3. Ibid., 1:285.

4. Henry Theodore Tuckerman, *The Life of Silas Talbot,* 240.

5. *London Courant and Westminster Chronicle,* 29 December 1780; Footner, *Sailor of Fortune,* 76.

6. Footner, *Sailor of Fortune,* 78–79.

7. Thomas Bradford Papers, Pennsylvania Historical Society, British naval prisoners' correspondence, 1:70; Footner, *Sailor of Fortune,* 83.

Chapter 4. Home: The *Hyder-Ally*

1. M. Barney, *Memoir,* 100–101.

2. Historians have not definitively identified this mysterious woman, although some believe she was a mistress of the emperor.

3. John Trumbull, *Reminiscences of His Own Times,* 80–89.

4. Ibid., 82.

5. Charles Henry Lincoln, *Naval Records of the American Revolution,* no. 41, 1:348; Footner, *Sailor of Fortune,* 102.

6. Fred Lewis Pattee, ed., *The Poems of Philip Freneau,* 2:149–53; M. Barney, *Memoir,* 119.

7. Lincoln, *Naval Records of the American Revolution,* no. 41, 1:348.

8. The Pennsylvania legislature did not officially pass the resolution authorizing the purchase of the *Hyder-Ally* for the defense of the Delaware until 9 April 1782. Thus it was not the property of the commonwealth when it won its most famous battle.

9. M. Barney, *Memoir,* 112–17 and appendix 1, 303; Marion V. Brewington, "The Battle of Delaware Bay, 1782," 432.

10. *Niles' Weekly Register,* 13 November 1813, 5:190; M. Barney, *Memoir,* 116.

11. James Fenimore Cooper, *The History of the Navy of the United States of America,* 120.

12. Footner, *Sailor of Fortune,* 114.

13. Pattee, *Poems,* 149–53, 170–80; M. Barney, *Memoir,* 120–22; "Captain Barney's Victory over the *General Monk,*" microfilm no. 50508, American Antiquarian Society, Worcester, Mass.

14. Pennsylvania Archives, 5:9.

CHAPTER 5. FINALE: END OF A FIRST CAREER

1. M. Barney, *Memoir*, 124–25.
2. Ibid., 125.
3. E. James Ferguson and John Catanzariti, eds., *Papers of Robert Morris, 1781–1784*, 5:217–18.
4. Pennsylvania Archives, 1:9.
5. M. Barney, *Memoir*, 134.
6. Ibid., 137.
7. John Kenedy, *The American Songster*, 114–16.
8. The King's Passport, no. 137, in Lincoln, *Naval Records of the American Revolution*, 2:413.
9. M. Barney, *Memoir*, 141.
10. Pennsylvania Archives, 1:9.
11. M. Barney, *Memoir*, 144.
12. (Mrs.) Reginald De Koven, *The Life and Letters of John Paul Jones*, 1:239.
13. Many references to this dispatch and subsequent dispatches involving Barney and the *General Washington* are found in Edmund C. Burnett, ed., *Letters of Members of the Continental Congress*, 6:70–75, 463, 465, 469, 472.
14. M. Barney, *Memoir*, 146.
15. Footner, *Sailor of Fortune*, 132.
16. M. Barney, *Memoir*, 150.
17. Ibid., 150–51.

CHAPTER 6. MERCHANT AND POLITICIAN

1. M. Barney, *Memoir*, 156.
2. *Maryland Gazette and Baltimore Advertiser*, 2 May 1788.
3. John C. Fitzpatrick, ed., *The Diaries of George Washington: 1748–1799*, 9 July 1788, 3:365.
4. George Washington to William Smith and others, 8 January 1788, in *The Writings of George Washington*, ed. John C. Fitzpatrick, 3:516.
5. Footner, *Sailor of Fortune*, 165.
6. Scharf, *Chronicles*, 250–51.
7. Fitzpatrick, *Washington Diaries*, 24 July 1788, 3:394–95.
8. William Wright Abbot, ed., *The Papers of George Washington*, Presidential series, entry of 17 April 1789, 2:64.
9. Ann Hollingsworth Wharton, *Martha Washington*, 187–90.
10. Scharf, *Chronicles*, 252–54.
11. Tench Coxe to Barney, 19 August 1790, in *The Papers of George Washington*, ed. Dorothy Twohig, Presidential series, 6:438, n. 3.
12. Irving King, *Washington's Coast Guard*, 27, 79; Edward Beck, "Joshua Barney," 1:632–35.

13. Ibid

14. Barney to Washington, 15 September 1790, in Twohig, *Washington Papers,* 6:437–38.

15. Hamilton to Washington, 29 September 1790, in Syrett and Cooke, *Hamilton Papers,* 7:78.

16. James McHenry to Hamilton, 3 January 1791, in Syrett and Cooke, *Hamilton Papers,* 7:409–10. Barney's petition for compensation was presented to the House of Representatives on 12 January 1791, but the bill was defeated (*House Journal* 1:353, 385).

17. Barney to Washington, 15 September 1790, in Syrett and Cooke, *Hamilton Papers,* 13:58; Twohig, *Washington Papers,* 6:437–38.

18. Twohig, *Washington Papers,* 7:391–92; Footner, *Sailor of Fortune,* 172–73.

19. Gustavus Vasa, "The Story of Olaudah Equiano (also known as Gustavus Vassa)," in *The Slave's Narratives,* ed. Charles T. Davis and Henry Louis Gates Jr., provides an autobiographical account written in 1814 of the capture, separation, and transport of a slave.

20. Twohig, *Washington Papers* 6:438, note, autographed signed letter, Library of Congress, George Washington Papers.

21. Ibid., 7:391–92.

22. Barney to Washington, 21 February 1791, in Abbot, *Washington Papers,* 7:391–93.

23. M. Barney, *Memoir,* 174–75.

24. Thomas Mason, Robert A. Rutland, and Jeanne K. Sisson, *The Papers of James Mason,* 5:280–81; Archives of Island Records of 1794, Island Record Office, Spanish Town, Jamaica, W.I.

25. Barney to Edmund Randolph, 27 March 1794, quoted in Footner, *Sailor of Fortune,* 187.

26. Ibid., 187.

27. Twohig, *Washington Papers,* Journal Proceedings 1793–1797, 287.

28. Footner, *Sailor of Fortune,* 187–88.

29. Randolph to Hamilton, 16 June 1794, in Syrett and Cooke, *Hamilton Papers,* 16:490. The secretary of state denied fiscal responsibility for $575.05 to John Hollins of Baltimore for the hiring of the *Slavery* for Barney's rescue. Although the president had ordered a ship to be sent, evidently payment was not to come from the budget of the Department of State.

CHAPTER 7. FRANCE: CAPITAINE DE VAISSEAU DU PREMIER

1. William M. Fowler Jr., *Silas Talbot,* 92.

2. Footner, *Sailor of Fortune,* 93.

3. M. Barney, *Memoir,* 327–28.

4. Footner, *Sailor of Fortune,* 202.

5. Hunter Miller, *Treaties and Other International Acts of the United States of America,* 2:261.

6. Hamilton to Phineas Bond, 15 September 1796, in Syrett and Cooke, *Hamilton Papers,* 20:325–27.

7. G. La Roërie and J. Vivielle, *Navires et Marins,* vol. 2, pl. 7, costume de marins française, no. 1, matelot, 1792.

8. Footner, *Sailor of Fortune,* 208.

9. *Annals of Congress,* 1796 (opening of the second session of the Fourth Congress); Fitzpatrick, *Writings of Washington,* 35:314.

10. Footner, *Sailor of Fortune,* 208.

11. Maclay, *History of the United States Navy from 1775 to 1898,* 1:164.

12. Extract of a letter from an unidentified gentlemen from New York regarding capture by the French privateer *Flower of the Sea,* 2 September 1798, in Dudley W. Knox, ed., *Naval Documents Related to the Quasi-War between the United States and France,* 1:200.

13. Benjamin Stoddert to Thomas Truxtun, 7 March 1799, in ibid., 1:427.

14. Footner, *Sailor of Fortune,* 226.

Chapter 8. Rebirth of a Patriot

1. Madison to Jefferson, 18 August and 22 September 1804, quoted in Irving Bryant, *James Madison,* 4:228.

2. "Amendatory Report of the Committee of Elections, 7 December 1807, House of Representatives, 10th Congress of the United States," in Early American Imprints, Microfilm, American Antiquarian Society, Worcester, Mass., 1970.

3. Register of Saint Paul's Church, 24 April 1809, Maryland Historical Society, Baltimore, Md.

4. Barney to Jefferson, 4 July 1807, Jefferson Correspondence, Library of Congress.

5. Campaign quotes, *Baltimore Whig,* 5 September, 17 September, 3 October 1810.

6. Ibid.

7. Barney to James Monroe, 14 April 1811, Monroe Correspondence, Library of Congress.

8. Christopher Deshon to Barney, 11 July 1812, quoted in Jerome Garitee, *The Republic's Private Navy,* 62–63.

9. For political reasons, the coveted number 1 commission was also issued to James McCulloch, the collector of customs for Baltimore, and George Stiles, a prominent merchant and subsequent mayor of Baltimore. Ibid., 152.

10. M. Barney, *Memoir,* 282–84.

11. Ibid., 282.

12. Log of the *Rossie,* U.S. Naval Academy Library, Annapolis, Md.; William S. Dudley, *The Naval War of 1812,* 1:248–60.

13. John P. Cranwell and William B. Crane, *Men of Marque: A History of Private Armed Vessels out of Baltimore during the War of 1812,* 68; Horace Beck, *Folklore and the Sea,* 325.

14. Dudley, *Naval War of 1812,* 1:449.

15. Garitee, *Private Navy,* 217.

16. Dudley, *Naval War of 1812,* 1:449.

17. Ibid., 1:248–60.

18. Garitee, *Private Navy,* 187.

19. Ibid., 100.

20. John A. McManemin, *Captains of the Privateers of the War of 1812,* 89.

CHAPTER 9. DEFENSE OF TIDEWATER MARYLAND

1. George Armistead to Samuel Smith, n.d., Samuel Smith Papers, 1813, Maryland Historical Society; Walter Lord, *The Dawn's Early Light,* 274.

2. The bill for both flags was $574.44. The receipt for this payment is preserved in the Star Spangled Banner Museum in Baltimore, Md.

3. Gilbert Auchinleck, *A History of the War between Great Britain and the United States during the Years 1812, 1813, and 1814,* 43; Barney to John Paul Jones, 4 July 1813, in Dudley, *Naval War of 1812,* 2:374–76.

4. Footner, *Sailor of Fortune,* 262.

5. Jones to Barney, in Dudley, *Naval War of 1812,* 2:376–77.

6. *Baltimore American and Commercial Advertiser,* 25 December 1813.

7. Donald Shomette, *Flotilla: Battle for the Patuxent,* 33.

8. Letters of the Officers of Ships of War, Naval Registry Office, London.

9. There is no record of the first name of the Mr. Parran in this incident. According to Maryland census records of 1814, he may have been John Parran, a resolute Federalist from the southern Maryland peninsula, or an outspoken relative, Dr. Thomas Parran, a Revolutionary War veteran.

10. Shomette, *Flotilla,* 106.

11. Ibid., 80; Barney to Louis Barney, 22 June 1814, Dreer Collection, Pennsylvania Historical Society, Philadelphia.

12. Shomette, *Flotilla,* 95.

13. Ibid., 97.

14. Ibid., 105.

15. Footner, *Sailor of Fortune,* 290; Barney-Wilson letters, *Baltimore Federal Gazette,* 16, 17 February 1815.

16. M. Barney, *Memoir,* 316–17.

17. Anthony S. Pitch, *The Burning of Washington: The British Invasion of 1814,* 85.

18. Cooper, *History of the Navy,* 337.

19. Gaillard Hunt, ed., *First Forty Years of Washington Society in the Family Letters of Margaret Bayard Smith,* 113.

20. Shomette, *Flotilla*, 191.
21. Quoted in Footner, *Sailor of Fortune*, 285.
22. *Niles' Weekly Register*, 7:24.
23. Cooper, *The History of the Navy of the United States of America*, 340.
24. For a brief time in 1914 a "Star Spangled" 4,200-pound nun buoy marked the putative spot on the Patapsco River where Key observed the bombardment of Fort McHenry and penned his poem.
25. Cooper, *The History of the Navy of the United States of America*, 340.

CHAPTER 10. TWILIGHT OF THE COMMODORE

1. M. Barney, *Memoir*, 318–19.
2. An Act, U.S. House of Representatives, 2 November 1814, *Annals of Congress*, Microfilm, American Antiquarian Society, 1976; Footner, *Sailor of Fortune*, 293.
3. Quoted in M. Barney, *Memoir*, 272; Footner, *Sailor of Fortune*, 294.
4. Footner, *Sailor of Fortune*, 295.
5. Ibid., 297.
6. Ibid.
7. Ibid.
8. Ibid.
9. Joshua Barney to Commodore Jacob Lew, 23 January 1815, Crowninshield Papers, Box 8, Peabody-Essex Museum, Salem, Mass.
10. William M. Fowler Jr., *Jack Tars and Commodores*, 261.
11. Footner, *Sailor of Fortune*, 300.
12. Ibid., 300.
13. M. Barney, *Memoir*, 286.
14. Hopwood, "The Laws of the Navy," in Leland P. Lovette, *Naval Customs, Traditions and Usage*, 380.

EPILOGUE

1. C. C. March, comp., *Official Records of the Union and Confederate Navies in the War of Rebellion*, ser. 2, vol. 1, pts. 1–4, 62–63; Report of the damage sustained by the USS *Commodore Barney*, in ibid., ser. 1, 9:247–48.
2. James L. Mooney et al., eds., *Dictionary of American Naval Fighting Ships*, 1:96–97.
3. Ibid., 97.
4. Richard Sharpe, ed., *Jane's Fighting Ships 1991–92*, 94th ed., 373.

~⊰ Bibliography ⊱~

Manuscript Collections

Archives of Island Records, Spanish Town, Jamaica
   Archives of Island Records of 1794
Daughters of the American Revolution Library, Washington, D.C.
   Joshua Barney, Autobiography
Library of Congress, Washington, D.C.
   Defence of the Chesapeake, by Joshua Barney, Manuscripts Division
   Thomas Jefferson Correspondence
Maryland Historical Society, Baltimore
   Register of Saint Paul's Church
   Samuel Smith Papers
Naval Registry Office, London, England
   Letters of the Officers of Ships of War
   The British in America, Letters
Peabody-Essex Museum, Salem, Massachusetts
   Crowninshield Papers
Pennsylvania Archives, Philadelphia
Pennsylvania Historical Society, Philadelphia
   Barney Papers, Dreer Collection
   Thomas Bradford Papers
Star Spangled Banner Museum, Baltimore, Maryland
   Receipt for Sewing Flag
U.S. Naval Academy Library, Annapolis, Maryland
   Log of the *Rossie*

Newspapers

Baltimore American and Commercial Advertiser
Baltimore Federal Gazette
Baltimore Whig

London Courant and Westminister Chronicle
Maryland Gazette and Baltimore Advertiser
Niles' Weekly Register

PUBLISHED WORKS

Abbot, William Wright, et al., eds. *The Papers of George Washington*. Presidential series. vols. 1-4. Charlottesville: University Press of Virginia, 1987.

Adams, Henry. *The History of the United States of America*. Volumes covering the first and second administrations of James Madison, 1809–13, 1813–17. New York: Charles Scribner's Sons, 1891.

Adams, William Frederick. *Commodore Joshua Barney*. Springfield, Mass.: privately printed, 1912. (This work is a genealogy of the Barney family.)

Ansted, A. *A Dictionary of Sea Terms*. Glasgow, U.K.: James Brown and Son, 1919.

Auchinleck, Gilbert. *A History of the War between Great Britain and the United States during the Years 1812, 1813, and 1814*. 1855. Reprint. Toronto: Arms and Armor Press and Pendragon House, 1972.

Axelrad, Jacob. *Philip Freneau: Champion of Democracy*. Austin: University of Texas Press, 1967.

Barney, Mary. *Biographical Memoir of the Late Joshua Barney. From Autobiographical Notes and Journals in Possession of His Family, and Other Authentic Sources*. Boston: Gray and Bowen, 1832.

Beck, Edward. "Joshua Barney." In *Dictionary of American Biography*, vol. 1, ed. Allen Johnson and Dumas Maloner. New York: Charles Scribner's Sons, 1943.

Beck, Horace. *Folklore and the Sea*. Middletown, Conn.: Mystic Seaport–Wesleyan University Press, 1973.

Bemis, Samuel Flagg. *The Diplomacy of the American Revolution*. New York: D. Appleton-Century, 1935.

Bixby, W. K. *Letters and Recollections of George Washington*. New York: Page and Company, 1906.

Boyd, Julian P., ed. *The Papers of Thomas Jefferson*. 21 vols. Princeton: Princeton University Press, 1950.

Bradford, James C. *Command under Sail: Makers of the American Naval Tradition, 1775–1850*. Annapolis: Naval Institute Press, 1985.

Bryant, Irving. *James Madison*. Indianapolis: Bobbs-Merrill, 1961.

Brewington, Marion V. "The Battle of Delaware Bay, 1782." *U.S. Naval Institute Proceedings* 65, no. 2 (1941): 432.

Burnett, Edmund C., ed., *Letters of Members of the Continental Congress*. 10 vols. Baltimore: Lord Baltimore Press, 1934.

Butterfield, L. H., ed. *Diary and Autobiography of John Adams*. Cambridge: Belknap Press of Harvard University Press, 1961.

"Captain Barney's Victory over the *General Monk*." Microfilm no. 50508, American Antiquarian Society, Worcester, Mass.

Carroll, John Alexander, and Mary Wells Ashworth. *George Washington*. Vol. 7. New York: Charles Scribner's Sons, 1957.

Chapelle, Howard I. *The History of the American Sailing Navy: The Ships and Their Development*. New York: Bonanza Books, 1949.

Clark, William B., et al., eds. *Naval Documents of the American Revolution*. 9 vols. to date. Washington, D.C.: U.S. Government Printing Office, 1964–.

Coggins, Jack. *Ships and Seamen of the American Revolution*. Harrisburg, Pa.: Stackpole Books, 1969.

Commager, Henry Steele, and Richard B. Morris. *The Spirit of 'Seventy-six: The Story of the American Revolution as Told by Participants*. New York: Bobbs-Merrill, 1958.

Cooper, James Fenimore. *The History of the United States Navy*. Philadelphia: Thomas, Cowperthwait and Company, 1845.

Cordingly, David. *Under the Black Flag*. New York: Random House, 1995.

Cranwell, John P., and William B. Crane. *Men of Marque: A History of Private Armed Vessels out of Baltimore during the War of 1812*. New York: W. W. Norton, 1940.

Crawford, Michael J. *Naval Documents of the American Revolution*. October 1, 1777–December 31, 1777. Washington, D.C.: Naval Historical Center, Department of the Navy, 1996.

Davis, Charles T., and Henry Louis Gates Jr., eds. *The Slave's Narrative*. New York: Oxford University Press, 1985.

De Koven, (Mrs.) Reginald. *The Life and Letters of John Paul Jones*. 2 vols. New York: Charles Scribner's Sons, 1913.

de Selincourt, Aubrey. *The Book of the Sea*. New York: W. W. Norton, 1961.

Dudley, William S. *The Naval War of 1812*. 2 vols. to date. Washington, D.C.: Naval Historical Center, Department of the Navy, 1985, 1992.

Durant, Will, and Ariel Durant. *The Age of Napoleon: A History of European Civilization from 1789 to 1815*. New York: Simon and Schuster, 1975.

Early American Imprints. Microfilm. Worcester, Mass.: American Antiquarian Society, 1970.

Ellis, Joseph J. *The American Sphinx: The Character of Thomas Jefferson*. New York: Alfred A. Knopf, 1996.

Ferguson, E. James, and John Catanzariti, eds. *The Papers of Robert Morris, 1781–1784*. 8 vols. to date. Pittsburgh: University of Pittsburgh Press, 1973–.

Fitzpatrick, John C., ed. *The Diaries of George Washington, 1748–1799*. 4 vols. Boston: Houghton Mifflin, 1925.

_____, ed. *Writings of George Washington*. 39 vols. Washington, D.C.: Government Printing Office, 1931–44.

Footner, Hulbert. *Sailor of Fortune: The Life and Adventures of Commodore Joshua Barney*. New York: Harper Brothers, 1940.

Fowler, William M. Jr. *Jack Tars and Commodores: The American Navy, 1783–1815*. Boston: Houghton Mifflin, 1984.

_____. *Silas Talbot: Captain of Old Ironsides*. Mystic, Conn.: Mystic Seaport Press, 1995.

Frost, John. *The Book of the Navy*. New York: D. Appleton and Company, 1842.

_____. *The Pictorial Book of the Commodores: Lives of the Distinguished Commodores of the United States Navy*. New York: Nafts and Cornish, 1845.

Garitee, Jerome R. *The Republic's Private Navy*. Mystic, Conn.: Mystic Seaport Press, 1977.

Gould, Rupert T. *The Marine Chronometer: Its History and Development*. Greenwich, England: National Maritime Museum, 1923. Reprint. Antique Collectors Club, Suffolk, England: Woodbridge, 1989.

Graham, G. S. "Considerations on the War of American Independence." *Bulletin of the Institute of Historical Research* 22 (1949): 23.

Greene, George Washington. *Historical View of the American Revolution*. Boston: Ticknor and Fields, 1865.

Gutridge, Leonard F., and Jay D. Smith. *The Commodores: The U.S. Navy in the Age of Sail*. New York: Harper and Row, 1969.

Harrison, Peleg D. *The Stars and Stripes and Other American Flags*. Boston: Little, Brown, 1906.

Herold, J. Christopher. *The Age of Napoleon*. New York: American Heritage, 1963.

Hunt, Gaillard, ed. *First Forty Years of Washington Society in the Family Letters of Margaret Bayard Smith*. New York: Scribner, 1906.

Jameson, J. F. "St. Eustatius in the American Revolution." *American Historical Review* 8 (1903): 691.

Kenedy, John. *The American Songster*. 3d ed. Baltimore: John Kenedy, 1830.

Kennedy, Paul. *The Rise and Fall of British Naval Mastery*. New York: Charles Scribner's Sons, 1976.

King, Dean. *A Sea of Words*. New York: Henry Holt, 1995.

King, Irving. *Washington's Coast Guard*. Annapolis: Naval Institute Press, 1978.

Knox, Dudley W., ed. *Naval Documents Related to the Quasi-War between the United States and France*. Washington, D.C.: Office of Naval Records and Library, Department of the Navy, 1935–38.

Langguth, A. J. *Patriots: The Men Who Started the American Revolution*. New York: Simon and Schuster, 1988.

Langley, Harold D. *Social Reform in the United States Navy, 1798–1862*. Urbana: University of Illinois Press, 1967.

La Roërie, G., and J. Vivielle. *Navires et Marins*. 2 vols. Paris: Duchartre and Van Buggenhoudt, 1930.

Lincoln, Charles Henry. *Naval Records of the American Revolution 1775–1788*. Manuscripts Division, Library of Congress. Washington, D.C.: Government Printing Office, 1906.

Lloyd, Allen. *The Scorching of Washington: The War of 1812*. Washington, D.C.: Robert B. Luce, 1974.

Lord, Walter. *The Dawn's Early Light*. New York: W. W. Norton, 1972.

Lovette, Leland P. *Naval Customs, Traditions and Usage*. Annapolis: Naval Institute Press, 1939.

Maclay, Edgar Stanton. *A History of American Privateers*. New York: D. Appleton and Company, 1899.

———. *A History of the United States Navy from 1775 to 1898*. 2 vols. New York: D. Appleton and Company, 1898.

March, C. C., comp. *Official Records of the Union and Confederate Navies in the War of Rebellion*. 30 vols. Washington, D.C.: Government Printing Office, 1894–1922.

Mason, Thomas A., Robert A. Rutland, and Jeanne K. Sisson, eds. *The Papers of James Madison*. 17 vols. to date. Charlottesville: University Press of Virginia, 1962–.

McManemin, John A. *Captains of the Privateers of the War of 1812*. Springdale, N.J.: HoHoKus, 1994.

Melville, Herman. *White Jacket; or The World in a Man-of-War*. New York: Grove Press, [1850].

Miller, Hunter. *Treaties and Other International Acts of the United States of America, 1776–1863*. 8 vols. Washington, D.C.: Government Printing Office, 1931–48.

Mooney, James L., et al., eds. *Dictionary of American Naval Fighting Ships*. 8 vols. Washington, D.C.: Naval Historical Center, 1959–81.

Morison, Samuel Eliot. *John Paul Jones*. Boston: Little, Brown, 1959.

Norton, Louis Arthur. "The Second Captain: Silas Talbot of the USS *Constitution*." *Sea History* 81 (1997): 37–39.

Ott, Thomas O. *The Haitian Revolution, 1789–1804*. Knoxville: University of Tennessee Press, 1973.

Paine, Ralph D. *The Fight for a Free Sea: A Chronicle of the War of 1812*. New Haven: Yale University Press, 1921.

———. *Joshua Barney: Forgotten Hero of the Blue Water*. New York: Century, 1924.

Pattee, Fred Lewis, ed. *The Poems of Philip Freneau, Poet of the American Revolution*. 3 vols. Princeton, N.J.: Princeton Historical Association, 1902–7.

Peterson, Charles J. *The American Navy*. Philadelphia: James B. Smith and Company, 1858.

Petrie, Charles. *King Charles III of Spain*. New York: John Day, 1971.

Pitch, Anthony S. *The Burning of Washington: The British Invasion of 1814*. Annapolis: Naval Institute Press, 1998.

Pool, J. Laurence. *Fighting Ships of the Revolution on Long Island Sound, 1775–1783*. Torrington, Conn.: Rainbow Press, 1990.

Potter, E. B. *Sea Power: A Naval History*. Annapolis: Naval Institute Press, 1981.

Preston, Anthony, David Lyons, and John H. Batchelor. *Navies of the American Revolution*. New York: Prentice-Hall, 1975.

Scharf, J. Thomas. *Chronicles of Baltimore*. Baltimore: Turnbull Brothers, 1874.

Seward, Desmond. *Napoleon's Family*. New York: Viking Penguin, 1986.

Sharpe, Richard, ed. *Jane's Fighting Ships 1991–92*, 94th ed. Surrey, England: Jane's Information Group, 1991.

Shay, Frank. *An American Sailor's Treasury*. New York: W. W. Norton, 1948.

Shomette, Donald G. *Flotilla: Battle for the Patuxent*. Solomons, Md.: Calvert Marine Museum Press, 1981.

Sioussat, Annie Leakin. *Old Baltimore*. New York: Macmillan, 1931.

Smith, Page. *A New Age Now Begins*. New York: McGraw-Hill, 1976.

Sobel, Dava. *Longitude: The True Story of the Lone Genius Who Solved the Greatest Scientific Problem of His Time*. New York: Walker, 1995.

Sprout, Harold, and Margaret Sprout. *The Rise of American Naval Power*. London: Oxford University Press, 1939.

Stacton, David. *The Bonapartes*. New York: Simon and Schuster, 1966.

Statham, E. P. *Privateers and Privateering*. New York: James Pott and Company, 1910.

Sternlicht, Sanford, and Edwin M. James. *U.S.F. Constellation: "Yankee Racehorse."* Cockeyville, Md.: Liberty Publishing Company, 1981.

Syrett, David, and R. L. DiNiro. *The Commissioned Sea Officers of the Royal Navy: 1660–1815*. Aldershot, England: Scolar Press for the Navy Records Society; Brookfield, Vt.: Ashgate, 1994.

Syrett, Harold C., and Jacob E. Cooke, eds. *The Papers of Alexander Hamilton*. 27 vols. New York: Columbia University Press, 1961–87.

Trumbull, John. *Reminiscences of His Own Times from 1756 to 1841*. New York: Wiley and Putnam, 1841.

Tuchman, Barbara W. *The First Salute*. New York: Alfred Knopf, 1988.

Tuckerman, Henry Theodore. *The Life of Silas Talbot, a Commodore in the Navy of the United States*. New York: J. C. Riker, 1850.

Twohig, Dorothy, ed. *The Journals of the Proceedings of the President, 1793–1797*. Charlottesville: University Press of Virginia, 1981.

———, ed. *The Papers of George Washington*. Presidential series, vols. 5–7. Charlottesville: University Press of Virginia, 1987.

U.S. Congress. *Annals. Debates and Proceedings in the Congress of the United States, 1789–1824*. 42 vols. Washington, D.C.: Gales and Seaton, 1834–73.

Vassa, Gustavus. *The Interesting Narrative of the Life of Olaudah Equianon, or Gustavus Vassa*. London: Cradock and Joy, 1814.

Wells, Gerard. *Naval Customs and Traditions*. London: Philip Allan, Camelot Press, 1930.

Wharton, Ann Hollingsworth. *Martha Washington*. New York: Charles Scribner's Sons, 1897.

~~ *Further Reading* ~~

As preparation for writing a new biography of Joshua Barney I explored several old biographies as well as numerous related books. The commodore's daughter-in-law, Mary Barney, wrote *Biographical Memoir of the Late Joshua Barney* (1832). This book is unique because women rarely wrote biographies of military men in the early part of the nineteenth century. The work chronicles events that, at the time, were relatively recent history, events that the commodore and his family passed on to Mrs. Barney. Although these accounts are written in an atavistic style, they are colorful and occasionally charming. One may, however, question the reliability of Mary Barney as a primary source. She had a vested interest in making her father-in-law appear heroic. Also, she had to depend on an aged Barney for his recollections of events, particularly those of his early years. Although Mrs. Barney was not a historian, she did supply some documentary evidence of the reported accounts in an appendix. It should be noted that many corroborating primary source documents were not available to her at the time she wrote the biography. This memoir may not be completely accurate, but it is obligatory reading for a historian doing research on Joshua Barney's life.

A second biography written 102 years later, *Joshua Barney: Forgotten Hero of the Blue Water*, by Ralph D. Paine (1924), is pleasant reading. Unfortunately this book is not at all scholarly, presenting Barney's life in a quasi-historical novel format. Paine's book appears to be based almost entirely on Mary Barney's work, and it depicts the commodore as an even larger-than-life figure than the original work. The book's major contribution was in resurrecting a nearly forgotten hero.

The most recent biography, *Sailor of Fortune: The Life and Adventures of Commodore Joshua Barney* (1940), by Hulbert Footner, is very detailed and is the most erudite of the three. The background research is adequate for the time, but additional data have become available since it was written, and some details are in need of correction. In addition, Footner's attention to minutiae makes for dry reading. Perhaps the book's biggest flaw is its overly narrative style. It fails to critically examine Barney's life and demonstrate his influence on the significant events happening around him.

A fourth work, William Adams's *Commodore Joshua Barney* (1912), is a genealogy and says very little about the events in Barney's life or his character.

Barney's biographers may have been few, but the events in which he participated have captured the attention of numerous historians. The most useful and engaging recent work is Donald Shomette's *Flotilla: Battle for the Patuxent* (1981), which explores the 1814 Maryland Peninsula campaign leading to the Battle of Bladensburg. Shomette weaves Barney into the fascinating fabric of the military campaign and gives insight into Barney's thinking and interactions with both his commanders and his flotillamen.

Barney's 1794 refusal of a captain's commission in the U.S. Navy because of bruised pride was likely the pivotal event in his career. It turned on his strange relationship with Silas Talbot, whose life is chronicled in William Fowler's excellent biography, *Silas Talbot: Captain of Old Ironsides* (1995). Except for brief references, comments about Joshua Barney appear on only one page:

> [Talbot] held a commission as a captain in the Continental navy that was dated 19 September 1779, but he never sailed in command of a Continental vessel. . . . Joshua Barney had technically never risen above [lieutenant during the war but] had in fact commanded the Continental ship *General Washington*, as Talbot had good reason to recall, and was referred to in that capacity as Captain. Accordingly, he [Barney] informed [Henry] Knox that he and not Talbot deserved to be number three. When Knox refused to alter rankings Barney refused the commission and went off in a huff to serve in the French Navy.

Fowler may have dismissed this event too hastily. The two men must have known one another quite well. They were imprisoned together on the *Jersey*, sailed as prisoners on the *Yarmouth*, and were incarcerated at the same time at Old Mill Prison in Plymouth, England. After declining appointment as one of the first six American naval captains, Barney did accept a commission in the French navy, but only after long negotiations, and hardly "in a huff." Ironically, Barney's rivalry with Talbot cost him far more than Talbot's dispute over Truxtun's position in seniority cost Talbot. Talbot complained, but he did not resign his commission, certainly a more reasoned move.

Joshua Barney appears in many books on the early navy, but not as a prominent figure. These secondary sources nevertheless provide an excellent backdrop to Barney's career. Nathan Miller's *Sea of Glory: The Continental Navy Fights for Independence, 1775–1783* (1974) and William M. Fowler Jr.'s *Jack Tars and Commodores: The American Navy, 1783–1815* (1984) are well-written narrative accounts of operations by the Continental navy and other maritime aspects of the American Revolution at sea through the early history of the U.S. Navy. John W. Jackson's *The Pennsylvania Navy: 1775–1781* (1974) describes, as its subtitle says, "The Defense of the Delaware [River]," but it also paints a useful picture of maritime Philadelphia, where Barney served during much of the war. Similarly, the essays in *Chesapeake Bay in the American Revolution* (1981), edited by Ernest M. Eller, describe events in the region around Barney's home port of Baltimore. Richard Buel Jr., in his recent work *In Irons* (1998), portrays the economic pressures between Britain and its American colonies that led to the development of the Continental navy. Buel cleverly weaves a complex tapestry of the military and commercial struggles that led to the improbable outcome of the Revolution.

The Quasi-War with France has received less attention from historians than either the Revolutionary War or the War of 1812, but Alexander DeConde's *The Quasi-War* (1966) is a good source for diplomatic events. Michael Palmer's *Stoddert's War* (1987) is particularly detailed in covering U.S. naval operations, especially in the West Indies.

The War of 1812 has been a popular subject for historians, which makes it difficult for one to be selective in identifying source materials. William Dudley's two-volume *The Naval War of 1812* (1985, 1992) is an important source of documentary materials about the naval history of the conflict. Donald Hickey's *The War of 1812* (1989) is a solid overview of the war, while Walter Lord's *The Dawn's Early Light* (1972) focuses on the Chesapeake invasion. Although Lord is inaccurate in some historical details, the book is very good reading. Jerome Garitee, in *The Republic's Private Navy* (1977), gives a scholarly account of privateering around Baltimore during that time and describes Barney as a central figure. Anthony Pitch's *The Burning of Washington: The British Invasion of 1814* (1998) gives a scholarly account of the events leading to the invasion of Washington, including the

Battle of Bladensburg. A reader seeking organized primary sources can turn to the ten-volume series *Naval Documents of the American Revolution*. A dated but still useful source on the administration of the early navy is Charles O. Paullin's *The Navy of the American Revolution: Its Administration, Its Policy, and Its Achievements* (1906).

Finally, an excellent overview of the diverse personalities that comprised the leadership of the nascent American navy is *Command under Sail* (1985), edited by James Bradford. The first two sections of the book, titled "The Struggle for Independence" and "Baptism by Fire," cover the Revolutionary War and the War of 1812, respectively. These collected biographical sketches give insight into the problems of naval command and describe the skills necessary to engage in battle during the age of sail, the Barney era. Although these chapters lack depth, they contain an extraordinary amount of information that direct the reader to useful primary and secondary source material.

The following is a reading list of secondary sources that are directly related to Barney or provide background material.

REVOLUTIONARY WAR

Buel, Richard Jr. *In Irons.* New Haven: Yale University Press, 1998.

Dupuy, Trevor Nevitt, and Grace R. Hayes. *The Military History of the Revolutionary War Naval Battles.* New York: Watts, 1970.

Eller, Ernest McNeill, ed. *Chesapeake Bay in the American Revolution.* Centreville, Md.: Tidewater Publications, 1981.

Jackson, John W. *The Pennsylvania Navy 1775–1781: The Defense of the Delaware.* New Brunswick: Rutgers University Press, 1974.

Larrabee, Harold Atkins. *Decision at the Chesapeake: 1775–1783 Campaign.* New York: C. N. Potter, 1964.

Miller, Nathan. *Sea of Glory: The Continental Navy Fights for Independence, 1775–1783.* New York: David McKay, 1974.

QUASI-WAR WITH FRANCE

Palmer, Michael A. *Stoddert's War: Naval Operations during the Quasi-War with France: 1798–1801.* Columbia: University of South Carolina Press, 1987.

WAR OF 1812

DeConde, Alexander. *The Quasi-War: The Politics and Diplomacy of the Undeclared War with France, 1798–1801.* New York: Scribner, 1966.

Hickey, Donald. *The War of 1812: A Forgotten Conflict.* Urbana: University of Illinois Press, 1989.

·∼❧ *Index* ❧∼·

abolitionists, 109, 110–11. *See also* slavery/slavetrading

Adams, John, 66–67, 107, 145

Admiralty Court, 121

Alexander, Charles, 22

Algiers, 127

Alicante (Spain), 10

Allibone, William, 73

American colonies: autonomy of individual states, 15; declare independence, 26; maritime trade in, 1–2, 3, 4, 14–15; New England's influence in, 18; revolution commences within, 12. *See also* Continental navy

Andrea Doria, 26–30, 34

Antoinette, Marie, 91

apprenticeships, 3, 4–6

Ardent, 40–41

Armistead, George, 168–69

Baltimore (Maryland): 1814 defense of, 184–86, 189; growth of, 101, 108–9, 168; politics in, 155; privateering in, 159

Barbary coast, 10–12, 127

barge design, 170–71

Barney, 201, 202

Barney, Anne (Bedford) (wife), 47, 70, 156

Barney, Caroline (daughter), 101

Barney, Frances Holland (Watts) (mother), 2

Barney, Harriet (Coale) (second wife), 156

Barney, John (son), 101

Barney, Joshua: and American flags, 14, 18–19, 132–33, 169, 189; on *Andrea Doria*, 26–30; apprenticeships of, 3, 4–6; barge design of, 170–71; in Belgium, 65–66; at Bladensburg, 179–83, 191–92; business ventures of, 100–101, 109–16, 119–20, 141; captured on *Charming Molly*, 50–51; captured on *Thomas*, 31–32; captured on *Virginia*, 37; captures *General Monk*, 76–78; childhood of, 2–3; commands *General Washington*, 85–99; commands *Hyder-Ally*, 72–84; commands *Rossie*, 160–67; commands *Sampson*, 112–23; commands *Sidney*, 1–2, 6–13; commissioned a lieutenant on *Sachem*, 25–26; declines commission in Revenue Cutter Service, 108; declines commission in U.S. Navy, 128–30; delivers news of Peace of Paris, 92–93; death of,

221

About the Author

Louis Arthur Norton, a native of the seaport of Gloucester, Massachusetts, is a professor emeritus at the University of Connecticut Health Center at Farmington. He received his education at Bowdoin College and Harvard University and pursued his graduate studies in American maritime history at the University of Connecticut at Storrs. Professor Norton is the author of many publications in the maritime field.